Yale Southeast Asia Studies, 6

Editorial Committee

Harry J. Benda
Harold C. Conklin
Karl J. Pelzer
Robert O. Tilman

A Guide to Reference Materials on
Southeast Asia

Based on the Collections in the
Yale and Cornell University Libraries

Compiled by
Donald Clay Johnson

New Haven and London, Yale University Press, 1970

Copyright © 1970 by Yale University.
All rights reserved. This book may not be
reproduced, in whole or in part, in any form
(except by reviewers for the public press),
without written permission from the publishers.
Library of Congress catalog card number: 75–104616
Standard book number: 300–01277–2
set in Documentary type,
and printed in the United States of America by
Murray Printing Co., Forge Village, Mass.
Distributed in Great Britain, Europe, Asia, and
Africa by Yale University Press Ltd., London; in
Canada by McGill-Queen's University Press, Montreal; and
in Mexico by Centro Interamericano de Libros
Académicos, Mexico City.

This work is dedicated to
Professor John M. Echols,
friend of librarians and libraries
dealing with Southeast Asia

CONTENTS

Preface		ix
A.	Bibliographies and Catalogs	1
B.	Published Catalogs of Library Resources	11
C.	Newspaper and Periodical Guides	20
D.	Biographies	24
E.	Almanacs, Encyclopedias, Handbooks, and Other General Compendiums of Information	29
F.	Guidebooks	36
G.	Social Science	43
H.	Law and Political Science	45
I.	Economics	50
J.	History	52
K.	Anthropology	55
L.	Education (Including Theses)	58
M.	Geography and Gazetteers	61
N.	Atlases and Map Bibliographies	65
O.	Language and Literature	69
P.	Dictionaries	73
Q.	Archeology	99
R.	Religion	101
S.	Other Materials Dealing with the Humanities	103
T.	Libraries and the Book Trade	104
U.	Agriculture	106
V.	Natural Sciences	108
W.	General Statistics	112
X.	Agricultural Statistics	121
Y.	Commercial Statistics	125
Z.	Demographic Statistics	137
Index		143

PREFACE

Reference librarians such as Kroeger, Mudge, and Winchell have provided librarians and scholars with excellent general reference guides that can be used to locate a limited number of reference works in the various area studies. No one, however, has attempted to compile a comprehensive guide to reference materials that deal with Southeast Asia. In the present work I have tried to provide such a guide.

Reference work with the Yale Southeast Asia Collection has shown me that users (including myself) are not aware of the number or variety of reference aids dealing with Southeast Asia that are available in a collection like Yale's. With the expansion of the Southeast Asia program at Yale, the problem has become more complex as additional faculty have introduced new courses, and students have in turn begun to look for new and different types of materials. Accordingly, I began assembling a list of reference sources dealing either exclusively or primarily with Southeast Asia, imagining that the maximum number of titles I should find would be between 500 and 750, and that such a list could be reproduced cheaply for distribution to interested individuals.

I was able to locate 750 titles with comparative ease, however, and it soon became apparent that a comprehensive list would be much longer than I had first thought. I determined to continue until I had succeeded in compiling a reasonably complete list of reference works dealing with Southeast Asia.

Initially I listed the holdings of the libraries at Yale. Since Cornell University also has an active Southeast Asia program and significant library holdings on Southeast Asia, I felt that the list should be expanded to include the holdings of that collection as well. A timely grant from the Yale Southeast Asia Studies program enabled me to go to Ithaca to survey the Cornell holdings. This enlarged the list considerably. After rechecking the Yale catalog against the additional materials found at Cornell, I was able to organize the work in its present form.

I have tried to list all reference sources dealing with Southeast Asia found in either the Yale or Cornell libraries, or in both. Because of typographical limitations, I have included only works printed in the Roman alphabet, or having a title page in the Roman alphabet. Works not held by either Cornell or Yale are omitted.

In general, only separately published works are included. Exceptions have sometimes been made for monographic works published as special issues of journals (e.g. Beda Lim's bibliography of Malaya, item AM7), and for a few special reference guides published as a chapter or part of another title.

Government publications are included, with the exception of publications of the United Nations, which are omitted. General worldwide compendia such as the Statesman's Yearbook are also omitted.

Although the table of contents will reveal the general sequence of subjects, a few words are in order regarding the arrangement of titles. Each citation is preceded by a classification notation. The first letter of this notation designates a broad subject area, and the second letter generally designates a country of Southeast Asia. The numbers of each notation designate the order of items within a subject category. Thus a general bibliography on Southeast Asia will be given the notation AA and will be included in the section of general bibliographies, while a general bibliography of Malaya will be found in section AM, one of Thailand in section AT, and so on. A bibliography of the social sciences in Thailand, however, would be found in section GT (Social Science–Thailand) and a bibliography of political science dealing with Thailand in section HT (Political Science–Thailand).

Holdings are indicated by the location symbols "C" (for Cornell) and "Y" (for Yale) at the end of each citation.

The form of entry used conforms with that found in the public catalog at Yale, and in general follows standard United States cataloging practice as found in such works as the <u>National Union Catalog</u>. If the Cornell entry for a given title differs from the Yale entry, a note at the end of the citation provides the Cornell entry.

Within subdivisions the arrangement is chronological. I felt that this arrangement would offer several advantages over the usual listing alphabetically by author, for it (1) brings related works published contemporaneously together; (2) enables librarians engaged in collection building to locate the most recent publications within a given subject, so that these materials can be ordered promptly, before, one hopes, they have gone out of print; (3) provides a means of cross-checking entries in bookdealers' catalogs by date, since these catalogs often have non-standard entries.

It was sometimes necessary to place certain works arbitrarily in one section rather than in another. All works dealing with statistics were placed in the statistics sections (letters W-Z) rather than with the subject. Thus a work on Burmese social science statistics would be found in section WB (General Statistics-Burma) rather than in section BG (Social Sciences-Burma). Similarly, atlases are grouped in section N, so that a linguistic atlas of the Philippines would be found in section NP (Atlases-Philippines) rather than in OP (Languages and Literature-Philippines).

If a work dealt with two countries of Southeast Asia it was placed in the general section of that subject, except for titles dealing with the countries formerly in Indochina, which were placed in an Indochina section. Books dealing with more than two subjects were placed in the most appropriate general subject area, rather than with one of the subjects. A work dealing with two subjects was placed with the subject mentioned first, and a cross reference was inserted at the second subject.

The work of many people goes into the compilation of a list like this one. I should like to thank Professor John M. Echols of Cornell University, to whom this work is dedicated, for patiently reading the manuscript and pointing out errors in the spelling of entries in foreign languages. Mr. Giok Po Oey, Southeast Asia Librarian at Cornell, was most helpful during my stay in Ithaca and generously gave time to assist me in using the Cornell libraries. Mr. John K. Musgrave, Southeast Asia Bibliographer at the University of Michigan, was the first to suggest that the work be published, and he worked actively for its publication. Professor Robert O. Tilman of Yale, while serving as Acting Director of the Southeast Asia Studies program, provided financial assistance which enabled me to visit Cornell. The staff of the Southeast Asia Collection at Yale, in particular the librarian, Miss Lian Tie Kho, were most helpful during the compilation of the work, particularly in providing linguistic assistance. Miss F. Bernice Field, Associate Librarian for Technical Services at Yale, provided constant encouragement, which was particularly welcome during the typing of the manuscript. Mr. Robert Balay, Head of the Reference Department at Yale, offered suggestions regarding the format of the work and the index.

D.C.J.

New Haven, Connecticut
September 1969

ABBREVIATIONS

The following list gives the abbreviations most commonly used in the text. Infrequently used special language abbreviations are not included. There may be several possible expanded spellings of a given abbreviation, depending upon context; e.g. "trans." may mean either "translated" or "translator," and "Dept." may stand for the English "Department" or French "Département."

Aum.	Augmented	ℓ	Leaves
Bearb.	Bearbeitet	Mij.	Maatschappij
C	Cornell	Min.	Ministry
Cal.	California	Ned.	Nederlands
Col.	Columns, colored (in section "N" only)	Pr.	Press
		Prelim.	Preliminary
Cong.	Congress	Pub.	Publication
Cor.	Corrected	Rev.	Revised
Dept.	Department	Ser.	Series
Div.	Division	Sess.	Session
Enl.	Enlarged	Tip.	Tipografia
Fed.	Federation	Tr., or trans.	Translated
FMS	Federated Malay States	Uitg.	Uitgave
Fr.	Friar	Univ.	University
GPO	Government Printing Office	V.	Volume
Herz.	Herzien	Verb.	Verbeterde
HRAF	Human Relations Area Files	Verm.	Vermeerderd
Impr.	Imprint	Y	Yale
Kon.	Koninklijk		

A—BIBLIOGRAPHIES AND CATALOGS

AA—GENERAL BIBLIOGRAPHIES

AA1. Books and articles on Oriental subjects published in Japan. Tokyo, Toho Gakkai. v.1- annual. C, Y
[Cornell entry: Tohogakkai.]

AA2. ZENKER, JULIUS THEODOR. Bibliotheca orientalis. Leipzig, Engelman, 1846-61. 2v. in 1. C, Y

AA3. Bibliotheca orientalis; or, A complete list of books, papers, serials, and essays published in England and the colonies, Germany and France on the history, languages, religions, antiquities, literature and geography of the East. London, Trübner, 1876-83. 8v. Y

AA4. Orientalische Bibliographie. Berlin, Reuther, 1882-1922, 1928. 26v. in 14. C, Y

AA5. ACADEMIA DE LA HISTORIA, MADRID. BIBLIOTECA. Bibliografía hispano-oriental, apuntes para un catálogo de los documentos referentes a Indias orientales (China, Japón, Cochinchina, etc.) que se conservan en las colecciones de la Academia de la historia; por Antonio R. Rodríguez Moñino. Madrid, Tip. de Archivos, 1931. 59p. Y

AA6. Bulletin of Far Eastern bibliography. Washington, Committees on Far Eastern studies of the American Council of Learned Societies, 1936-40. 5v. C, Y
[Continued in the Far Eastern Quarterly.]

AA7. Journal of Asian studies. Ann Arbor, 1941- C, Y
[Includes Bibliography of Asian Studies, formerly Far Eastern bibliography.]
[See also AA6]

AA8. TOKYO. NAN'YO KEIZAI KENKYUSHO. Nan'yô kankei tosho mokuroku. Tokyo, 1941. 50p. (Its Nan'yô shiryô, 1) Y

AA9. NIHON TAKUSHOKU KYOKAI, TOKYO. Nampô bunken mokuroku. Tokyo, 1942. 238p. C, Y

AA10. TAIHEIYO KYOKAI, TOKYO. Nan'yô bunken mokuroku, edited by Uehara Hitoshi. Zôho dai 2 han. Tokyo, Chûô Kôronsha, 1942. 198p. (Taikeiyô mondai kenkyû sôsho) Y

AA11. ALLIED FORCES. An annotated bibliography of the Southwest Pacific and adjacent areas. 1944-45. 4v. Y
[Contents: v.1. Netherlands and British East Indies and the Philippine Islands. —v.2. The Mandated territory of New Guinea, Papua, the British Solomon Islands, the New Hebrides and Micronesia. — v.3. Malaya, Thailand, Indochina, the China Coast and the Japanese Empire. —v.4. Supplement to volumes 1-3.]

AA12. ROYAL COMMONWEALTH SOCIETY. LIBRARY. The Pacific region: a bibliography of the Pacific and East Indian islands exclusive of Japan by Evans Lewin. London, 1944. 2, 75p. (Royal Empire Society bibliographies, no. 11) C, Y

AA13. U.S. LIBRARY OF CONGRESS. ORIENTALIA DIVISION. Southeast Asia, 1935-45; a selected list of reference books compiled by Cecil Hobbs. Washington, 1946. 86p. C, Y

AA14. Asien-Bibliographie. Frankenau/Hessen, Asien-Bücherei, 1949-54. 6v. C
[Superseded by: Bibliographia asiatica.]

AA15. EMBREE, JOHN FEE. A selected bibliography on Southeast Asia. New York, Institute of Pacific Relations, 1950. 15p. C
AA16. U.S. LIBRARY OF CONGRESS. ORIENTALIA DIVISION. Southeast Asia; an annotated bibliography of selected reference sources compiled by Cecil Hobbs. Washington, 1952. 163p. C, Y
AA17. AMERICAN INSTITUTE OF PACIFIC RELATIONS.
Southeast Asia; a selected bibliography. New York, 1955. 30ℓ C
AA18. KOKURITSU KOKKAI TOSHOKAN, TOKYO. IPPAN KOSABU. Tonan Ajia kankei shiryo sogo mokuroku. Tokyo, 1955. 129p. C
AA19. GARDE, P.K. Directory of reference works published in Asia. Paris, UNESCO, 1956. 139p. (UNESCO bibliographical handbook, 5) C, Y
AA20. IRIKURA, JAMES K. Southeast Asia; selected annotated bibliography of Japanese publications. New Haven, Southeast Asia Studies, Yale Univ., 1956. 544p. (Behavior science bibliographies) C, Y
AA21. KAFTON, MIROSLAV. Indie-Barma-Indonesie; výběrový seznam literatury. Prague, Universitni Knihovna v Praze, 1956. 16p. (Čteme a studujeme, rok 1956, sešit 3) C
AA22. LASKER, BRUNO. Books on Southeast Asia; a selected bibliography. New York, American Institute of Pacific Relations, 1956. 43p. Y
[This is the 4th rev. ed. of the earlier IPR bibliography on Southeast Asia prepared by John F. Embree, 1950, rev. by Bruno Lasker, 1952, and reissued January 1955.]
AA23. EMBREE, JOHN FEE. Books on Southeast Asia; a select bibliography compiled with a foreword by Bruno Lasker. 4th. rev. ed. May 1956, with a supplement covering the period May 1956 to May 1957. New York, American Institute of Pacific Relations, 1957. 50p. C
AA24. FREI, ERNEST J. Bibliographies of Southeast Asia and Pacific areas. Quezon, Univ. of the Philippines, 1958. 33p. (Bibliographical Society of the Philippines Occasional papers, 1) C, Y
AA25. McVEY, RUTH THOMAS. Bibliography of Soviet publications on Southeast Asia as listed in the Library of Congress Monthly index of Russian acquisitions. Ithaca, 1959. 109p. (Cornell Univ. Southeast Asia Program. Data Paper no. 34) C, Y
AA26. HART, DONN V. A preliminary list of Southeast Asian bibliographies. n.p. 1959. 11ℓ C
AA27. HSU, YUN-CH'IAO. Preliminary bibliography of the Southeast Asian studies.
[In Nanyang University, Singapore. Institute of Southeast Asia. Bulletin. (Nan Yang yen chiu) no. 1 (1959) pp. 1-160.] C, Y
AA28. INDIAN COUNCIL OF WORLD AFFAIRS. Documentation on Asia. New Delhi, Allied Publishers, 1960- C, Y
[Supersedes its Documents on Asian affairs.]
AA29. HART, DONN V. A selective bibliography of the State University College of Forestry, Syracuse, New York, related to Burma, Thailand, Malaya, Indochina, Indonesia and the Philippines. Syracuse, 1961. 1, 14ℓ C
AA30. HORNE, NORMAN P. A guide to published United States government publications pertaining to Southeast Asia, 1893-1941. Washington, 1961. 147ℓ C
[Master's thesis in Library Science at Catholic University.]
AA31. CAMMACK, FLOYD M. Pacific island bibliography by Floyd M. Cammack and Shiro Saito. New York, Scarecrow Pr., 1962. 421p. C, Y
AA32. AJIA KEIZAI KENKYUJO, TOKYO. Documentary materials in Asian countries; report of a survey by a study group of the Institute of Asian

Economic Affairs. Tokyo, Institute of Asian Economic Affairs, 1963. 198p. C, Y

AA33. KYRIAK, THEODORE E. Asia: A bibliography. Annapolis, Research and Microfilm Publications, 1963-64. 3v. C, Y
["Guide to contents of a collection of US-JPRS translations in the social sciences emanating from Asian countries other than Communist China and exclusive of Near East."]

AA34. AJIA KEIZAI KENKYUJO, TOKYO. Union catalogue of documentary materials on Southeast Asia. Tokyo, Institute of Asian Economic Affairs, 1964. 5v. in 2. C, Y

AA35. KYRIAK, THEODORE E. China and Asia, exclusive of Near East. Annapolis, Research and Microfilm Publications, 1964- C, Y
[Supersedes his Asia: A bibliography, and continues the numbering.]

AA36. U.S. LIBRARY OF CONGRESS. ORIENTALIA DIVISION. Southeast Asia; an annotated bibliography of selected reference sources in western languages. Rev. and enl. Compiled by Cecil Hobbs. Washington, 1964. 180p. C, Y

AA37. ERICKSON, G. E. Southeast Asia. San Francisco, Clark Air Force Base Library, 1965. vii, 95p. (PACAF basic bibliographies) Y

AA38. BRUSSELS. UNIVERSITÉ LIBRE. CENTRE D'ÉTUDE DU SUD-EST ASIATIQUE. Premiers éléments bibliographiques relatifs aux problèmes actuels du sud-est de l'Asie. Brussels, 1966. 515p. Y

AA39. NUNN, GODFREY RAYMOND. South and Southeast Asia, a bibliography of bibliographies. Honolulu, East-West Center Library, 1966. v, 59ℓ (Hawaii. Univ., Honolulu. East-West Center. Library. Occasional paper, no. 4) C, Y

AA40. YUNESUKO HIGASHI AJIA BUNKA KENKYU SENTA, TOKYO. A survey of bibliographies in western languages concerning East and Southeast Asian studies, compiled by Tokihiko Tanaka, edited by Kazuo Enoki. Tokyo, 1966. 227p. (Its bibliography, no. 4) Y

AA41. AKADEMIIA NAUK SSSR. INSTITUT NARODOV AZII. Selections from the holdings in Oriental studies in the great libraries of the Soviet Union, articles and notes, compiled by A. S. Tveritinova, translated by Ruth M. Denney. Honolulu, Institute of Advanced Projects, East-West Center, 1967. 115ℓ (Hawaii. Univ., Honolulu. Center for Cultural and Technical Interchange between East and West. Institute of Advanced Projects. Research Translations. Occasional papers. Translation series, no. 19) C, Y

AA42. TERNAUX-COMPANS, HENRI. Bibliothèque asiatique et africaine; ou, Catalogue des ouvrages relatifs à l'Asie et à l'Afrique qui ont paru depuis la découverte de l'imprimerie jusqu'en 1700. Amsterdam, Grüner, 1968. 347p. Y
[Reprint of 1841 edition.]

AB—BURMA

AB1. The world of books. Rangoon, Burma Book Club, 1925- monthly. C, Y

AB2. U.S. DEPT. OF STATE. DIVISION OF RESEARCH FOR FAR EAST. Selected bibliography of English language publications on Burma. Washington, 1951. 4ℓ (Its DRF information paper no. 452) C

AB3. FISHER, JOSEPH. Research bibliography of books, documents and pamphlets on Burma. Rangoon, Rangoon-Hopkins Center for Southeast Asian Studies, 1953. 63ℓ C

AB4. NEW YORK UNIVERSITY. BURMA RESEARCH PROJECT. Annotated bibliography of Burma. New Haven, HRAF, 1956. 230p. (Behavior science bibliographies) C, Y

AB5. NEW YORK UNIVERSITY. BURMA RESEARCH PROJECT. Japanese and Chinese language sources on Burma, an annotated bibliography. New Haven, HRAF, 1957. 122p. (Behavior science bibliographies) C, Y

AB6. FRANCE. DIRECTION DE LA DOCUMENTATION. L'Union Birmanie. Paris, 1963. 28p. (Notes et études documentaires no. 3004) C

AB7. TRAGER, FRANK NEWTON. Furnivall of Burma; an annotated bibliography of the works of John S. Furnivall. Detroit, Cellar Book Shop, 1963. 51p. (Yale Univ. Graduate School. Southeast Asia Studies. Bibliography Series, no. 8) C, Y

AC—CAMBODIA

AC1. CHICAGO. UNIVERSITY. Bibliography of Cambodia prepared by HRAF Cambodia Research Project at the University of Chicago. New Haven, HRAF, 1956. 17p. (Behavior science bibliographies) C

AH—INDOCHINA

AH1. CORDIER, HENRI. Bibliotheca indosinica; dictionnaire bibliographique des ouvrages relatifs à la péninsule indochinoise. Paris, Leroux, 1912-32. 4v. (Pub. de l'École Française d'Extrême-Orient v. 15-18 bis) C, Y

AH2. BOUDET, PAUL. Pour mieux connaître l'Indochine; essai d'une bibliographie. Hanoi, Impr. d'Extrême-Orient, 1922. 92p. Y

AH3. INDOCHINA, FRENCH. DIRECTION DES ARCHIVES ET DES BIBLIOTHÈQUES. Bibliographie de l'Indochine française. Hanoi, 1924- C

AH4. BOUDET, PAUL. Bibliographie de l'Indochine française, 1913-1926— par Paul Boudet et Remy Bourgeois. Hanoi, Impr. d'Extrême-Orient, 1929-67. 5v. in 4. C, Y

AH5. HARVARD UNIVERSITY. LIBRARY. Indochina: selected list of references, Widener library, Harvard Univ., Cambridge, Mass. Cambridge, 194? 108ℓ C, Y

AH6. U.S. LIBRARY OF CONGRESS. REFERENCE DEPT. Indochina; a bibliography of the land and people, compiled by Cecil C. Hobbs. Washington, 1950. 367p. C, Y

AH7. AUVADE, ROBERT. Bibliographie critique des oeuvres parues sur l'Indochine française: un siècle d'histoire et d'enseignement. Paris, Maisonneuve, 1965. 153p. C, Y

AI—INDONESIA

AI 1. GUNUNG AGUNG, DJAKARTA. Daftar buku-buku. Djakarta. v.1- C

AI 2. Catalogus dari buku-buku jang diterbitkan di Indonesia, 1870-1937— Bandung, Gedung Buku Nasional. v.1-
[Cornell entry: Ockeloen, G.]
[Title varies slightly.]

AI 3. CHIJS, JACOBUS ANNE VAN DER. Proeve eener Nederlandsch.Indische Bibliographie (1659-1870). Batavia, Bruining, 1875. 325p. (Bataviaasch Genootschap van Kunsten en Wetenschappen: Verhandelingen. v.37)
Supplement I 1880. 95p. (v.39)
Supplement II 1903. 64p. (v.55)
C, Y

AI 4. JOUSTRA, M. Literatuuroverzicht der Bataklanden. Leiden, Becherer, 1907. 180p. C, Y

AI 5. AMSTERDAM. BALI INSTITUUT. Bali en Lombok; overzicht der literatuur omtrent deze eilanden tot einde 1919, door C. Lekkerkerker. Rijs-

wijk, Blankwaardt & Schoonhoven, 1920. 456p. C, Y
[Cornell entry: Bali-Instituut. Amsterdam.]

AI 6. ZUID SUMATRA INSTITUUT. Zuid-Sumatra, overzicht van de literatuur der gewesten Bengkoelen, Djambi, de Lampongsche districten en Palembang door J. W. J. Wellan en O. L. Helfrich. The Hague, Smits, 1923-28. 2v. (Uitgave van het Zuid-Sumatra Instituut) C, Y

AI 7. JOUSTRA, M. Overzicht der literatuur betreffende Minangkabau. Amsterdam, Minangkabau Instituut, 1924. 162p. (Minangkabau Instituut, Amsterdam. Uitgaaf, no. 2) C, Y

AI 8. ADRIANI, NICOLAUS. Lijst van de geschriften van dr N. Adriani. Leiden, Brill, 1928. 12p. C

AI 9. MOLUKKEN-INSTITUUT, AMSTERDAM. Overzicht van de literatuur betreffende de Molukken. Amsterdam, Molukken-instituut, 1928-35. 2v. C, Y
[Title varies slightly.]

AI 10. Bibliotheca javanica. Weltevreden, Albrecht, 1930- C, Y

AI 11. TAIHEIYO KYOKAI, TOKYO. Ranryô Indo (Nan'yô ippan o fukumete) bunken sô mokuroku. Tokyo, 1940. 49p. Y

AI 12. U.S. LIBRARY OF CONGRESS. DIVISION OF BIBLIOGRAPHY. The Netherlands East Indies; a selected list of references compiled by Helen F. Conover under the direction of Florence S. Hellman. Washington, 1942. 46p. C, Y

AI 13. U.S. LIBRARY OF CONGRESS. GENERAL REFERENCE AND BIBLIOGRAPHY DIVISION. NETHERLANDS STUDIES UNIT. Netherlands East Indies; a bibliography of books published after 1930, and periodical articles after 1932 available in U.S. libraries. Washington, 1945. 208p. C, Y

AI 14. INDONESIA. KEMENTERIAN PENDIDIKAN, PENGADJARAN DAN KEBUDAJAAN. PERPUSTAKAAN PERGURUAN. Daftar buku2 (Balai Pustaka). Djakarta, 195? v.1- C

AI 15. U.S. DEPT. of STATE. DIVISION OF RESEARCH FOR FAR EAST. Selected bibliography of English-language publications on Indonesia. Washington, 1950. 6ℓ (Its DRF information paper no. 372) C

AI 16. Buku baru. Het nieuwe boek. Bibliographisch tijdschrift voor Indonesie. Medan, 1951- C

AI 17. Bibliografi nasional Indonesia. Djakarta, Kantor Bibliografi Nasional, 1953- C

AI 18. GUNUNG AGUNG, DJAKARTA. Daftar buku untuk sekolah rendah (bahasa Indonesia). Djakarta, 1953. 68p. C

AI 19. INDONESIA. KANTOR BIBLIOGRAFI NASIONAL. Berita bulanan. Djakarta, 1953- Monthly. Y

AI 20. CANBERRA, AUSTRALIA. NATIONAL LIBRARY. Indonesia. Canberra, 1954. 1v. (Its select bibliographies, general series, no. 3) C, Y

AI 21. Berita bibliografi. Djakarta, Gunung Agung, 1955- Monthly. C, Y
[Supersedes Catalogus dari buku-buku jang diterbitkan di Indonesia.]

AI 22. INDONESIA. KANTOR BIBLIOGRAFI NASIONAL. Social science bibliography for Southeast Asia: Indonesia. Djakarta, 1955. ii, 65p. C

AI 23. PAMERAN BUKU INDONESIA, SINGAPORE AND KUALA LUMPUR, 1956. Daftar buku jang dewasa ini diperedarkan dalam perdagangan di Indonesia. Djakarta, 1956. 101p. C

AI 24. U.S. DEPT. OF STATE. DIVISION OF RESEARCH FOR FAR EAST. Selected bibliography of English language publications on Indonesia. Washington, 1956. 7ℓ (DRF information paper 372R) C, Y

AI 25. GUNUNG AGUNG. Sekedar tentang bibliografi nasional dengan tambahan teks bahasa Inggeris. Some notes on current national bibliographical and other documental activities in Indonesia. Djakarta, 1960. 36p. C

AI 26. JONES, GARTH N. Bibliography; publications in English on Indonesian social, political, economic life and institutions. Jogjakarta, Univ. of Gadjah Mada, 1960. 1v. C

AI 27. ECHOLS, JOHN M. Preliminary checklist of Indonesian imprints during the Japanese period, March 1942-August 1945, with annotations. Ithaca, Cornell Univ. Southeast Asia Program, 1963. 56p. (Cornell Univ. Modern Indonesia Project. Bibliography series) C, Y

AI 28. DJAKARTA. LEMBAGA EKONOMI DAN KEMASJARAKATAN NASIONAL PERPUSTAKAAN. Bibliografi-indeks. Beberapa buku2 dan artikel2 dalam lapangan ekonomi dan kemasjarakatan termasuk politik, diterbitkan Djuli 1964 s/d Agustus 1965, termasuk djuga perdagangan umum dan management. Djakarta, 1965. 20p. C

AI 29. ECHOLS, JOHN M. Preliminary checklist of Indonesian imprints, 1945-49, with Cornell University holdings. Ithaca, Cornell Univ. Southeast Asia Program, 1965. 186p. (Cornell Univ. Modern Indonesia Project. Bibliography series) C, Y

AI 30. INDONESIA. BIRO PERPUSTAKAAN. Bibliografi nasional Indonesia, kumulasi 1945-63. Djakarta, 1965. 2v. C

AL — LAOS

AL1. KÉNE, THAO. Bibliographie du Laos. Vientiane, Edition du Comité Littéraire, 1958. 68, 7ℓ C, Y

AL2. McKINSTRY, JOHN. Bibliography of Laos and ethnically related areas to 1961. Los Angeles, Univ. of Cal. at Los Angeles, Dept. of Anthropology, Laos Project, 1961. 91ℓ (California. Univ. Univ. at Los Angeles, Dept. of Anthropology, Laos Project, paper no. 22) C, Y

AL3. McKINSTRY, JOHN. Bibliography of Laos and ethnically related areas to 1961. Berkeley, Center for Southeast Asia Studies, 1962. 89ℓ C, Y

AL4. LAFONT, PIERRE BERNARD. Bibliographie du Laos. Paris, 1964. 269p. (Publications de l'École Française d'Extrême-Orient, v.50) C, Y

AM — MALAYSIA-SINGAPORE

AM1. MALAYA (FED.) PERMANENT MISSION TO THE UNITED NATIONS. Reading list. n.p. v.1- C

AM2. ROBSON, J. H. M. Malaya; bibliography. Kuala Lumpur, FMS Pr., 1938. 49p. C

AM3. ROBSON, J. H. M. A bibliography of Malaya, also a short list of books relating to North Borneo and Sarawak. Kuala Lumpur, 1941. 54p. C

AM4. U.S. LIBRARY OF CONGRESS. DIVISION OF BIBLIOGRAPHY. British Malaya and British North Borneo: a bibliographical list, compiled by Florence S. Hellman. Washington, 1943. 103p. C, Y

AM5. CHEESEMAN, HAROLD AMBROSE ROBINSON. Bibliography of Malaya; being a classified list of books wholly or partly in English relating to the Federation of Malaya and Singapore. London, Published for the British Association of Malaya by Longmans, Green, 1959. 234p. C, Y

AM6. MILLS, LENNOX ALGERNON. British Malaya, 1824-67, edited for reprinting with a bibliography of writings in English on British Malaya, 1786-1867 by C. M. Turnbull, and a new chapter on European influence in the Malay Peninsula, 1511-1786 by D.K. Bassett. Singapore, Royal Asiatic Society, 1961. 424p. (Journal of the Malayan Branch, Royal Asiatic Society, v.33, pt. 3, 1960 no. 191) C, Y

AM7. LIM, BEDA. Malaya; a background bibliography. Kuala Lumpur, Royal Asiatic Society, 1962. 199p. (Journal of the Malayan Branch, Royal Asiatic Society, v.35, pts. 2-3, nos. 198/99) C, Y

AM8. COTTER CONRAD PATRICK. North Borneo, Brunei and Sarawak; a bibliography or [i.e. of] English language, historical, administrative and ethnographic sources. n.p. 1963. 33, 5ℓ C

AM9. MALAYA (FED.) EMBASSY. U.S. Getting to know the Federation of Malaya. Washington, 1963. 6ℓ (Its catalog no. 2) C

AM10. SINGAPORE (CITY) NATIONAL LIBRARY. Books about Malaysia. Singapore, National Library, 1963. 22p. C

AM11. SINGAPORE. (CITY) NATIONAL LIBRARY. Books about Malaysia. Rev. with additions, 1964. Singapore, 1964. 29p. C

AM12. Sabah materials; non-government publications. Kuching, 1965. 16, 2p. C

AM13. SINGAPORE (CITY) NATIONAL LIBRARY. Books about Singapore and Malaysia. Singapore, 1965. 40p. C, Y

AM14. SINGAPORE (CITY) NATIONAL LIBRARY. Daftar buku2 dalam bahasa kebangsaan yang terpileh dari buku2 di-Perpustakaan Negara untok orang2 dewasa. Singapore, 1965. 37p. C

AM15. LONDON. COMMONWEALTH INSTITUTE. Malaysia and Singapore, selected reading lists for advanced study. London, 1967. 15p. C

AP—PHILIPPINES

AP1. Tagala bibliography. Manila, Ayuda. v.1- C
      [Title varies: -106, Bibliographic list.]

AP2. LECLERC, CHARLES. Bibliotheca Americana; catalogue raisonné d'une très-précieuse collection des livres anciens et modernes sur l'Amérique et les Philippines. Paris, Maisonneuve, 1867. 407p. C, Y

AP3. LECLERC, CHARLES. Bibliotheca Americana, histoire, géographie, voyages, archéologie et linguistique des deux Amériques et des îles Philippines. Paris, Maisonneuve, 1878. 737p. C, Y

AP4. BLUMENTRITT, F. Vocabular einzelner Ausdrücke und Redensarten, welche dem Spanischen der philippinischen Inseln eigenthümlich sind; mit einem Anhange: Bibliotheca philippina. Leitmeritz, 1882-85. 2v. Y

AP5. RETANA Y GAMBOA, WENCESLAO EMILIO. Bibliográfia de Mindanao (epitome). Madrid, Viuda de M. Minuesa de los Rios, 1894. 69p. C, Y

AP6. RETANA Y GAMBOA, WENCESLAO EMILIO. Epítome de la bibliográfia general de Filipinas. Parte primera: Obras que posee el autor. Madrid, Viuda de M. Minuesa de los Rios, 1895-98. 4pts. Y

AP7. MEDINA, JOSE TORIBIO. La imprenta en Manila desde sus origenes Hasta 1810. Santiago de Chile, Impreso y grabado en case del autor, 1896. 280p.
      Adiciones y ampliaciones. 1904. 203p. C, Y

AP8. MEDINA, JOSE TORIBIO. Bibliográfia española de las islas Filipinas (1523-1810). Santiago de Chile, Cervantes, 1897-98. 556p. C, Y

AP9. RETANA Y GAMBOA, WENCESLAO EMILIO. La imprenta en Filipinas; adiciones y observaciones a la Imprenta en Manila de D. J. T. Medina. Madrid, Viuda de M. Minuesa de los Rios, 1897. 276p. Y

AP10. RETANA Y GAMBOA, WENCESLAO EMILIO. Catálogo abreviado de la biblioteca filipina de W. E. Retana. Madrid, Viuda de M. Minuesa de los Rios, 1898. 652p. Y

AP11. JOSEPHSON, AKSEL GUSTAV S. Bibliographies of the Philippine Islands, chronological checklist. Boston, Boston Book Co., 1899. 8p. Y
      [Reprinted from the Bulletin of bibliography vol. 2, no.1, 1899.]

AP12. MIDDLETON, THOMAS COOKE. Some notes on the bibliography of the Philippines. Philadelphia, Free Library, 1900. 58p. Y
[Reprinted from Bulletin of the Free Library of Philadelphia no. 4.]

AP13. RETANA Y GAMBOA, WENCESLAO EMILIO. Catálogo de obras filipinas que ofrece en venta W. E. Retana. Madrid, 1902. 160p. Y

AP14. U.S. LIBRARY OF CONGRESS. Bibliography of the Philippine Islands. Washington, GPO, 1903. 397, 439p. C, Y
[57th Cong., 2d. sess. Senate Doc. no. 74.]

AP15. PÉREZ, ANGEL. Adiciones y continuación de "La imprenta en Manila" de D. J. T. Medina; ó rarezas y curiosidades bibliográficas filipinas de las bibliotecas de esta capital, por los PP. Fr. Angel Pérez y Fr. Cecilio Guëmes, Agustinos. Manila, Santos y Bernal, 1904. 620p. Y

AP16. BLAIR, EMMA HELEN. The Philippine Islands, 1493-1803, by Emma Helen Blair and James Alexander Robertson. Cleveland, Clark, 1908. 55v. C, Y
[v.53 bibliography.]

AP17. RETANA Y GAMBOA, WENCESLAO EMILIO. Tablas cronológica y alfabética de imprentas é impresores de Filipinas (1593-1898). Madrid, Suarez, 1908. 114p. C, Y

AP18. ROBERTSON, JAMES ALEXANDER. Bibliography of the Philippine Islands, printed and manuscript, preceded by a descriptive account of the most important archives and collections containing Philippina. Cleveland, Clark, 1908. 437p. Y

AP19. RETANA Y GAMBOA, WENCESLAO EMILIO. Origenes de la imprenta filipina; investigaciones históricas, bibliográficas y tipográficas. Madrid, Suarez, 1911. 204p. C, Y

AP20. PHILIPPINE ISLANDS. LEGISLATURE, 1914. PHILIPPINE ASSEMBLY. Vida y obras de Ferdinand Blumentritt, folleto preparado por la secretaria de la Asamblea filipinia. Manila, GPO, 1914. 89p. Y
["Catalogo bibliografico de las obras del Prof. Dr. Ferdinand Blumentritt" pp. 45-85.]

AP21. MAGGS BROS. LONDON. Bibliotheca americana. London, 1922- C, Y
[pts. 1, 3 and 4 have title: Bibliotheca americana et philippina.]

AP22. U.S. LIBRARY OF CONGRESS. DIVISION OF BIBLIOGRAPHY. A selected list of references on the Philippine Islands, supplementing previous lists, compiled by Ann Duncan Brown. Washington, 1935. 43p. C, Y

AP23. EAST AND WEST ASSOCIATION, NEW YORK. What to read about the Philippines. New York, 1942. 8v. in 1. C, Y

AP24. JACQUET, CONSTANT H. The Philippines, a selected list of references. New York, Missionary Research Library, 1955. 10ℓ C

AP25. CHICAGO. UNIVERSITY. PHILIPPINE STUDIES PROGRAM. Selected bibliography of the Philippines, topically arranged and annotated, prepared by Philippine Studies Program, The University of Chicago, Fred Eggan, Director. Prelim. ed. New Haven, HRAF, 1956. 138p. (Behavior science bibliographies) C, Y

AP26. PHILIPPINES (REP.) BUREAU OF PUBLIC AFFAIRS. Books copyrighted, published in the Philippines 1945-57. Manila, 1957. 143ℓ C

AP27. HOUSTON, CHARLES ORVILLE. Philippine bibliography. Manila, Univ. of Manila, 1960- C, Y
[Contents. —v.1. An annotated preliminary bibliography of Philippine bibliographies since 1900.]

AP28. Philippine books and pamphlets, 1955-60. n.p. 1960. 1v. (Bibliography bulletin, v.1, no.1) C

AP29.   SAITO, SHIRO. The Philippines, a review of bibliographies. Honolulu, East-West Center Library, Univ. of Hawaii, 1960. 80p. (Hawaii. Univ., Honolulu. East-West Center. Library. Occasional paper, no. 5) C, Y

AP30.   INSTITUTE OF PHILIPPINE CULTURE. IPC Manila area study series. Manila, 1963– C, Y
[Cornell entry: Quezon, Philippines. Ateneo de Manila. Institute of Philippine Culture.]

AP31.   Philippine bibliography. Diliman, Univ. of the Philippines Library, 1963/64– Y

AP32.   QUIRINO, CARLOS. Regésto guión catálogo de los documentos existentes en México sobre Filipinas compilado por Carlos Quirino y dr. Abraham Laygo. Manila, El Comité de Amistad Filipino-Méxicana, 1965. 541p. Y

AT — THAILAND

AT1.   CORNELL UNIVERSITY. SOUTHEAST ASIA PROGRAM. Bibliography of Thailand; a selected list of books and articles with annotations by the staff of the Cornell Thailand research project. Ithaca, 1956. iv, 65, 5ℓ (Its Data paper no. 20) C, Y
[Cornell entry: Cornell University. Thailand Project.]

AT2.   KAWABE, TOSHIO. Bibliography of Thai studies. Tokyo, Tokyo Univ. of Foreign Studies, Institute of Foreign Affairs, 1957. ii, 75p. C, Y

AT3.   MASON, JOHN BROWN. Thailand bibliography by John Brown Mason and H. Carroll Parish. Gainesville, Dept. of Reference and Bibliography, Univ. of Florida Libraries, 1958. 247p. (Florida. Univ., Gainesville. Libraries. Bibliographic series, no. 4) C, Y

AT4.   BANGKOK. CHULALONGKORN UNIVERSITY. CENTRAL LIBRARY. Bibliography of material about Thailand in western languages. Bangkok, 1960. 325p. C, Y
[Cornell entry: Bangkok, Thailand. Chulalongkon Mahawitthayalai. Ho Samut Klong.]

AT5.   CORNELL UNIVERSITY. THAILAND PROJECT. Bibliography of the Cornell Thailand Project, 1947–62. Ithaca, 1962. 18ℓ C

AT6.   U.S. MILITARY ASSISTANCE INSTITUTE. LIBRARY. Suggested reading list on Thailand. 4th. rev. Arlington, Va., 1963. 36p. C

AT7.   CORNELL UNIVERSITY. THAILAND PROJECT. Bibliography of materials relating to Thailand and project personnel. Ithaca, Dept. of Anthropology and Southeast Asia Program, Dept. of Asian Studies, Cornell Univ., 1964. 32ℓ C, Y

AT8.   Annotated bibliography of Northeast Thailand. Bangkok, Joint Thai–U.S. Military Research and Development Center, 1967– Y

AT9.   CORNELL UNIVERSITY. THAILAND PROJECT. Bibliography of materials relating to Thailand and project personnel, 1947–67, reissued with addenda. Ithaca, 1967. vi, 40ℓ C

AV — VIETNAM

AV1.   GASPARDONE, EMILE. Bibliographie annamite. Hanoi, 1935. 173p. C, Y
[Reprinted from Bulletin de l'École française d'Extrême-Orient, XXXIV–1, 1934.]

AV2.   VIETNAM. DAI-SU-QUAN. FRANCE. Liste des ouvrages sur Vietnam et l'Indochine. Paris, 1955. 15p. C

AV3.   AMBEKAR, C. G. Viet-Nam; a reading list. n.p. 1958. 42p. C, Y

AV4.   MICHIGAN. STATE UNIVERSITY, EAST LANSING. VIETNAM PROJECT. What to read on Vietnam; a selected annotated bibliography. New York, Institute of Pacific Relations, 1959. 67p. C, Y

AV5.   MICHIGAN. STATE UNIVERSITY, EAST LANSING. VIETNAM PROJECT. What to read on Vietnam; a selected annotated bibliography. 2d. ed., with a supplement covering the period November 1958 to October 1959. New York, Institute of Pacific Relations, 1960. 73ℓ C, Y

AV6.   Vietnam; a checklist. New York, American Friends of Vietnam, 1961– C

AV7.   ANDREATTA, LOUIS. Vietnam 1961, a checklist. New York, American Friends of Vietnam, 1962. 6ℓ Y

AV8.   U.S. DEPT. OF STATE. OFFICE OF INTELLIGENCE RESEARCH AND ANALYSIS. EXTERNAL RESEARCH STAFF. The Republic of Vietnam (South Vietnam); a bibliography. Washington, 1963. 2pts. in 1v. (<u>Its</u> External research paper, 143) C, Y

AV9.   COATES, JOSEPH. Bibliography of Vietnam. Washington, Institute for Defense Analysis, 1964. vi, 52p. C

AV10. U.S. DEPT. OF STATE. EXTERNAL RESEARCH DIVISION. The Democratic Republic of Viet-Nam (North Viet-Nam); a bibliography. Washington, 1964. 21p. (<u>Its</u> External research paper 142) C

AV11. TRAN-THI-KIMSA. Bibliography on Vietnam, 1954–1964. Thu' tich ve Viet-Nam, 1954–1964. Saigon, National Institute of Administration, 1965. 255p. C, Y

AV12. U.S. MILITARY ASSISTANCE INSTITUTE. LIBRARY. Vietnam; a selected bibliography. Arlington, Va., 1965. 42ℓ C

AV13. POLIN, CHARLOTTE. Recommended books from and about Vietnam. New York, U.S. Committee to aid the National Liberation Front of South Vietnam, 1966. 15p. C

B— PUBLISHED CATALOGS OF LIBRARY RESOURCES
Catalogs of Published Materials

BA— LIBRARIES IN THE UNITED STATES

BA1. U.S. LIBRARY OF CONGRESS. A list of books (with references to periodicals) on the Philippine Islands in the Library of Congress by A. P. C. Griffin. Washington, GPO, 1903. 397p. C, Y
[Reprint of part I of "Bibliography of the Philippine Islands" published as Senate doc. no. 74, 57th Cong. 2d. sess. Part II of that document is "Biblioteca filipina," por T. H. Pardo de Tavera.]

BA2. AYER, EDWARD EVERETT. Books, maps, and manuscripts on the Phillippine [sic] Islands from the library of Mr. Edward E. Ayer, exhibited at the Chicago historical society, December 28-30, 1904. Chicago, 1904. 4p. Y

BA3. AMERICAN ORIENTAL SOCIETY. LIBRARY. Catalog of the library, edited by Elizabeth Strout. New Haven, Yale Univ. Pr., 1930. 308p. C, Y

BA4. IRIKURA, JAMES K. Annotated bibliography of Japanese works on Southeast Asia at the Sterling Library, Yale University. New Haven, 1952. 47ℓ Y

BA5. U.S. LIBRARY OF CONGRESS. ORIENTALIA DIVISION. Southern Asia accessions list. Washington, 1952-60. 9v. C, Y

BA6. OEY, GIOK PO. Survey of Chinese language materials on Southeast Asia in the Hoover Institute and Library. Ithaca, Cornell Univ., Southeast Asia Program, 1953. 73p. (Cornell Univ. Southeast Asia Program. Data Paper no. 8) C, Y

BA7. STANFORD UNIVERSITY. HOOVER INSTITUTION ON WAR, REVOLUTION AND PEACE. Indonesian language publications in the Hoover Library. Stanford, 1953. 21ℓ C

BA8. LIETZ, PAUL S. Calendar of Philippine documents in the Ayer collection of the Newberry Library. Chicago, Newberry Library, 1956. 259p. C, Y

BA9. CORNELL UNIVERSITY. LIBRARIES. A bibliography of Indonesian government documents and selected Indonesian writings on government in the Cornell University Library. Ithaca, Cornell Univ., Southeast Asia Program, 1958. 58ℓ (Cornell Univ., Southeast Asia Program. Data paper, no. 31) C, Y
[Cornell entry: Lev, Daniel Saul.]

BA10. CORNELL UNIVERSITY. SOUTHEAST ASIA PROGRAM. Southeast Asia accessions list. Ithaca, Cornell Univ., Southeast Asia Program, 1959- C, Y

BA11. NEWBERRY LIBRARY, CHICAGO. A catalogue of printed materials relating to the Philippine Islands, 1519-1900 in the Newberry Library compiled by Doris Varner Welsh. Chicago, 1959. 179p. C, Y

BA12. NEW YORK (CITY) PUBLIC LIBRARY. REFERENCE DEPT. Dictionary catalog of the oriental collection. Boston, Hall, 1960. 16v. C, Y
[Cornell entry: New York. Public Library.]

BA13. ECHOLS, JOHN M. A survey of Asian materials in the Syracuse University library with some recommendations. Ithaca, 1961. iii, 33ℓ C

BA14. KEYES, JANE GODFREY. A bibliography of North Vietnamese publications in the Cornell University Library. Ithaca, Cornell Univ., Southeast

Asia Program, 1962. 116p. (Cornell Univ., Southeast Asia Program. Data paper, no. 47) C, Y
[Cornell entry: Keyes, Elizabeth Jane (Godfrey).]

BA15. CORNELL UNIVERSITY. LIBRARIES. Catalogue of Thai language holdings in the Cornell University libraries through 1964, compiled by Frances A. Bernath. Ithaca, Cornell Univ., Southeast Asia Program, 1964. 236p. (Cornell Univ., Southeast Asia Program. Data paper, no. 54) C, Y

BA16. U.S. LIBRARY OF CONGRESS. AMERICAN LIBRARIES BOOK PROCUREMENT CENTER, DJAKARTA. Accessions list, Indonesia. Djakarta, 1964- C, Y

BA17. U.S. LIBRARY OF CONGRESS. ORIENTALIA DIVISION. Southeast Asia subject catalog at the Library of Congress. Washington, 1965. 27 reels of microfilm. C, Y

BA18. KEYES, JANE GODFREY. A bibliography of western language publications concerning North Vietnam in the Cornell University Library; supplement of Data paper 47. Ithaca, Cornell Univ., Southeast Asia Program, 1966. 280p. (Cornell Univ., Southeast Asia Program. Data paper, no. 63) C, Y
[Cornell entry: Keyes, Elizabeth Jane (Godfrey).]

BA19. LEIGH, MICHAEL B. Checklist of holdings on Borneo in the Cornell University libraries. Ithaca, Cornell Univ., Southeast Asia Program, 1966. 62ℓ (Cornell Univ. Southeast Asia Program. Data paper, no. 62) C, Y

BA20. ILLINOIS. NORTHERN ILLINOIS UNIVERSITY, DEKALB. LIBRARY. List of Southeast Asian holdings in the Swen Franklin Parson Library, compiled by the Center for Southeast Asian Studies, Northern Illinois University. DeKalb, 1967. 86ℓ Y

BA21. HARVARD UNIVERSITY. LIBRARY. Southern Asia: Afghanistan, Bhutan, Burma, Cambodia, Ceylon, India, Laos, Malaya, Nepal, Pakistan, Sikkim, Singapore, Thailand, Vietnam. Cambridge, Distributed by Harvard Univ. Pr., 1968. 534p. (Its Widener Library shelflist, 19) C, Y

BA22. ILLINOIS. NORTHERN ILLINOIS UNIVERSITY, DEKALB. LIBRARY. Revised list of Southeast Asia holdings in the Swen Franklin Parson Library, compiled by Southeast Asia Library and Center for Southeast Asian Studies. DeKalb, 1968. 285ℓ Y

See also AI 29

BB—EUROPEAN LIBRARIES, EXCLUDING THE NETHERLANDS

BB1. RETANA Y GAMBOA, WENCESLAO EMILIO. Aparato bibliográfico de la historia general de Filipinas deducido de la colección que posee en Barcelona la Compañia General de Tabacos de dichas islas. Madrid, M. Minuesa de los Rios, 1906. 3v C, Y

BB2. BRITISH MUSEUM. DEPT. OF ORIENTAL PRINTED BOOKS AND MANUSCRIPTS. A catalogue of the Burmese books in the British Museum by L.D. Barnett. London, 1913. 346 columns. C, Y

BB3. SPAIN. ARCHIVO GENERAL DE INDIAS, SEVILLE. Catálogo de los documentos relativos a las islas Filipinas existentes en el Archivo de Indias de Sevilla, pr. d. Pedro Torres y Lanzas. Obra editada por la Compañía general de tabacos de Filipinas como testimonio de afecto al archipiélago Magallánico. Barcelona, Impr. de la viuda de L. Tasso, 1928-34 [i.e. 1936] 5v. in 6. C, Y

BB4. ROYAL COMMONWEALTH SOCIETY, LONDON. LIBRARY. Subject catalogue of the library of the Royal Empire Society, formerly Royal Colonial Institute, by Evans Lewin. London, 1930-37. 4v. C, Y
[v.4 Mediterranean colonies, Middle East, Indian Empire, Burma, Ceylon, British Malaya, East Indian Islands and the Far East.]

BB5. ROYAL ASIATIC SOCIETY OF GREAT BRITAIN AND IRELAND. LIBRARY. Catalogue of printed books published before 1932 in the library. London, 1940. 541p. C, Y

BB6. MADRID. BIBLIOTECA NACIONAL. Catálogo de obras iberoamericans y filipinas de la Biblioteca Nacional de Madrid, redactado y ordenado por Luisa Cuesta, Modersta Cuesta. Madrid, Biblioteca Nacional, 1953. 322p. (Catálogos de archivos y bibliotecas) C, Y

BB7. PARIS. BIBLIOTHÈQUE NATIONALE. DÉPARTEMENT DES MANUSCRITS. Catalogue du fonds khmer, par Au Chieng. Paris, GPO, 1953. 307p. C, Y

BB8. BEATTY, SIR ALFRED CHESTER. A catalogue of the Batak manuscripts, including two Javanese manuscripts and a Balinese painting by P. Voorhoeve. Dublin, Hodges Figgis, 1961. 167p. C, Y

BB9. LONDON. UNIVERSITY. SCHOOL OF ORIENTAL AND AFRICAN STUDIES. LIBRARY. Library catalog. Boston, Hall, 1963. 28v. C, Y

BC—LIBRARIES IN THE NETHERLANDS

BC1. NETHERLANDS (KINGDOM, 1815-) DEPARTEMENT VAN ZAKEN OVERZEE. BIBLIOTHEEK. Catalogus van de boeken en kaarten, uitmakende de bibliotheek van het Departement van Koloniën, met een alphabetisch register. The Hague, 1884. 711p.
Vervolg, 1-3. The Hague, 1887-91. 3v. C

BC2. HAGUE. KOLONIALE BIBLIOTHEEK. Catalogus der Koloniale Bibliotheek van het Kon. Instituut voor de Taal-, Land- en Volkenkunde van Ned. Indië en het Indisch Genootschap, door G. P. Rouffaer en W. C. Muller. The Hague, Nijhoff, 1908. 1053p.
Supplement, door W. C. Muller. The Hague, Nijhoff, 1915-66. 4v. C, Y
[Cornell entry: Instituut voor Taal-, Land- en Volkenkunde.]

BC3. KONINKLIJK INSTITUUT VOOR DE TROPEN. AFDELING TROPISCHE PRODUCTEN. BIBLIOTHEEK, HAARLEM. Catalogus der boekverzameling. Nieuwe uitg. Haarlem, De Erven Loosjes, 1908. 208p. Eerste supplement van Juni 1908 tot Mei 1911. Haarlem, Ketting, 1911. vii, 70p. Y

BC4. NETHERLANDS (KINGDOM, 1815-) DEPARTEMENT VAN ZAKEN OVERZEE. BIBLIOTHEEK. Overzicht van de literatuur betreffende Nieuw-Guinea, aanwezig in de Bibliotheek van het Ministerie voor Uniezaken en Overzeese Rijksdelen. The Hague, 1952-53. 2v. in 1. C, Y

BC5. VROMANS, A. G. De Indische collectie van het Rijksinstituut voor Oorlogsdocumentatie te Amsterdam. Amsterdam, 1955. 39p. C, Y

BC6. NETHERLANDS (KINGDOM, 1815-) RIJKSARCHIEF, THE HAGUE. Collecties 2de afdeling betrekking hebbende op Oost-Indië. The Hague, 1962. 29ℓ Y

BD—LIBRARIES IN BURMA

BD1. BURMA. GOVERNMENT BOOK DEPOT. Catalogue of books and maps in stock at the Government book depot, Rangoon. Rangoon, GPO. v.1- semi-annual. C, Y
[Cornell entry: Burma (Union) Government Book Depot.]

BD2. BURMA. SECRETARIAT LIBRARY, RANGOON. Revised catalogue of books in the Burma secretariat library. Rangoon, 1896. 1v. Y

BD3. BURMA. PUBLIC WORKS DEPT. SECRETARIAT LIBRARY. Catalogue of books, reports, periodicals, etc., in the Burma public works secretariat library. Rangoon, 1900. ii, 58ℓ
Additions and alterations, list no. 1-9, July 1900-July 1902. Y

BD4. THEBAW, KING OF BURMA. Catalogue of Pali and Burmese books and manuscripts belonging to the library of the late King of Burma and found in the palace at Mandalay in 1886. Rangoon, 1910. 113p. C, Y
[Cornell entry: title.]

BD5. BURMA (UNION) HISTORICAL COMMISSION. LIBRARY. A catalogue of Chinese books in the library of the Burma Historical Commission. Rangoon, 1961. 119p. C

BE — LIBRARIES IN INDONESIA

BE1. LEMBAGA KEBUDAJAAN INDONESIA. PERPUSTAKAAN. Lijst van aanwinsten. Batavia. v.1- C

BE2. LEMBAGA KEBUDAJAAN INDONESIA. PERPUSTAKAAN. Tambahan buku2 baru. Acquisitions of new books. Djakarta. v.1- C

BE3. LEMBAGA KEBUDAJAAN INDONESIA. PERPUSTAKAAN. Bibliothecae Societatis artium scientiarumque quae Bataviae floret catalogus systematicus. Bataviae, Lange, 1853. 156p. Y

BE4. LEMBAGA KEBUDAJAAN INDONESIA. PERPUSTAKAAN. Katalogus der boekwerken waarmede 's Genootschaps bibliotheek verrijkt is sedert de laatste opgave, voor komende in dℓ. XXIV(1), opgemaakt door J. Munnich. Batavia, Lange, 1853. 10p. (Verhandelingen van het Bataviaasch Genootschap van Kunsten en Wetenschappen, deel 25, 3. stuk) C

BE5. LEMBAGA KEBUDAJAAN INDONESIA. PERPUSTAKAAN. Catalogus der Bibliotheek van het Bataviaasch Genootschap van Kunsten en Wetenschappen door J. A. van der Chijs. Batavia, Lange, 1864. 487p.
Eerste vervolg catalogus der Bibliotheek en catalogus der Maleische, Javaansche en Kawi handschriften van het Bataviaasch Genootschap van Kunsten en Wetenschappen. Batavia, Bruining & Wijt, 1872. 118, 46p.
Tweede vervolg-catalogus der Bibliotheek van het Bataviaasch Genootschap van Kunsten en Wetenschappen. Batavia, Bruining, 1877. 217p. C, Y
[Cornell entry: Chijs, . . .]

BE6. CHIJS, JACOBUS ANNE VAN DER. Inventaris van 's lands archief te Batavia (1602-1816). Zamengsteld en uitgegeven op last van de Nederlandsch-Indisch regering. Batavia, GPO, 1882. 477p. C, Y
[Cornell entry: Indonesia Arsip Nasional.]

BE7. DUTCH EAST INDIES. ALGEMENE SECRETARIE. Catalogus van de boekerij der Algemeene secretarie. Batavia, GPO, 1899. 291p. Y

BE8. ATJEH EN ONDERHOORIGHEDEN (RESIDENCY). AMBTELIJKE BOEKERIJ, BANDA ATJEH. Catalogus der Ambtelijke Boekerij van het Gewestelijke Bureau te Koeta-Radja. Koeta-Radja, 1915. 29p. (Geschriften over Atjeh, v.5, no. 3) C

BE9. OOSTKUST VAN SUMATRA-INSTITUUT. Catalogus van het Deli-archief. Amsterdam, de Bussy, 1917. 107p. C, Y

BE10. LEMBAGA KEBUDAJAAN INDONESIA. Register op de Verhandelingen van het Bataviaasch Genootschap, deel LVI (5e stuk)- LXI (1907-1919) en het Tijdschrift voor Indische taal-, land- en volkenkunde, deel LI-LVIII (1909-1919). Weltevreden, N.V. uitg. mij. "Papyrus," 1920. 81, 14p. C, Y

BE11. LEMBAGA KEBUDAJAAN INDONESIA. PERPUSTAKAAN. Javaansche bibliographie, gegrond op de boekwerken in die taal- aanwezig in de

BE12. Boekerij van het Bataviaasch Genootschap van Kunsten en Wetenschappen door Poerwa Soewignja en Wirawangsa. Batavia, Bataviaasch Genootschap van Kunsten en Wetenschappen, 1920-21. 2v. C, Y

BE12. MOLUCCAS (RESIDENCY) GEWESTELIJKE BIBLIOTHEEK. Catalogus van de Gewestelijke bibliotheek ten kantore van den Resident der Molukken te Amboina. 2. druk. Amboina, 1937. 304p. C

BE13. LEMBAGA KEBUDAJAAN INDONESIA. PERPUSTAKAAN. Catalogus der bibliotheek, F-G: Geschiedenis. Bandoeng, Nix, 1940. 474 columns. C, Y

BE14. DJAKARTA. CENTRALE NATUURWETENSCHAPPELIJKE BIBLIOTHEEK. Centrale catalogus, samengesteld door W. van der Bragghen. With summaries in English. Batavia, 1948. 42p. (Organisatie voor Natuurwetenschappelijk Onderzoek. Bulletin, no. 2) Supplement. Bandung, 1950. 17p. (Organisation for scientific research. Bulletin, no. 6) Y

BE15. DJAKARTA. PERPUSTAKAAN SEDJARAH POLITIK DAN SOSIAL. Daftar penerbitan pemerintah Republik Indonesia; suatu usaha pertjobaan; dikumpulkan dan disusun dibawah pengawasan Rusina Sjahrial-Pamuntjak. Djakarta, 1964. 56ℓ C, Y

BE16. DJAKARTA. LEMBAGA EKONOMI DAN KEMASJARAKATAN NASIONAL. Katalogus perpustakaan; daftar buku2 dan madjalah, 1963-64. Djakarta, 1965. 1v. C

BF — LIBRARIES IN LAOS

BF1. LUANG PRABANG (CITY) BIBLIOTHÈQUE ROYALE. Catalogue par M. Meillier. Hanoi-Haiphong, Impr. d'Extrême-Orient, 1918. 42ℓ

BG — LIBRARIES IN MALAYSIA-SINGAPORE

BG1. IPOH, MALAYSIA. PUBLIC LIBRARY. Accession list. Ipoh. v.1- C

BG2. RAFFLES MUSEUM AND LIBRARY, SINGAPORE. Catalogue of the Raffles Library, Singapore, 1900. Singapore, American Mission Pr., 1905. 636p. C

BG3. RAFFLES MUSEUM AND LIBRARY, SINGAPORE. A descriptive catalogue of the books relating to Malaysia in the Raffles Museum and Library, Singapore, compiled by Padma Daniel. Singapore, 1941. 125p. (Journal of the Malayan Branch of the Royal Asiatic Society, v.19, pt.3) C, Y

BG4. SINGAPORE (CITY) UNIVERSITY. LIBRARY. Catalogue of the Chinese collection. Singapore, Univ. of Malaya Pr., 1956- C, Y

BG5. SINGAPORE (CITY) NATIONAL LIBRARY. Southeast Asia collection. Singapore, 1964. 15p. C

BG6. SINGAPORE (CITY) UNIVERSITY. LIBRARY. Bibliography of literature on Malaysia in English in the University of Singapore Library. Singapore, 1965. 5ℓ C

BG7. IPOH, MALAYSIA. FREE PUBLIC LIBRARY. Malaysiana Collections. Ipoh, 1967. 102p. C, Y

BG8. NADANASABAPATHY, V. Scientific, technical and agricultural reference works in the University of Malaya Library. Kuala Lumpur, 1967. 78p. C, Y

[Cornell entry: Kuala Lumpur, Malaya. Univ. of Malaya. Library.]

BH — LIBRARIES IN THE PHILIPPINES

BH1. MANILA. NATIONAL LIBRARY. Monthly bulletin. v.1-4; Sept. 1912- Aug. 1916. Manila, GPO, 1912-16. 4v. in 2. Y

BH2. QUEZON, PHILIPPINES. UNIVERSITY OF THE PHILIPPINES. LIBRARY.

	A list of main library books and pamphlets on Southeast Asia. Quezon City, 1957– C
BH3.	QUEZON, PHILIPPINES. UNIVERSITY OF THE PHILIPPINES. LIBRARY. Classified list of Filipiniana books and pamphlets in the main library, University of the Philippines, as of December 1958. Quezon City, Univ. of the Philippines, 1959. 358p. C, Y
BH4.	MANILA. FAR EASTERN UNIVERSITY. LIBRARY. Classified list of Filipiniana books and pamphlets in the Filipiniana Section, Far Eastern University, as of December 1960. Manila, Far Eastern Univ., 1960. 254ℓ C
BH5.	AYALA Y COMPAÑÍA, LIBRARY. Classified list of Filipiniana holdings of the Ayala y Compañía Library as of December 1960. Makati, 1961. x, 74, 35ℓ C
BH6.	LOPEZ MEMORIAL MUSEUM. MANILA. Early Philippine imprints in the Lopez Memorial Museum. Manila, 1961. vii, 45p. C [Cornell entry: Manila. Lopez . . .]
BH7.	LOPEZ MEMORIAL MUSEUM, MANILA. Catalogue of Filipiniana materials in the Lopez Memorial Museum. Manila, 1962– C, Y [Cornell entry: Manila. Lopez . . .]
BH8.	PACIS, MIGUEL B. The Filipiniana division and its books. 4th revision. Vintar, Ilocos, Norte, 1962. 48ℓ Y [Deals with the Philippine Bureau of Public Libraries.]

BI— LIBRARIES IN THAILAND

BI 1.	BANGKOK, NATIONAL LIBRARY. List of the Pali and Sanskrit books and manuscripts in the Vajiranana national library. Bangkok, 1921. 153p. Y

BJ— LIBRARIES IN VIETNAM

BJ1.	SAIGON. HOC-VIEN QUOC-GIA HANH-CHANH. THU-VIEN. Ban tong-ke phan-loai sach thu-vien. Classified catalog of books in the library. 2d. ed. Saigon, 1959. 366p. C
BJ2.	SAIGON. HOC-VIEN QUOC-GIA HANH-CHANG. THU-VIEN. Ban tong-ke phan-loai sach thu-vien. Classified catalog of books in the library. Saigon, 1960. 606p. C
BJ3.	SAIGON. NHA VAN-KHO VA THU-VIEN QUOC GIA. Sach moi. Nouvelles acquisitions. New acquisitions. Saigon, 1962– C, Y

<u>See also</u> HV2

Catalogs of Manuscripts

BL— LIBRARIES IN THE UNITED STATES

BL1.	NEWBERRY LIBRARY, CHICAGO. EDWARD E. AYER COLLECTION. Checklist of manuscripts in the Edward E. Ayer collection, compiled by Ruth Lapham Butler. Chicago, 1937. 295p. C, Y

BM— LIBRARIES IN EUROPE (EXCLUDING THE NETHERLANDS)

BM1.	RETANA Y GAMBOA, WENCESLAO EMILIO. Archivo del bibliofilo filipino; recopilación de documentos históricos, científicos, literarios y políticos y estudios bibliográficos. Madrid, Viuda de M. Minuesa de los Rios, 1895–1905. 5v. C, Y
BM2.	PARIS. BIBLIOTHÈQUE NATIONALE. DEPT. DES MANUSCRITS. Catalogue sommaire des manuscrits indiens, indo-chinois et malayo-

BM3.   polynésiens par Antoine Cabaton. Paris, Leroux, 1912. 319p. C, Y
GT. BRIT. INDIA OFFICE. LIBRARY. Catalogue of the manuscripts in European languages belonging to the library of the India Office. London, Oxford Univ. Pr., 1916-37. 3v. Y

BM4.   GT. BRIT. COMMONWEALTH RELATIONS OFFICE. INDIA OFFICE LIBRARY. Index of post-1937 European manuscript accessions. Boston, Hall 1964. 156p. Y
[A supplement to BM3.]

BM5.   WAINWRIGHT, M. D. A guide to western manuscripts and documents in the British Isles relating to South and Southeast Asia, compiled by M. D. Wainwright and Noel Matthews. London, Oxford Univ. Pr. 1965. 532p. C, Y

BM6.   COPENHAGEN. KONGELIGE BIBLIOTEK. Catalogue of Oriental manuscripts, xylographs, etc. in Danish collections. Copenhagen, Royal Library, 1966- Y
[Vol. 2 pt. 2 Catalogue des manuscrits en pali, laotien et siamois provenant de la Thailande, par George Coedès.]

BN—LIBRARIES IN THE NETHERLANDS

BN1.   LEYDEN. RIJKSUNIVERSITEIT. BIBLIOTHEEK. Catalogus codicum orientalium Bibliothecae Academiae Lugduno Batavae. Lugduni Batavorum, Brill, 1851-77. 6v. C, Y

BN2.   MATTHES, BENJAMIN FREDERIK. Kort verslag aangaande alle mij in Europa bekende Makassaarsche en Boeginesche handschriften, vooral die van het Nederlandsch Bijbelgenootschap te Amsterdam. Amsterdam, Spin, 1875. 101p. C, Y

BN3.   LEYDEN. RIJKSUNIVERSITEIT. BIBLIOTHEEK. Catalogus van de Javaansche en Madoereesche handschriften der Leidsche Universiteitsbibliotheek, door A. C. Vreede. Leiden, Brill, 1892. 434p. Supplement door H. H. Juynboll. Leiden, Brill, 1907-11. 2v. C, Y

BN4.   LEYDEN. RIJKSUNIVERSITEIT. BIBLIOTHEEK. Catalogus van de Maleische en Sundaneesche handschriften der Leidsche universiteitsbibliotheek door dr. H. H. Juynboll. Leiden, Brill, 1899. 356p. C, Y

BN5.   LEYDEN. RIJKSUNIVERSITEIT. BIBLIOTHEEK. Beschrijving der Javaansche, Balineesche en Sasaksche handschriften aangetroffen in de nalatenschap van Dr. H. N. van der Tuuk. Batavia, GPO, 1901-26. 4v. C, Y

BN6.   LEYDEN. RIJKSUNIVERSITEIT. BIBLIOTHEEK. Supplement op den catalogus van de Sundaneesche handschriften en catalogus van de Balineesche en Sasaksche handschriften der Leidsche universiteitsbibliotheek, door H. H. Juynboll. Leiden, Brill, 1912. 224p. Y

BN7.   LEYDEN. RIJKSUNIVERSITEIT. BIBLIOTHEEK. Supplement-catalogus der Maleische en Minangkabausch handschriften in de Leidsche universiteits-bibliotheek, door Dr. Ph. S. van Ronkel. Leiden, Brill, 1921. 316p. C, Y
[Supplements BN4.]

BN8.   RONKEL, PHILLIPUS SAMUEL VAN. Bericht aangaande de jongste aanwinst van Maleische handschriften in het buitenland (Cambridge). Amsterdam, 1925. 16p. (Koninklijke Akademie van Wetenschappen. Afdeeling Letterkunde. Mededeeling. Deel 59, ser. A. no.8) Y

BN9.   LEYDEN. RIJKSUNIVERSITEIT. BIBLIOTHEEK. Catalogus van de boeginese, tot de La Galigo-cyclus behorende handschriften van Jajasan

Matthes (Matthesstichting) te Makassar (Indonesia) door R. A. Kern. Makassar, Jajasan Matthes, 1954. 268p. C, Y
[Cornell entry: Kem, R.A.]

BN10. INSTITUUT VOOR TAAL-, LAND- EN VOLKENKUNDE. Catalogus van de handschriften in Westerse talen toebehorende aan het Koninklijk Instituut voor Taal-, Land- en Volkenkunde. The Hague, Nijhoff, 1963. 169p. C

BN11. INSTITUUT VOOR TAAL-, LAND- EN VOLKENKUNDE. Catalogus van de handschriften in Westerse talen toebehorende aan het Koninklijk Instituut voor Taal-, Land- en Volkenkunde. The Hague, Nijhoff, 1963. 172p. C

BN12. PIGEAUD, THEODOOR. Literature of Java, catalogue raisonné of Javanese manuscripts in the library of the University of Leiden and other public collections in the Netherlands. Leiden, 1967- 3v. (Codices manuscripti, Univ. of Leiden 9) C, Y

BP— LIBRARIES IN SOUTHEAST ASIA (EXCLUDING INDONESIA)

BP1. SAIGON. VIEN KHAO CO. Liste des microfilms reçus de L'EFEO. Saigon, 19?? 27ℓ C

BP2. KÉNE, THAO. Catalogue des manuscrits de la littérature du Laos. Vientiane, Comité littéraire lao, Ministère de l'education nationale, 1958. 43ℓ (Éditions du Comité littéraire) C

BP3. SINGAPORE (CITY) UNIVERSITY. LIBRARY. List of students' theses deposited in the University Library. Singapore, 1962. 16ℓ C
[Cornell entry: Singapore. University. Library.]

BP4. SINGAPORE (CITY) UNIVERSITY. LIBRARY. Microfilm holdings in the field of Southeast Asia Studies (non-scientific), 1963. Singapore, 1963. 11ℓ C

BP5. KUALA LUMPUR, MALAYA. UNIVERSITY OF MALAYA. Malay manuscripts; a bibliographical guide compiled by Joseph H. Howard. Kuala Lumpur, 1966. 96p. C, Y
[Cornell entry: Howard, Joseph H.]

BR— LIBRARIES IN INDONESIA

BR1. LEMBAGA KEBUDAJAAN INDONESIA. PERPUSTAKAAN. Codicum arabicorum in bibliotheca Societatis artium et scientiarum quae Bataviae floret asservatorum catalogum, inchoatum a doct. R. Friederich. Batavia, Bruining & Wijt, 1873. 154p.
Supplement. Batavia, Albrect, 1913. 554p. C, Y

BR2. BERG, LODEWIJK WILLEM CHRISTIAAN VAN DEN. Verslag van eene verzameling Maleische, Arabische, Javaansche en andere handschriften, door de regeering van Nederlandsch Indië aan het Bataviaasch Genootschap van Kunsten en Wetenschappen ter bewaring afgestaan. Batavia, Bruining, 1877. xi, 62p. C, Y

BR3. LEMBAGA KEBUDAJAAN INDONESIA. MUSEUM. Catalogus der Maleische handschriften in het Museum van het Bataviaasch Genootschap van Kunsten en Wetenschappen door S. van Ronkel. Batavia, Albrecht, 1909. 546p. (Verhandelingen van het Koninklijk Bataviaasch Genootschap van Kunsten en Wetenschappen, deel 57) C

BR4. NATUURWETENSCHAPPELIJKE RAAD VOOR NEDERLANDSCH-INDIË. Catalogue of manuscripts, old curious and more recent and richly illustrated books concerning the study of science in the Dutch East Indies, exhibited in the Technical high school at Bandoeng for the occasion of the fourth Pacific science congress to be held in that city from May 18th to 25th, 1929. Compiled and described by Dr. H. C. A. Muller. Weltevreden, Emmink, 1929. 38p. Y

BR5. POERBATJARAKA, RADEN MAS NGABEI. Beschrijving der handschriften. Bandung, Nix, 1940. 114p. Y

BR6. POERBATJARAKA, RADEN MAS NGABEI. Indonesische handschriften. Bandung, Nix, 1950. 207p. C, Y
[Cornell entry: Purbatjaraka, . . .]

C—NEWSPAPER AND PERIODICAL GUIDES

CA—GENERAL GUIDES TO THE AREA

CA1. CROW, CARL, INC., FIRM, ADVERTISING AGENTS, SHANGHAI. Newspaper directory of China (including Hong Kong) with check list of newspapers and periodicals published in Japan, Chosen, Java, Sumatra, Borneo, Siam, Singapore and Federated Malay States. Shanghai, Crow, 1931– C, Y

CA2. RANGANATHAN, SHIYALI RAMAMRITA. Union catalogue of learned periodical publications in South Asia, published with the assistance of UNESCO. Delhi, Indian Library Assoc., 1953– (Indian Library Association. English ser. 7) C
[Lists holdings in libraries of Indonesia, Malaya, Thailand, and Burma.]

CA3. KOKURITSU KOKKAI TOSHAKAN. TOKYO. IPPAN KOSABU. List of periodicals published in the Southeast Asia, British Borneo, Cambodia, Ceylon, Hongkong, India, Indonesia, Laos, Malaya, Pakistan, Philippines, Singapore, Thailand, and Viet-Nam. Tokyo, 1954. 117p. C

CA4. LONDON. UNIVERSITY. SCHOOL OF ORIENTAL AND AFRICAN STUDIES. LIBRARY. The Far East and Southeast Asia; cumulated list of periodical articles. London, 1954/55– C, Y
[An annual cumulation kept up to date by monthly issues entitled: Monthly list of periodical articles on the Far East and Southeast Asia.]

CA5. BEHN, HANS ULRICH. Presse/Rundfunk/Fernsehen in Asien und Afrika; eine Bibliographie in-und ausländischer Fachliteratur (Zeitschriftenartikel, Monographien, Bücher), zusammengestellt und erläutert von Hans Ulrich Behn. Bonn, 1965. 117ℓ (Studien und Berichte aus dem Forschungsinstitut der Friedrich-Ebert-Stiftung) C, Y

CA6. FEUEREISEN, FRITZ. Die Presse in Asien und Ozeanien; ein Handbuch für Wirtschaft und Werbung. Bearb. von Fritz Feuereisen und Ernst Schmacke. München-Pullach, Verlag Dokumentation, 1968. 303p. Y

CA7. NANYANG UNIVERSITY, SINGAPORE. NAN-YANG YEN CHIU SO. Index to Chinese periodical literature on Southeast Asia, 1905–1966. Singapore, Institute of Southeast Asia, Nanyang University, 1968. 363p. Y

CB—BURMA

CB1. BURMA (UNION) MINISTRY OF INFORMATION. Notes of foreign publications. Washington, Dept. of State, 1950. 6ℓ C
[List of the newspapers and periodicals published in Burma in the English, Burmese, Chinese, Urdu, Hindi, Tamil, and Telegu languages.]

CI—INDONESIA

CI 1. INDONESIA. DEPARTEMEN PENERANGAN. Daftar harian dan madjalah seluruh Indonesia. Djakarta, v.1– C, Y

CI 2. Repertorium op de literatuur betreffende de Nederlandsche Koloniën, voor zoover zij verspreid is in tijdschriften en mengelwerken, samengesteld door Alexander Hartmann. The Hague, Nijhoff, 1895. 454p. 8 supplements issued 1901–35. C, Y

CI 3. LEMBAGA KEBUDAJAAN INDONESIA. Register op de artikelen voorkomende in het Tijdschrift voor Indische taal-, land- en volkenkunde, en de Verhandelingen van het Bataviaasch genootschap van kunsten en wetenschappen, loopende tot het jaar 1907, benevens eene inhoudsopgave tevens

	prijslijst van 's Genootschaps uitgaven bijgewerkt tot Juni 1908, door D. van Hinloopen Labberton. Batavia, Albrecht, 1908. 3, 276, 98p. C, Y
CI 4.	Nijhoff's index op Nederlandse en Vlaamse periodieken. The Hague, Nijhoff, 1909- Y [Title varies.]
CI 5.	LEMBAGA KEBUDAJAAN INDONESIA. Inhoudsopgave der Javaansche couranten in de bibliotheek van het Bataviaasch Genootschap van Kunsten en Wetenschappen, door Raden Poerwa Soewignja. Batavia, Drukkerij Papyrus, 1911. 156p. C
CI 6.	NETHERLANDS (KINGDOM, 1815-) REGERINGSVOORLICHTINGSDIENST, DJAKARTA. Perslijst Indonesië; een nominatieve opgave van in Indonesië verschijnende periodieken. List of publications; list of dailies and periodicals published in Indonesia. Batavia, GPO, 1948-49. 2v. C
CI 7.	AMSTERDAM. RIJKSINSTITUUT VOOR OORLOGSDOCUMENTATIE. Voorlopige lijst van tidjschriften dag en nieuwsbladen, Indische collectie. Amsterdam, 1954. 31ℓ C
CI 8.	CORNELL UNIVERSITY. LIBRARY. Bibliography of Indonesian publications: newspapers, non-government periodicals and bulletins, 1945-58 at Cornell University compiled by Benedict R. Anderson. Ithaca, Southeast Asia Program, Cornell Univ., 1959. 69p. (Cornell Univ. Southeast Asia Program. Data paper, no. 33) C, Y [Cornell entry: Anderson, Benedict R.]
CI 9.	Index of Indonesian learned periodicals. Indeks madjalah ilmiah. Djakarta, 1960- annual. Y [1960-65 issued as Madjelis Ilmu Pengetahuan Indonesia; 1966- as Pusat Dokumentasi Ilmiah Nasional.] [Title varies: 1960, Indonesian scientific periodical index.]
CI 10.	INDONESIA. BIRO PERPUSTAKAAN. Checklist of serials in Indonesian libraries. Katalogus induk sementara madjalah pada perpustakaan di Indonesia. Djakarta, 1962. 3v. C, Y
CI 11.	CORNELL UNIVERSITY. LIBRARIES. A guide to Indonesian serials, 1945-65 in the Cornell University Library by Yvonne Thung and John M. Echols. Ithaca, Cornell Univ. Modern Indonesia Program, 1966. 151p. (Cornell Univ. Modern Indonesia Project. Bibliography series) C, Y [Cornell entry: Thung, Yvonne.]

See also VI 13, VI 14, VI 15

CM— GUIDES TO MALAYSIA-SINGAPORE

CM1.	SINGAPORE. MINISTRY OF CULTURE. Digest of Malay, Chinese and Tamil press. Singapore. v.1- weekly. C
CM2.	SINGAPORE. PUBLIC RELATIONS OFFICE. Singapore news summary. Singapore, 1953- C
CM3.	SINGAPORE. PUBLIC RELATIONS OFFICE. Weekly digest of non-English press. Singapore, 1953- C
CM4.	KUALA LUMPUR, MALAYA. RUBBER RESEARCH INSTITUTE OF MALAYA. LIBRARY. List of journal holdings. Kuala Lumpur, 1960. 1v. C
CM5.	ROFF, WILLIAM R. Guide to Malay periodicals, 1876-1941, with details of known holdings in Malaya. Singapore, 1961. 46p. (Papers on Southeast Asian subjects, no. 4) C, Y
CM6.	SINGAPORE (CITY) UNIVERSITY. LIBRARY. Checklist of current serials, April 1962. Singapore, 1962. 85p. C, Y
CM7.	HAZRA, NIRANJAN K. Malaysian serials; a checklist of current official series of the Malaysian Government by Niranjan K. Hazra and Edwin Lee

Siew Cheng. Singapore, Univ. of Singapore, Center for Southeast Asia Studies in the Social Sciences, 1963. 18p. C

CM8. SINGAPORE (CITY) UNIVERSITY. LIBRARY. List of English, Chinese, Malay and Arabic newspapers in the library of the University of Singapore. Singapore, 1963. 5ℓ C

CM9. SARAWAK. INFORMATION SERVICE. Sarawak newspapers, 1964. Kuching, 1964. 19ℓ C

CM10. SINGAPORE (CITY) POLYTECHNIC. LIBRARY. List of current periodicals. Singapore, 1964. 22p. C

CM11. KUALA LUMPUR, MALAYA. UNIVERSITY OF MALAYA. Guide to current Malaysian serials, compiled by L. J. Harris. Kuala Lumpur, Univ. of Malaya Library, 1967. xi, 73p. Y

CM12. SINGAPORE (CITY) UNIVERSITY. LIBRARY. Checklist of current serials in the University of Singapore Library, 1967. Singapore, 1967. 109p. C

CP— PHILIPPINES

CP1. AYER, FIRM, NEWSPAPER ADVERTISING AGENTS, PHILADELPHIA. N. W. Ayer and Son's directory of newspapers and periodicals. Philadelphia, Ayer, 1880– annual. C, Y
[Special supplement beginning 1903 lists Philippine newspapers.]

CP2. RETANA Y GAMBOA, WENCESLAO EMILIO. El periodismo filipino. Noticias para su historia (1811–94). Apuntes bibliográficos, indicaciones biográficas, notas críticas, semblanzas, anécdotas. Madrid, Minuesa de los Rios, 1895. 646, 2p. C, Y

CP3. QUEZON, PHILIPPINES. UNIVERSITY OF THE PHILIPPINES. INSTITUTE OF PUBLIC ADMINISTRATION. Union list of serials of selected special libraries in the Philippines. Prelim. listing. Manila, 1953. 192ℓ C, Y
[Cornell entry: Quezon, Philippines. Univ. of the Philippines. Interdepartmental reference service.]

CP4. PHILIPPINES (REP.) INSTITUTE OF NATIONAL LANGUAGE. Tagalog periodical literature, compiled by Teodoro A. Agoncillo. Manila, 1953. 264p. C, Y

CP5. QUEZON, PHILIPPINES. UNIVERSITY OF THE PHILIPPINES. INTERDEPARTMENTAL REFERENCE SERVICE. Index to Philippine periodicals. Manila, 1955/56– C, Y
[Cornell entry: title]

CP6. QUEZON, PHILIPPINES. UNIVERSITY OF THE PHILIPPINES. INSTITUTE OF PUBLIC ADMINISTRATION. Union list of serials of government agency libraries of the Philippines. Manila, 1955. 623p. C, Y
[See note CP3.]

CP7. HART, DONN V. An annotated guide to current Philippine periodicals by Donn V. Hart and Quintin A. Eala. New Haven, Southeast Asia Studies, Yale Univ., 1957. 116p. (Yale Univ. Graduate School. Southeast Asia Studies. Bibliography Series, no. 4) C, Y

CP8. QUEZON, PHILIPPINES. UNIVERSITY OF THE PHILIPPINES. INSTITUTE OF PUBLIC ADMINISTRATION. Union list of serials of government agency libraries of the Philippines. Rev. and enl. ed. Manila, 1960. 911 p. C, Y
[See note CP3.]

CP9. ILUSTRACIÓN FILIPINA, PERIÓDICO QUINCENAL. (INDEXES). Index to Ilustración filipina; an author and subject index, March 1859–Dec. 1860, compiled by Isagani R. Medina. Quezon City, Library, Univ. of the Philip-

	pines Library. Research guide, no. 2) C. Y
CP10.	CASTRO, JOSE LUNA. The Manila Times journalism manual. Manila, Manila Times, 1963. 331p. C, Y
CP11.	QUEZON, PHILIPPINES. UNIVERSITY OF THE PHILIPPINES. LIBRARY. Union checklist of Filipiniana serials in the libraries of the University of the Philippines, as of 1962. Quezon City, 1963. 287ℓ (<u>Its</u> research guide, no. 3) C, Y
CP12.	SAITO, SHIRO. Philippine newspapers in selected American libraries; a union list. Honolulu, East-West Center Library, 1966. xi, 46ℓ (Hawaii. University. East-West Center. Library. Occasional papers, no. 6) C, Y

CT — THAILAND

CT1.	U.S. INFORMATION SERVICE, BANGKOK. English digest, The Bangkok Chinese press. Bangkok, 1957– C

CV — VIETNAM

CV1.	NGUYEN-XUAN-DAO. Bibliography of periodicals published in Viet Nam prepared by Nguyen Xuan Dao and Richard K. Gardner. East Lansing, Michigan State Univ., 1958. 8ℓ C
CV2.	PARKS, ORAL E. Recent articles on Vietnam, an annotated bibliography by O. E. Parks and M.J. Reban. East Lansing, Michigan State Univ., Vietnam Project, 1958. 25p. C
CV3.	Tin sach. Saigon, Trung-Tam VanBut Viet-Nam. v.1– monthly. C, Y [Title varies: –June 1964, Nguyet san tin sach.]
CV4.	TRAN-THI-KIMSA. Muc-luc Phan-tich tap-chi Viet-ngu, 1954–1964. A guide to Vietnamese periodical literature, 1954–1964. Saigon, Hoc-vien Quoc-gia Hanh-chanh, 1965. 318p. C, Y

D — BIOGRAPHIES

DA — GENERAL BIOGRAPHIES

DA1. SOUTHEAST ASIA DEVELOPMENT ADVISORY GROUP. Directory. New York, Asia Society. v.1- C, Y

DA2. FOREIGN AREA FELLOWSHIP PROGRAM. Directory, foreign area fellows. New York, 1952/59- C, Y

DA3. Asia who's who. Hong Kong, Pan-Asia Newspaper Alliance, 1957- C, Y

DA4. VALENZUELA, WILFREDO P. Know them; a book of biographies. Manila, Dotela, 1958- Y

DA5. ROYAL COMMONWEALTH SOCIETY. LIBRARY. Biography catalogue of the library of the Royal Commonwealth society by Donald H. Simpson. London, 1961. 511p. C, Y

DB — BURMA

DB1. BURMA. Quarterly civil list for Burma. Rangoon, 18?? Y

DB2. India office and Burma office list. London, Harrison, 18?? C, Y

DB3. Who's who in India, Burma and Ceylon, edited and compiled by Thomas Peters. 9th ed. Poona, Sun, 1938. 818, 48, xxiiip. Y

DB4. Who's who in Burma. Rangoon, People's literature committee and house, 1961- triennial. C, Y

DC — CAMBODIA

DC1. Personalités du Cambodge. Phnom-Penh, Réalités Cambodgiennes, 1963- annual. C

DC2. Les élites khmères. Phnom-Penh, Université bouddhique Preah Sihanouk Raj, 1965. 195p. (Culture et civilisation, no. 8) C

DH — INDOCHINA

DH1. BREBION, ANTOINE. Dictionnaire de bio-bibliographie générale, ancienne et moderne de l'Indochine française. Paris, Société d' Éditions Géographiques, Maritimes, et Coloniales, 1935. 446p. (Académie des sciences coloniales. Annales. Tome 8) C, Y

DH2. U.S. DEPT. OF STATE. OFFICE OF INTELLIGENCE AND RESEARCH ANALYSIS. Biographical information on prominent nationalist leaders in French Indochina. Washington, 1945. 90p. (Its R & A 3336) C, Y

DI — INDONESIA

DI 1. Almanak en naamregister van Nederlandsch Indie voor het jaar. Batavia. v.1- C

DI 2. Naam- en ranglijst der officieren van het Nederlandsche leger en van dat in Nederlandsch Oost-Indië, alsmede van de landmacht in West-Indië. Gorinchem, Noorduyn. v.1- annual. Y

DI 3. Naam-boek der hoge Indische regeering te Batavia en daar buiten. Mitsgaders van de ambtenaren en bedienden, zoo als dezelve in weezen waaren op den laatsten December 1804. Als mede van de gouverneurs, directeurs, commandeurs en verdere opperhoofden en mindere bedienden by de respective comptoiren in Indië. Benevens de lysten van de persoonen die gerepatrieerd, of naar de buiten comptoiren vertrokken, of overleden zyn. Amsterdam, Gulik, 1805. 173p. C

DI 4.   LEMBAGA KEBUDAJAAN INDONESIA. Naamlijst der leden van het Bataviaasch Genootschap van Kunsten en Wetenschappen. Batavia, Lange, 1849. 9p. (Verhandelingen van het Bataviaasch Genootschap van Kunsten en Wetenschappen, deel 22, 2. stuk) C

DI 5.   LEMBAGA KEBUDAJAAN INDONESIA. Naamlijst der leden van het Bataviaasch Genootschap van Kunsten en Wetenschappen. Batavia, Lange, 1852. 8p. (Verhandelingen van het Bataviaasch Genootschap van Kunsten en Wetenschappen, deel 24, 3. stuk) C

DI 6.   LEMBAGA KEBUDAJAAN INDONESIA. Naamlijst der leden van het Bataviaasch Genootschap van Kunsten en Wetenschappen. Batavia, Lange, 1853. 6p. (Verhandelingen van het Bataviaasch Genootschap van Kunsten en Wetenschappen, deel 25, 2. stuk) C

DI 7.   BRUIJN, CASPAR ADAM LAURENS VAN TROOSTENBURG DE. Biographisch woordenboek van Oost-Indische predikanten. Nijmegen, Milborn, 1893. 521p. Y

DI 8.   HOUTEN, H. VAN. Bepalingen op het houden der registers van den burgerlijken stand in Nederlandsch-Indië. n.p. 1912. 313p. C

DI 9.   WALL, VICTOR IDO VAN DE. Indische landhuizen en hun geschiedenis. Batavia, Kolff, 1932. 1v. C, Y

DI 10. BLOYS VAN TRESLONG PRINS, PAUL CONSTANT. Genealogische en heraldische gedenkwaardigheden betreffende Europeanen op Java. Batavia, Albrecht, 1934–39. 4v. C, Y

DI 11. De Indische navorscher. Batavia, 1934– monthly. Y

DI 12. Orang Indonesia jang terkemoeka di Djawa. Djakarta, Gunseikanbu, 1944. 552p. C, Y

DI 13. NETHERLANDS (KINGDOM, 1815–) REGEERINGSVOORLICHTINGSDIENST, DJAKARTA. Personalia van staatkundige eenheden (Regeringen Volksvertegenwoordiging) in Indonesië. Batavia, 1949. 62p. C

DI 14. TJIPTONING. Apa dan siapa. Jogjakarta, Kedaulatan Rakjat, 1951. 173p. C, Y

DI 15. COLORADO. UNIVERSITY. INSTITUTE OF ASIATIC AFFAIRS. Directory of Chinese personal names in Indonesia. Washington, External Research Staff, Office of Intelligence Research, Dept. of State, 1953. 117p. Key to romanization of Chinese personal names in Indonesia. n.p. 195? 33p. C, Y

DI 16. Dimanakah alamatnja? Sukabumi, Riaks, 1955. 98p. C

DI 17. PARLAUNGAN. Hasil rakjat memilih tokoh-tokoh parlemen. Hasil pemilihan umum pertama, 1955 di Republik Indonesia. Djakarta, Gita, 1956. 429p. C, Y

DI 18. INDONESIA. KEMENTERIAN PENERANGAN. List of members of the Provisional Supreme Advisory Council and members of the National Planning Council. Djakarta, 1959. 4p. (Its Special release on current Indonesian affairs, no. 75)

DI 19. KOCH, DANIEL MARCELLUS GEORGE. Batig slot; figuren uit het oude Indië. Amsterdam, De Brug-Djambatan, 1960. 212p. (Van gisteren tot morgen, 3) C, Y

See also HI 1.

DL— LAOS

DL1.   LAOS (KINGDOM) MINISTÈRE DES AFFAIRES ÉTRANGÈRES. DIRECTION DU PROTOCOLE. Liste des personnalités lao. Vientiane. v.1–
        C

DL2. SITHIBOURN, SITHAT. Biographies des personnalités du Royaume du Laos. Vientiane, 1960. 1v. C

DM — MALAYSIA-SINGAPORE

DM1. Directory of the State of Singapore including trade index and biographical section. London. v.1– C

DM2. KUCHING, SARAWAK. RURAL DISTRICT COUNCIL. List of councillors and meetings. Kuching. v.1– Y

DM3. MALAYA (FED.) Staff list. Kuala Lumpur. v.1– annual. C, Y

DM4. Personages in Malaysia and Singapore. Kuala Lumpur, The Ford Foundation. v.1– C

DM5. ROTARY INTERNATIONAL DISTRICT 46. Directory. Penang, Rotary Club of Penang. v.1– Y

DM6. SABAH. Civil service staff list; divisions I & II. Jesselton. v.1– annual. Y

DM7. SABAH. Directory; legislative assembly, cabinet, ministries, councils, boards, committees, etc. Jesselton. v.1– C

DM8. SARAWAK. Government staff list. Kuching. v.1– C, Y
[Cornell entry for title: Staff list.]

DM9. SINGAPORE. Directory of Istana Negara, judicial, cabinet, Legislative Assembly, Public Service Commission, audit, ministries, Industrial Arbitration Court, statutory boards, advisory committees, universities, polytechnic, Commonwealth representatives and foreign consuls. Singapore. v.1– C, Y
[Title varies: Distribution of work in government offices, councils, consulates and University of Malaya.]

DM10. SINGAPORE. COLONIAL SECRETARY'S OFFICE. Singapore establishment staff list. Singapore. v.1– Y

DM11. Singapore and Straits directory containing also directories of the Federated Malay States: Perak, Selangor, Negri Sembilan, and Pahang; Johore, Labuan, Brunei, British North Borneo, Sarawak, Sumatra (east coast), western and south-eastern Dutch Borneo, Riouw and dependencies, Saigon, Siam and Kedah. Singapore. v.1– annual. C

DM12. HALE, ABRAHAM. List of Malay proper names. Kuala Lumpur, GPO, 1925. 1, 1, 20p. Y

DM13. Biographies of prominent Chinese in Singapore, compiled under the direction of Victor Sim. Singapore, Nan Kok, 1950. 111, 111p. C

DM14. COLORADO. UNIVERSITY. INSTITUTE OF ASIATIC AFFAIRS. Directory of Chinese personal names in Singapore. Washington, Reproduced and distributed by External Research Staff, Office of Intelligence Research, Dept. of State, 1953. 236p. C, Y

DM15. Who's who in Malaysia. Kuala Lumpur, 1956– C, Y
[Title varies: 1956–1959/60. The leaders of Malaya and who's who.]

DM16. SINGAPORE. MINISTRY OF CULTURE. Biography service. Singapore, 1959–65. 1v. C

DM17. SARAWAK. INFORMATION SERVICE. Sarawak who's who. Kuching, 196? 25 C

DM18. SARAWAK ASSOCIATION. List of members, 1962. Kuching, 1962. 17p. C

DM19. MALAYSIA. PARLIAMENT. Names, addresses and telephone numbers of President and Members of Dewan Negara (Senate), Mr. Speaker and Members of Dewan Ra'ayat (House of Representatives). Kuala Lumpur, 1964–65. 6p. 16 C

DM20.   MALAYSIA. PARLIAMENT. SENATE. Names, addresses and telephone numbers of president and members of Dewan Negara, as at 20th Nov. 1964. Kuala Lumpur, 1964. 6ℓ C

DM21.   NATIONAL CHAMBER OF MALAYSIAN MANUFACTURES. Directory. Kuala Lumpur, 1964– Y

DM22.   SARAWAK. INFORMATION SERVICE. Lists of Sarawak councillors and report on the general elections 1963. Kuching, 1964. 50, 12, 3p. C

DM23.   MALAYSIA. PARLIAMENT. HOUSE OF REPRESENTATIVES. Names, addresses and telephone numbers of Mr. Speaker and members, as of 7th April, 1965. Kuala Lumpur, 1965. 17ℓ C

DP—PHILIPPINES

DP1.   Almanaque filipino i guia de forasteros para el año. Manila. v.1– C

DP2.   Guia de forasteros en Filipinas. Manila, Miguel Sanchez. v.1– C, Y
[Cornell entry: Calendario, manual, y guia de forasteros de las Islas Filipinas para el año.]

DP3.   PHILIPPINE ISLANDS. BUREAU OF CIVIL SERVICE. Official roster of officers and employees in the civil service of the Philippine Islands. Manila, GPO. v.1– C, Y

DP4.   PHILIPPINE ISLANDS. LEGISLATURE, 1916– HOUSE OF REPRESENTATIVES. Directorio oficial de la Cámara de representantes. Manila, GPO. v.1– Y

DP5.   PHILIPPINES (COMMONWEALTH) NATIONAL ASSEMBLY. HOUSE OF REPRESENTATIVES. Directorio Oficial. Manila, GPO. v.1– Y

DP6.   PHILIPPINES (REP.) COMMISSION ON ELECTIONS. List of female officials-elect. Manila. v.1– C

DP7.   Up-to-date Manila residential directory. Manila, Garcia. v.1– C, Y

DP8.   PHILIPPINE ISLANDS. BUREAU OF EDUCATION. List of Philippine baptismal names. Manila, GPO, 1905. 16p. (Its Bulletin, no. 9, 1905) Y

DP9.   PHILIPPINE ISLANDS. BUREAU OF EDUCATION. Official roster of the Bureau of education, corrected to March 1, 1906. Manila, GPO, 1906. 39p. (Its bulletin no. 25) Y

DP10.   PHILIPPINE ISLANDS. BUREAU OF CONSTABULARY. Official constabulary register for 1915. Manila, GPO, 1915. 1v Y

DP11.   NELLIST, GEORGE FERGUSON MITCHELL. Men of the Philippines, a biographical record of men of substantial achievement in the Philippine islands. Manila, Sugan News, 1931. 1v. C, Y

DP12.   NATIONAL RESEARCH COUNCIL OF THE PHILIPPINE ISLANDS. Report. Manila, 1935– Y
[List of charter members included in the report.]

DP13.   Who's who in the Philippines. A biographical dictionary of notable living men of the Philippine Islands. Manila, McCullough, 1936/37– Y

DP14.   PHILIPPINES (COMMONWEALTH) NATIONAL ASSEMBLY. Directorio oficial de la Asamblea nacional. Manila, GPO, 1938– Y

DP15.   PHILIPPINES (REP.) OFFICE OF PUBLIC INFORMATION. Official directory. Manila, GPO, 1946– C, Y

DP16.   PHILIPPINES (REP.) CONGRESS. HOUSE OF REPRESENTATIVES. Official directory. Manila, GPO, 1946/49– C, Y

DP17.   COLORADO. UNIVERSITY. INSTITUTE OF ASIATIC AFFAIRS. Directory of Chinese personal names in the Philippines. Washington, Reproduced and distributed by External Research Staff, Office of Intelligence

DP18.   Research, Dept. of State, 1953. 172p. (External research paper, no. 110) C, Y

DP18.   MANUEL, E. ARSENIO. Dictionary of Philippine biography. Quezon City, Filipiniana, 1955– C, Y

DP19.   Philippines who's who. Quezon City, Capitol, 1957– C, Y
[Cornell entry: Retizos, Isidoro L.]

DP20.   DAGUIO, ALFREDO O. Elective officials of the Philippines. Manila, Metro, 1963. 223p. C

DP21.   NICANOR, PRECIOSO M. Profiles of notable Filipinos in the U.S.A. New York, Pre-Mer, 1963– C, Y

DP22.   Philippine government elective officials. Manila, URERA, 1964– C, Y

DP23.   QUEZON, PHILIPPINES. UNIVERSITY OF THE PHILIPPINES. U.P. biographical directory. Quezon City, 1964– Y

DP24.   GARCIA, MAURO. Philippine pseudonyms, aliases, pen names, pet names, screen names and name aberrations. Manila, Bibliographical society of the Philippines, 1965. 157p. (Bibliographical society of the Philippines. Occasional papers, no. 4) C, Y

DP25.   PHILIPPINE COLLEGE OF SURGEONS, MANILA. Directory. Manila, 1966. 86p. Y

DP26.   The Philippine officials review. Pasay City, M & M, 1967– Y

DP27.   Women of distinction; biographical essays on outstanding Filipino women of the past and the present. Manila, 1967. 243p. Y

DT — THAILAND

DT1.   U.S. EMBASSY. THAILAND. Directory of American personnel, Embassy of the United States of America and U.S. Information Service Bangkok, Thailand. Bangkok. v.1– C

DT2.   COLORADO. UNIVERSITY. INSTITUTE OF ASIATIC AFFAIRS. Directory of Chinese personal names in Bangkok. Boulder, 1952. 147p. C, Y

DV — VIETNAM

DV1.   Who's who in Vietnam. Saigon, Vietnam Press, 1967. 1v. C, Y

E — ALMANACS, ENCYCLOPEDIAS, HANDBOOKS, AND OTHER GENERAL COMPENDIUMS OF INFORMATION

EA — GENERAL

EA1. HAMILTON, WALTER. A geographical, statistical and historical description of Hindostan, and the adjacent countries. London, 1820. 2v. C, Y

EA2. CRAWFURD, JOHN. A descriptive dictionary of the Indian islands and adjacent countries. London, Bradbury and Evans, 1856. 459p. C, Y

EA3. BALFOUR, EDWARD GREEN. Cyclopaedia of India and of eastern and southern Asia, commercial, industrial and scientific; products of the mineral, vegetable and animal kingdoms, useful arts and manufactures. Madras, 1857. 1v. Y

EA4. Directory and chronicle for China, Japan, Straits Settlements, Malaya, Siam, Korea, Indo-China, Netherlands Indies, Borneo, the Philippines with which are incorporated The China directory, The Hong Kong directory and Hong list for the Far East. Hong Kong, Hongkong Daily Pr., 1866-1941. annual. C, Y

EA5. BALFOUR, EDWARD GREEN. The cyclopaedia of India and of eastern and southern Asia, commercial, industrial, and scientific; products of the mineral, vegetable, and animal kingdoms, useful arts and manufactures. 3d ed. London, Quaritch, 1885. 3v. Y

EA6. YULE, HENRY. Hobson-Jobson; a glossary of colloquial Anglo-Indian words and phrases, and of kindred terms, etymological, historical, geographical and discursive, by Sir Henry Yule and A. C. Burnell. New edition by William Crooke. London, Murray, 1903. 1021p. C, Y

EA7. Asian annual; the "Eastern World" handbook. London, Eastern World, 1954- annual. C, Y

EA8. Worldmark encyclopedia of the nations: a practical guide to the geographic, historical, political, social and economic status of all nations, their international relationships, and the United Nations system. New York, Worldmark Pr., Harper, 1963. 5v. C, Y
[v.2. Asia and Australia]

EB — BURMA

EB1. BURMA (UNION) MINISTRY OF INFORMATION. Burma facts and figures. v.1- C

EB2. Thacker's Indian directory including Burma and Ceylon. Thacker's press and directories. v.1- Y

EB3. BURMA, LOWER. Handbook for British Burma compiled by G. E. Fryer. Moulmein, Whittam, 1867. 579p. Y

EB4. SCOTT, JAMES GEORGE. Burma: a handbook of practical information. London, Moring, 1906. 520p. C, Y

EB5. SCOTT, JAMES GEORGE. Burma, a handbook of practical information. 3d ed. rev. London, Moring, 1921. 536p. Y

EB6. Burma facts and figures. London, Longmans, Green, 1946. 47p. (Burma pamphlets, no.9) C, Y

EB7. BURMA (UNION) DEPT. OF INFORMATION AND BROADCASTING. Burma, a handbook on Burma with special reference to Burmese customs, culture, history, economic resources, education, famous pagodas and cities. Published on the occasion of the Chatta Sangayana (6th Buddhist

Synod). Rangoon, 1954. 46p. C, Y
[Cornell entry: Burma (Union) Ministry . . .]

EB8. NEW YORK UNIVERSITY. BURMA RESEARCH PROJECT. Burma. New Haven, 1956. 3v. (HRAF Subcontractor's monograph, no. 37) Y

EB9. Burma yearbook & directory. Rangoon. 1957/58– C

EB10. BURMA (UNION) MINISTRY OF INFORMATION. Burma, a handbook on Burma, with special reference to Burmese customs, history, economic resources, education, famous pagodas and cities, published on the occasion of the centenary of the founding of the Royal City of Mandalay, 1221–1321 B.E. (1859–1959). Rangoon, 1959. 196p. C

EB11. AMERICAN UNIVERSITY, WASHINGTON, D.C. FOREIGN AREAS STUDIES DIVISION. Area handbook for Burma. Washington, GPO, 1968. 375p. (DA Pam. no. 550–61) C, Y

EC — CAMBODIA

EC1. CAMBODIA. Annuaire du Cambodge. Phnom Penh. annual. Y
[Continued in: Indochina. Annuaire général de l'Indochine française.]

EC2. ZADROZNY, MITCHELL G. Area handbook on Cambodia. Prelim. ed. Chicago, Univ. of Chicago for HRAF, 1955. 391p. (HRAF Subcontractor's monograph, no. 21) C, Y
[Cornell entry: Chicago. University. Division of Social Sciences.]

EC3. STEINBERG, DAVID J. Cambodia; its people, its society, its culture. New Haven, HRAF, 1957. 345p. (Country survey series) C, Y

EC4. STEINBERG, DAVID J. Cambodia: its people, its society, its culture. Rev. for 1959 by Herbert H. Vreeland. New Haven, HRAF, 1959. 350p. (Survey of world cultures) C, Y

EC5. AMERICAN UNIVERSITY, WASHINGTON, D.C. FOREIGN AREAS STUDIES DIVISION. Area handbook for Cambodia by Frederick P. Munson. Washington, GPO, 1963. 415p. (Dept. of the Army pamphlet, no. 550–50) C, Y

EH — INDOCHINA

EH1. Annuaire de l'Indo-Chine. Hanoi. v.1– Y

EH2. Annuaire général, commercial, administratif et industiel de l'indo-chine. Hanoi. v.1– C, Y

EH3. TESTON, E. L'Indochine moderne, encyclopédie administrative, touristique, artistique et économique. Paris, Librairie de France, 1932. 1028p. C, Y

EH4. GREAT BRITAIN. NAVAL INTELLIGENCE DIVISION. Indo-China. Cambridge, 1943. 535p. (Geographical handbook series, B.R. 510) C, Y

EI — INDONESIA

Almanacs (Arranged alphabetically)

EI 1. Almanak. Jogjakarta. 1943. 242p. C

EI 2. Almanak Angkatan Perang. Djakarta, P.T. Usaha Pegawai Nasional. v.1– C

EI 3. Almanak Batak. Balige, Indra, 1965– C

EI 4. Almanak Dai Toa (Asia Timoer Raja) Medan. v.1– C

EI 5. Almanak en naamregister van Nederlandsch Indie voor het jaar. Batavia. v.1– C

EI 6. Almanak Hindu Bali. n.p. Dinas Agama Daerah Bali. v.1– C

EI 7. Almanak Malajoe. Jogjakarta. v.1– C
[Indonesian edition of Serat penanggalan Djawi]

EI 8. Almanak Mudjahidien. Djakarta, Jajasan Masdjid Mudjahidien. v.1- C
EI 9. Almanak nasional. Surabaja, Koemisi Penerbitan Almanak Nasional, 1942- C
EI 10. Almanak olahraga. Djakarta, 1962- C
EI 11. Almanak pembangunan. Djakarta. v.1- C
EI 11a. Almanak pers Indonesia. Djakarta, Jajasan Lembaga Pers dan Pendapat Umum, 1954/55- annual. C, Y
[PL 480 Indo-S-178]
EI 12. Almanak primbon Djawa. Solo, Sedu-budi. v.1- C, Y
EI 13. Almanak tani. Weltevreden, Balai Poestaka. v.1- C
EI 14. Almanak "Telaga Djaja" Jogjakarta, 1962- C
EI 15. Almanak "Tjerdas" Medan. v.1- C
EI 16. Almanak umum nasional. Djakarta. v.1- C
EI 17. Almanak van de Indologische Vereeniging. Delft, van Markens. 18??- 1896. C, Y
EI 18. DJAMBEK, SAÄDOEDDIN. Almanak Djamilijah. Djakarta, Tintomas, 1953. 51p. C, Y
[Cornell entry: Saaduddin Djambek]
EI 19. Indische cultuur-almanak. Amsterdam. v.1- C
EI 20. Java annual directory and almanac. Batavia. v.1- Y
EI 21. Utrechtse Indologen-Almanak. Utrecht, Utrechtse Indologen Vereniging, 1939- C, Y
EI 22. Volksalmanak Djawi. Batavia, Bale Poestaka. v.1- C, Y
EI 23. Volksalmanak Madhoera. Weltevreden, Balai Poestaka, 1921- C
EI 23a. Volksalmanak Melajoe. Weltevreden, Balai Poestaka, 1919- C
EI 24. Volksalmanak Soenda. Weltevreden, Bale Poestaka. v.1- C, Y
EI 25. ZEINI. Almanak seni 1957. Djakarta, Badan Musjawarat Kebudajaan Nasional, 1956. 184p. C, Y
[Cornell entry: title]

Other Materials

EI 26. DUTCH EAST INDIES. DEPARTEMENT VAN LANDBOUW, NIJVERHEID EN HANDEL. Handbook of the Netherlands East-Indies. Buitenzorg, Div. of commerce of the Dept. of Agriculture, Industry and Commerce. v.1- C, Y
[Title varies: 1916 and 1920, Yearbook of the Dutch East Indies.]
EI 27. Facts about Indonesia. Djakarta, Ministry of Information. v.1- C
EI 28. Encyclopaedie van Nederlandsch-Indië, met medewerking van verschillende ambtenaren, geleerden en officieren. The Hague, Nijhoff, 1895- 1905. 4v. C, Y
EI 29. LABBERTON, DIRK VAN HINLOOPERN. Geïllustreed handboek van Insulinde, zijnde een synthetische catalogus van den oeconomischen staat van den Nederlandsch-Indischen Archipel, naar de gegevens van de regeerings bureaux en bevoegde des kundigen op iedergebied. Amsterdam, Uitg. Mij. Vivat, 1910. 380, 16p. C, Y
EI 30. Encyclopaedie van Nederlandsch-Indië. 2. druk. met medewerking van verschillende geleerden ambtenaren en officieren. The Hague, Nijhoff, 1917-40. 9v. C, Y
EI 31. GREAT BRITAIN. ADMIRALTY. A manual of Netherlands India (Dutch East Indies). London, 1920. 548p. Y
EI 32. Encyclopaedie van Nederlandsch-Indië. Beknopte encyclopaedie van Nederlandsch-Indië, naar den 2. druk der Encyclopaedie van Nederlandsch-Indië bewerkt door T. J. Bezemer. The Hague, Nijhoff, 1921. 632p. C, Y

EI 33.   DUTCH EAST INDIES. DEPARTEMENT VAN LANDBOUW,
          NIJVERHEID EN HANDEL. AFDEELING HANDEL. Facts and figures
          about the Dutch East Indies. 3d ed. Buitenzorg, 1924. 40p. C
EI 34.   GONGGRIJP, GEORGE FRANÇOIS ELBERT. Geïllustreerde encyclo-
          paedie van Nederlandsch-Indië. Leiden, N.V. Leidsche Uitgeversmaat-
          schappij, 1934. 1582 col. C, Y
EI 35.   GREAT BRITAIN. NAVAL INTELLIGENCE DIVISION. Netherlands
          East Indies. Cambridge, 1944. 2v. (Geographical handbook series,
          B. R. 518-518A) C, Y
EI 36.   DUTCH EAST INDIES (NETHERLANDS INDIES CIVIL ADMINISTRATION).
          Handbook. n.p. 1945. 1v. Y
EI 37.   MUNAF, HUSAIN. Ensiklopedi-Indonesia, kumpulan pertama. Djakarta,
          Martaco, 195? 339p. C
EI 38.   ADINEGORO, DJAMALUDIN. Ensiklopedi umum dalam bahasa Indonesia.
          Djakarta, Bulan-Bintang, 1954. 404p. C
EI 39.   Ensiklopedia Indonesia. Bandung, N.V. Penerbitan, 1954-56. 3v. C,
          Y
EI 40.   YALE UNIVERSITY. GRADUATE SCHOOL. SOUTHEAST ASIA STUDIES.
          Area handbook on Indonesia. Prelim. ed. New Haven, Southeast Asia
          Studies, Yale Univ. for HRAF, 1956. 3v. (HRAF Subcontractor's mono-
          graph, no. 57) C, Y
          [Cornell entry: Yale University. Southeast Asia Studies.]
EI 41.   AMERICAN UNIVERSITY, WASHINGTON, D.C. FOREIGN AREAS STUDIES
          DIVISION. Area handbook for Indonesia. Prepared for the Dept. of the
          Army. Washington, GPO, 1964. 737p. (Dept. of the Army pamphlet no.
          550-39) C, Y
          [Updated version of the 1959 edition.]
EI 42.   SUPENO. Apakah artinja? Kamus populer, berisi pendjelasan kata-kata
          jang sering dipakai didalam rapat-rapat, pidato radio, surat kabar,
          madjalah dan lain-lain. Tjet. 7. Surabaja, Ksatrya, 1964. 418p. C, Y
EI 43.   NOEGROHO. Indonesia, facts and figures. Djakarta, 1967. 608p. C, Y
          [PL480 Indo-6274]

EL—LAOS

EL1.   HICKEY, GERALD CANNON. Area handbook on Laos. Prelim. ed.
         Chicago, Univ. of Chicago for HRAF, 1955. 328p. (HRAF Subcontractor's
         monograph, no. 23) Y
EL2.   AMERICAN UNIVERSITY, WASHINGTON, D.C. FOREIGN AREAS STUDIES
         DIVISION. Area handbook for Laos by T. D. Roberts, et. al. Washington,
         GPO, 1967. 349p. C, Y

EM—MALAYSIA

EM1.   Directory of Malaya. Singapore. v.1- C
EM2.   Directory of the State of Singapore including trade index and biographical
         section. London. v.1- C
EM2a.   Singapore facts and figures. Singapore, Ministry of Culture. v.1- C, Y
EM3.   Singapore year book. Singapore, GPO. v.1- C, Y
EM4.   STRAITS SETTLEMENTS. Blue book for the year. Singapore, GPO. v.1-
         C, Y
EM5.   The Straits times directory of Malaysia and Singapore. Singapore. v.1-
         C, Y
         [Title varies: The Straits times almanac, calendar and directory; -1964,
         The Straits times directory of Singapore and Malaya.]

EM6. DENNYS, NICHOLAS BELFIELD. A descriptive dictionary of British Malaya. London, London and China Telegraph, 1894. 423p. C, Y

EM7. BELFIELD, HENRY CONWAY. Handbook of the Federated Malay States. London, 1902. 170p. Y

EM8. BELFIELD, HENRY CONWAY. Handbook of the Federated Malay States. 3d ed. London, Stanford, 1906. 184p. Y

EM9. GRAHAM, WALTER ARMSTRONG. Kelantan; a state of the Malay Peninsula, a handbook of information. Glasgow, Maclehose, 1908. 139p. C, Y

EM10. Handbook to British Malaya. London, Malay States information agency, 1926– C, Y

EM11. Malayan year book containing information up to 31 December. Singapore, GPO, 1935– C

EM12. KAPLAN, IRVING. Area handbook on British Borneo. Prelim. ed. Chicago, Univ. of Chicago for HRAF, 1955. 443p. (HRAF Subcontractor's monograph, no. 14) Y

EM13. ROBERTS, CHESTER F. Area handbook on Malaya. Prelim. ed. Chicago, Univ. of Chicago for HRAF, 1955. 698p. (HRAF Subcontractor's monograph, no. 17) Y

EM14. HARRIS, GEORGE LAWRENCE. North Borneo, Brunei, Sarawak (British Borneo). New Haven, HRAF, 1956. 287p. (Country survey series, no. 2) C, Y

EM15. MALAYA (FED.) DEPT. OF INFORMATION. Information on the Federation of Malaya. Kuala Lumpur (?) 1957. 1v. (Its Reference papers nos. 1–16) C, Y
[Cornell entry for title: Reference papers.]

EM16. SA'AD SHUKRY BIN MUDA. Bahasa ber'adat; ensikelopidia. Kuala Lumpur, Federal Pub., 1960. vi, 73p. Y

EM17. SARAWAK. INFORMATION SERVICE. Information on Sarawak. Kuching, Borneo Literature Bureau, 1960. 178p. Y

EM18. MALAYSIA. Official yearbook. Kuala Lumpur, GPO, 1961– C, Y
[Entry 1961–6: Malaya (Fed.)]

EM19. Malaysia yearbook, 1963/64– Kuala Lumpur, Straits Times Press. C, Y
[Supersedes Federation of Malay yearbook.]

EM20. AMERICAN UNIVERSITY, WASHINGTON, D.C. FOREIGN AREA STUDIES DIVISION. Area handbook for Malaysia and Singapore. Washington, GPO, 1966. 745p. (Dept. of the Army pamphlet no. 550–45) C, Y

EP— PHILIPPINES

EP1. BUZETA, MANUEL. Diccionario geografico, estadístico, histórico, de las islas Filipinas, por Fr. Manuel Buzeta y Fr. Felipe Bravo. Madrid, de J. C. de la Peña, 1850–51. 2v. C, Y

EP2. Biblioteca histórica filipina: historias, crónicas, anales, memorias, relaciones, cartas, papeles sueltos y demas documentos históricos, todós inéditos y desconocidos, sobre la conquista militar, civilización cristiana, gobierno y administración de este archipiélago, escogidos en los archivos de sus conventos religiosos y establecimientos oficiales del estado y de los pueblos. Manila, Eco de Filipinas, 1892. 3v. C, Y

EP3. MARTÍNEZ DE ZÚÑIGA, JOAQUÍN. Estadismo de las islas Filipinas; ó, Mis viajes por este país, por el padre Fr. Joaquín Martínez de Zúñiga, Agustino calzado. Publica esta obra por primera vez extensamente anotada W. E. Retana. Madrid, Minuesa de los Rios, 1893. 2v. C, Y

EP4. BARANERA, FRANCISCO XAVIER. Handbook of the Philippine Islands, tr. from the Compendio de geografía with an historical sketch by A. Laist. Manila, Partier, 1899. 152p. C, Y

EP5. El archipiélago filipino. Coleccion de datos geográphicos, estadísticos, cronológicos y científicos, relativos al mismo, entresacados de anteriores obras ú obtenidos con la propia observación y estudio. Washington, GPO, 1900. 2v. C, Y

EP6. PARDO DE TAVERA, TRINIDAD HERMENEGILDO. Biblioteca filipina; o sea, catálogo razonado de todos los impresos, tanto insulares como extranjeros, relativos á la historia, la etnografía, la lingüística, la botánica, la fauna, la flora, la geología, la hidrografía, la geografía, la legislación, etc., de las islas Filipinas, de Joló y Marianas. Washington, GPO, 1903. 439p. C, Y
[57th Cong. 2d sess. Senate Doc. no. 74]
[Cornell entry: U.S. Library of Congress]

EP7. PHILIPPINE ISLANDS. LOUISIANA PURCHASE EXPOSITION BOARD. Official handbook of the Philippines and catalogue of the Philippine exhibit. Manila, GPO, 1903-04. 2v. Y

EP8. WRIGHT, HAMILTON MERCER. A handbook of the Philippines. Chicago, McClurg, 1907. 431p. C, Y

EP9. Enciclopedia filipino; política, administración, legislación comparada, historia, economía, legislación financiera, sociología. Manila, Morales, 1908. 1v. Y

EP10. National almanac and guide of the Philippine Islands. Manila, 1911- C

EP11. GALANG, ZOILO M. Encyclopedia of the Philippines; the library of Philippine literature, art and science. Manila, Philippine Education, 1936. 10v. C, Y

EP12. PHILIPPINES (COMMONWEALTH) DEPT. OF AGRICULTURE AND COMMERCE. Facts and figures about the Philippines. Manila, GPO, 1939. 102p. C, Y

EP13. PHILIPPINES (COMMONWEALTH) DEPT. OF AGRICULTURE AND COMMERCE. Facts and figures about the Philippines. Washington, Office of the resident commissioner of the Philippines, 1942. 64p. Y

EP14. PHILIPPINES (REP.) BUREAU OF THE CENSUS AND STATISTICS. Facts and figures about the Philippines. Manila, GPO, 1946/47- annual. C, Y
[Title varies: Facts and figures about the economic and social conditions of the Philippines.]

EP15. GALANG, ZOILO M. Encyclopedia of the Philippines. 3d ed. Manila, Floro, 1950-58. 20v. C

EP16. PHILIPPINE INFORMATION COUNCIL. The Philippines in facts and figures. Manila, 1950. 15 Y

EP17. PHILIPPINES (REP.) BUREAU OF LANDS. Handbook on Philippine land resources. Manila, 1954. 264 C

EP18. Juan's almanac. San Juan, Rizal, 1955- C

EP19. PHILIPPINES (REP.) OFFICE OF PUBLIC INFORMATION. The Philippines; a handbook of information. Manila, 1955. 110p. Y

EP20. PHILIPPINES (REP.) PHILIPPINE INFORMATION AGENCY. The Philippines; a handbook of information. Manila, 1955. 131p. C

EP21. CHICAGO. UNIVERSITY. PHILIPPINE STUDIES PROGRAM. Area handbook on the Philippines. Prelim. ed. New Haven. Univ. of Chicago for HRAF, 1956. 4v. (HRAF Subcontractor's monograph, no. 16) C, Y

EP22. PHILIPPINES (REP.) DEPT. OF FOREIGN AFFAIRS. DIVISION OF CULTURAL ACTIVITIES. The Philippines; a handbook of information. Re-

vised by the Division of Cultural Activities in cooperation with the National Economic Council. Manila, 1963. 104p. C, Y
[Earlier editions issued by the Philippine information agency.]
[Cornell entry: Philippines (Rep.) Dept. of Foreign Affairs.]

ET—THAILAND

ET1. The Bangkok calendar. Bangkok, Mission Press, 18?? annual. C, Y

ET2. THAILAND. MINISTRY OF NATIONAL DEVELOPMENT. DEPT. OF TECHNICAL AND ECONOMIC COOPERATION. Thailand, facts and figures. Bangkok. v.1– annual. C, Y

ET3. GRAHAM, WALTER ARMSTRONG. Siam; a handbook of practical, commercial, and political information. London, Moring, 1912. 637p. C, Y

ET4. Siam directory. Bangkok, Thai Co., 1947– annual. C, Y
[Title varies: Thai directory]

ET5. CORNELL UNIVERSITY. SOUTHEAST ASIA PROGRAM. Handbook on Thailand. Prelim. ed. New Haven, HRAF, 1956. 568p. (HRAF Subcontractor's monograph, no. 42) C, Y

ET6. BLANCHARD, WENDELL. Thailand; its people, its society, its culture. New Haven, HRAF, 1958. 528p. (Country survey series, v.8) C, Y

ET7. AMERICAN UNIVERSITY, WASHINGTON, D.C. FOREIGN AREAS STUDIES DIVISION. Area handbook for Thailand. Washington, 1963. 587p. C, Y

ET8. Thailand year book. Bangkok, Temple Publicity Services, 1964/65– C, Y

ET9. Thailand; facts and figures. Bangkok, 1965– annual. C, Y

ET10. AMERICAN UNIVERSITY, WASHINGTON, D.C. FOREIGN AREAS STUDIES DIVISION. Area handbook for Thailand. Washington, GPO, 1967. 555p. (Dept. of the Army pamphlet no. 550–53) C, Y

EV—VIETNAM

EV1. Annuaire général du Vietnam. Tong nien-giam Viet-Nam. General directory of Vietnam. Saigon, Bureaux d'études techniques et économiques, 19?? C

EV2. Nien-lich Cong-Dan. Saigon, 1960/61– C

EV3. AMERICAN UNIVERSITY, WASHINGTON, D.C. FOREIGN AREAS STUDIES DIVISION. Area handbook for Vietnam. Washington, 1962. 513p. C, Y

EV4. AMERICAN UNIVERSITY, WASHINGTON, D.C. FOREIGN AREAS STUDIES DIVISION. Area handbook for North Vietnam. Washington, GPO, 1967. 494p. (Dept. of the Army pamphlet 550–57) C, Y

EV5. AMERICAN UNIVERSITY, WASHINGTON, D.C. FOREIGN AREAS STUDIES DIVISION. Area handbook for South Vietnam. Washington, GPO, 1967. 510p. (Dept. of the Army pamphlet 550–55) C, Y

EV6. PHU NU MOI. Lich sach 1967, dac biet mua cuoi. Saigon, 1967. 96p. C

EV7. PHU NU NGAY MAI. Lich sach 1967. Saigon, 1967. 128p. C

F — GUIDEBOOKS

FA — GENERAL

FA1. MADROLLE, CLAUDIUS. De Marseille à Canton; guide du voyageur, Indo-chine, canal de Suez, Djibouti et Harar, Indes, Ceylan, Siam, Chine méridionale. Paris, Comité Asie française, 1902. 383p. Y

FA2. JAPAN. DEPT. OF RAILWAYS. An official guide to eastern Asia. 2d ed. Tokyo, 1920. 5v. Y
[v.5. East Indies including Philippine Islands, French Indo-China, Siam, Malay Peninsula, and Dutch East Indies.]

FA3. COOK, T., FIRM, PUBLISHERS, LONDON. Malaysia and Indo-China; information for visitors to British Malaya, Dutch-Indies (Java, Bali Sumatra, etc.), Siam, French Indo-China. Singapore, 1926. 164p. C

FA4. COOK, T., FIRM, PUBLISHERS, LONDON. Malaysia and Indo-China; information for visitors to British Malaya, Dutch-Indies (Java, Bali, Sumatra, etc.), Siam, French Indo-China. Singapore, 1929. 204p. C

FA5. The Golden guide to South and East Asia. Hongkong, Far Eastern Economic Review, 1961- annual. C, Y

FB — BURMA

FB1. Handbook for travellers in India, Pakistan, Burma and Ceylon. London, Murray, 1859- C, Y

FB2. COOK, T., FIRM, PUBLISHERS, LONDON. India, Burma and Ceylon, information for travellers and residents. London, 1898. 208p. Y

FB3. COOK, T., FIRM, PUBLISHERS, LONDON. India, Burma, Ceylon and South Africa, information for travellers and residents. London, 1902. 224p. Y

FB4. COOK, T., FIRM, PUBLISHERS, LONDON. India, Burma, and Ceylon, information for travellers and residents. London, 1913. 246p. Y

FB5. COOK, T., FIRM, PUBLISHERS, LONDON. India, Burma, and Ceylon, information for travellers and residents. London, 1921. 242p. Y

FB6. COOK, T., FIRM, PUBLISHERS, LONDON. India, Burma, and Ceylon, information for travellers and residents. London, 1925. 238p. Y

FB7. BURMA. Burma handbook. Simla, GPO, 1943. 126p. C

FB8. BURMA (UNION). The Kachin Hills manual, as corrected up to 3rd January 1948. Rangoon, GPO, 1959. 212p. C

FB9. Burma Bradshaw. Rangoon, 1952- C

FB10. BURMA (UNION) MINISTRY OF INFORMATION. Rangoon; a pocket guide with special references to history, places of interest, pagodas, weather, business establishments, postal and other useful information, and public services. 4th ed. Rangoon, 1954. 114p. C

FB11. BURMA (UNION) DEPT. OF INFORMATION AND BROADCASTING. Rangoon; a pocket guide with special references to history, places of interest, pagodas, weather, business establishments, postal and other useful information, and public services. 5th ed. Rangoon, 1954. 108p. Y

FB12. BURMA (UNION) MINISTRY OF INFORMATION. Rangoon, a pocket guide with special reference to history, weather, places of interest, pagodas, establishments and institutions, public services, and other useful information. 6th ed. Rangoon, 1956. 102p. C

FB13.   BURMA (UNION) MINISTRY OF INFORMATION. Rangoon, a pocket guide. 7th ed. Rangoon, 1959. 82p. C

FC — CAMBODIA

FC1.   MADROLLE, CLAUDIUS. To Angkor. Paris, Société d'éditions géographiques, maritimes et coloniales, 1939. 2, 84, 6p. (The Madrolle guides) C

FC2.   PARMENTIER, HENRI. Angkor a guide. 2nd ed. Saigon, Portail, 1950. 185p. C, Y

FC3.   PARMENTIER, HENRI. Angkor guide. Saigon, Portail, 1951. 149p. C

FC4.   SILPA BIRASRI. A visit to Khao Phra Vihorn. Bangkok, Fine Arts Dept. 1960. 32p. C

FC5.   SMITH, G. V. A Shell guide to Cambodia. Phnom Penh, Shell, 1966. 55p. C

FH — INDOCHINA

FH1.   MADROLLE, CLAUDIUS. L'Indochine française. Paris, Hachette, 1926–32. 2v. (Guides Madrolle) Y

FH2.   Guide G. B. indochinois, 1928–29. Hanoi, 1928. 236p. C

FH3.   ABOUT, PIERRE EDMOND. Indochine: Cochinchine, Annam, Tonkin, Cambodge, Laos. Rapis, Société d'éditions géographiques, maritimes et coloniales, 1931. 337p. (Guides des colonies françaises) C, Y

FH4.   MADROLLE, CLAUDIUS. Indochina; Cochinchina, Annam, Yünnan, Cambodia, Tonkin, Laos, Siam. Paris, Société d'éditions géographiques, maritimes et coloniales, 1939. 280p. (The Madrolle guides) C, Y

FH5.   MADROLLE, CLAUDIUS. Indochine du Nord; Tonkin, Annam, Laos, Yünnan, Hongkon, Koung-tcheou Wan. 3d ed. aug. Paris, Société d'éditions géographiques, maritimes et coloniales, 1939. 384p. C

FI — INDONESIA

FI 1.   MELVILL VAN CARNBEE, PIETER. The seaman's guide round Java by Baron Melvill of Carnbee and round the islands of Java by H. D. A. Smits. London, Printed for the Hydrographic Office, Admiralty, 1850. 252p. Y

FI 2.   MELVILL VAN CARNBEE, PIETER. Zeemans gids voor de vaarwaters rondom het eiland Java. Van wege de Commissie tot Verbetering der Oost-Indische Zeekaarten. 3 verb. uitg. Amsterdam, Hulst van Keulen, 1858. 116p. Y

FI 3.   SCHULZE, FEDOR. West-Java, traveller's guide for Batavia and from Batavia to the Preanger Regencies and Tjilatjap. Batavia, Visser, 1894. 83p. C, Y

FI 4.   BEMMELEN, JOHAN FRANS VAN. Uit Indië Reisindrukken en herinneringen uit onzen Archipel. Batavia, Kolff, 1895. 238p. C, Y

FI 5.   BEMMELEN JOHAN FRANS VAN. Guide to the Dutch East Indies, composed by invitation of the Koninklyke paketvaart maatschappij (Royal Steam Packet Company) by J. F. van Bemmelen and G. B. Hooyer. London, Luzac, 1897. 202p. Y

FI 6.   Java, the wonderful. Guide and tourist's handbook. Arnhem, Thieme, 19?? 102p. C

FI 7.   Latif, Isom. Peta. & petundjuk tamasja Djawa-Bali. Surabaja, Pembina, 19?? 30p. C

FI 8.   BEMMELEN, JOHAN FRANS VAN. Guide through Netherlands India by J. F. van Bemmelen and G. B. Hooyer. New ed. London, Cook, 1903. 201p. C

FI 9.   KONINKLIJKE PAKETVAART MAATSCHAPPIJ. Guide through Netherlands India. Amsterdam, de Bussy, 1911. 249p. Y
FI 10.   BRONDGEEST, HENRI. Reiswijzer voor Nederlandsche particulieren en Kunstenaars naar Nederlandsch Oost-Indië. Weltevreden, Visser, 1927. 99p. C
FI 11.   VEREENIGING TOERISTENVERKEER. Come to Java. 3d ed. 1926-27. Weltevreden, 1927. 329p. C
FI 12.   KONINKLIJKE VEREENIGING JAVA MOTOR CLUB, SEMARANG. Handboek voor toerisme in Nederlandsch-Indië. Semarang, 1929. 244p. C, Y
          [Cornell entry: Java Motor Club]
FI 13.   REITSMA, STEVEN ANNE. Van Stockum's travellers' handbook for the Dutch East Indies. The Hague, van Stockum, 1930. 613p. C, Y
FI 14.   RIJKEE, W. Naar Indië; beknopte gids voor hen die voor korte of lange tijd naar Indië gaan. Rijswijk, Kramers, 1936. 91p. C
FI 15.   Tourist guide to Central Java, in English and Indonesian. Semarang, Penerbit Gatot, 195? 224p. C
FI 16.   INDONESIA DEPARTEMEN PENERANGAN. Basic information on Indonesia. Djakarta, 1953. 204p. Y
FI 17.   MR. CHEN & CO. Guide to the main roads of Java, Madura, and Bali, for car owners and drivers, etc. Surabaja, 1953. 2 col. maps. C
FI 18.   INDONESIA. KEMENTERIAN PENERANGAN. Short guide: Djakarta, Bogor, Bandung. rev. ed. Djakarta, 1954. 125p. C
FI 19.   BAKOENOEN, PUB. SEMARANG. Buku petundjuk alamat dagang dan touris Djawa-Tengah, 1956. Semarang, 1956. 402p. C
FI 20.   INDONESIA. DEPARTEMEN PENERANGAN. Short guide: Djakarta, Bogor, Bandung. 4th ed. Djakarta, Min. of Information, 1956. 160p. C, Y
          [Cornell entry: Indonesia. Kementerian Penerangan.]
FI 21.   GARUDA INDONESIAN AIRWAYS. Indonesia, an invitation. Bandung, van Hoeve, 1956. 139p. C, Y
          [Cornell entry: title]
FI 22.   INDONESIA. DEWAN TOURISME. List of hotels and lodgements in Indonesia. Djakarta, 1958. 77p. C
FI 23.   KAELAN. Petundjuk tjandi: Mendut, Pawon, Barabudur. Jogjakarta, 1959. 159p. C
FI 23a.   ANANDA. Pedoman tamasja Djawa Timur/Bali. Djakarta, Keng Po, 196? 160p. C, Y
FI 24.   LATIF, ISOM. Peta kilometer 7 petundjuk tamasja Djawa-Bali. Djakarta, Pembina, 196? 40p. C, Y
FI 25.   SIMATUPANG, R. O. Pedoman tamasja Djawa Barat. Djakarta, Keng Po, 196? 88p. C
FI 26.   ANANDA. A handy guide for Java, Madura, and Bali. Djakarta, Kinta, 1962. 226p. C, Y
FI 27.   ATMADI, ENDANG T. Indonesia, general information and tourism by Endang T. Atmadi and Judith Waworuntu. Djakarta, 1962. 207p. (Wit Sidogura publications series, no. 621) C
FI 28.   Indonesia, an invitation. Rev. ed. The Hague, van Hoeve, 1963. 145p. C, Y

Bali

FI 29.   INDONESIA. KEMENTERIAN PENERANGAN. Bali, the isle of the gods. Djakarta, 1957. 95p. C

FI 30.   INDONESIA. KEMENTERIAN PENERANGAN. Bali; where, what, when, how. Djakarta, GPO, 1958. 63p. C
FI 31.   INDONESIA. KEMENTERIAN PENERANGAN. Bali, the isle of the gods. 2d ed. Djakarta, 1960. 92p. C
FI 32.   INDONESIA. DEPARTEMEN PENERANGAN. Bali, isle of temples and dances. 3d ed. Djakarta, 1962. 96p. C, Y
FI 33.   INDONESIA. BADAN PENJELENGGARA PARTISIPASI NEW YORK WORLD'S FAIR, 1964–65. Bali, isle of temples and dances. New York, 1964. 100p. C

Djakarta

FI 34.   Excursiegids voor Oud-Batavia. Batavia, 1947. 32p. C
FI 35.   GRENZENBERG, JOH. M. Gids voor Djakarta; petundjuk Djakarta. Djakarta, 195? 1v. C
FI 36.   DJAKARTA. DJAWATAN PENERANGAN. Pedoman Kota Djakarta. Djakarta, 1950. 1v. C
FI 37.   FULLER, MRS. CHARLES F. Introduction to Djakarta. n.p. 1956. 103p. C, Y
FI 38.   SIMATUPANG, R. O. Pedoman tamasja Djakarta & sekitarnja. Djakarta, Keng Po, 196? 160p. C, Y
FI 39.   Djakarta-Raja dengan Asian-Games. Semarang, Intrain, 1961. 170p. C
FI 40.   BAMBANG SUTARNO. Buku pedoman Djakarta. Guide book of Djakarta. Djakarta, Tarbijah, 1962. 35p. C
FI 41.   SIAGIAN, HARJATI. Djakarta guide; a year-round vacation city by Harjati and Gajus Siagion. Djakarta, Gunung Agung, 1962. 105p. C
FI 42.   PEMBINA. Peta Kota Djakarta, Kebajoran, Lampiran dari peta Djakarta & Kebajoran. Djakarta, 1963. 32p. C

Other Areas

FI 43.   VEREENIGING TOERISTENVERKEER. Short guide of Sumatra, with a more complete description of the Padang highlands. Batavia, Kolff, 1921. 176p. C
FI 44.   INDONESIA. KEMENTERIAN PENDIDIKAN. PENGADJARAN DAN KEBUDAJAAN. Pengantar singkat tjandi Borobudur. Jogjakarta, 1952. 11p. C
FI 45.   LATIF, ISOM. Map & tourist guide Djawa-Bali. Surabaja, Pembina, 196? 34p. C
FI 46.   Jogjakarta. Djakarta, GPO, 1960. 44p. C
FI 47.   SIMATUPANG, R. O. Pedoman tamasja Djawa Tengah. Djakarta, Keng Po, 1961. 204p. C, Y

FM—MALAYSIA

FM1.   Malaysia travel manual. Kuala Lumpur, Dept. of Tourism. v.1– C
FM2.   HARRISON, CUTHBERT WOODVILLE. An illustrated guide to the Federated Malay States. London, Malay States Information Agency, 1911. 358p. C, Y
FM3.   HARRISON, CUTHBERT WOODVILLE. An illustrated guide to the Federated Malay States. London, Malay States Information Agency, 1923. 377p. C, Y
FM4.   KANCHANANAGA, NAT THUAN. A Malayan all-in-one book of reference and guide. Singapore, Malayan Seminary Pr., 1934. 371, 7p. Y
FM5.   Willis's guide to Singapore and Malaya; with additional notes of interest to travellers to Hong Kong. Singapore, 1938. 139p. C

FM6.   AUTOMOBILE ASSOCIATION OF MALAYA. Handbook of the Automobile Association of Malaya. Singapore, 1942. xiii, 94p. C

FM7.   Travel information guide of Malaya. Penang, Morrison & Rose, 1948. 77p. C

FM8.   RAJARATNAM, S. Ipoh, where and what it is. Ipoh, Rotary Club of Ipoh, 1956. 41p. C

FM9.   SINGAPORE. DEPT. OF INFORMATION SERVICES. Malaya, a guide for businessmen and visitors, 1957. Singapore, 1957. 84p. Y

FM10. BRITISH OVERSEAS AIRWAYS CORPORATION. Malaya. London, Inter-Continental Air Guides, 1963. 56p. C

FM11. MALAYSIA. DEPT. OF TOURISM. Malaysia; visitors guide, hotel and rest house directory. Kuala Lumpur, 1963- C

FM12. MALAYSIAN AIRWAYS. The Malay Peninsula. London, Warner Publicity, 1964. 64p. C

Kuala Lumpur

FM13. Guide to Kuala Lumpur. Singapore, Moore, 1957. 81p. Y

FM14. PAPINEAU, ARISTIDE J. G. Guide to Kuala Lumpur, the Federal Capital. Singapore, 1963. 202p. C

Sabah

FM15. ROTARY CLUB, JESSELTON, NORTH BORNEO. Sabah story; a booklet on North Borneo. 2d ed. Jesselton, 1957. 47p. C

FM16. ROTARY CLUB, SANDAKAN, NORTH BORNEO. Tourist guide to Sandakan, North Borneo. Rev. ed. Sandakan, 1960. 64p. C

Singapore

FM17. SINGAPORE. SURVEY DEPT. Singapore guide and street directory. Singapore. v.1- C

FM18. Comprehensive directory of Singapore roads & streets, with postal district numbers and two official maps. Singapore, Jay, 19?? 68p. C

FM19. REITH, GEORGE MURRAY. Handbook to Singapore with map. 2d ed. rev. by Walter Makepeace. Singapore, Fraser and Neave, 1907. 133p. C, Y

FM20. ROTARY CLUB, SINGAPORE. A handbook of information presented by the Rotary Club and the Municipal Commissioners of the town of Singapore. Singapore, 1933. 112p. C, Y

FM21. PAPINEAU, ARISTIDE JOSEPH GUSTAV. Guide to Singapore and spotlight on Malaysia. Singapore, Andre Pub., 1947- C, Y
       [Title varies: Guide to Singapore.]

FM22. SINGAPORE. SURVEY DEPT. Street directory and guide to Singapore with sectional maps. New series. Singapore, 1954- Y

FM23. MILLER, HARRY, JOURNALIST. The traveller's guide to Singapore. Singapore, Moore, 1956. 120p. C, Y

FM24. SINGAPORE. DEPT. OF INFORMATION SERVICES. Traveller's guide to Singapore. Singapore, 1957. 76p. C, Y
       [Cornell entry: title]

FM25. BRITISH OVERSEAS AIRWAYS CORPORATION. Singapore. 3d ed. London, Inter-Continental Air Guides, 1963. 80p. C

FP — PHILIPPINES

FP1.   PHILIPPINE ISLANDS. Guia oficial de las islas Filipinas. Manila, 18??-98. C, Y

FP2. ESCOBAR Y LOZANO, JAIME. El indicador del viajero en las Islas Filipinas. Manila, Chofré, 1885. 175p. Y

FP3. BARANERA, FRANCISCO XAVIER. Compendio de geografia de las Islas Filipinas, Marianas, Joló y Carolinas. 3 ed. cor. y aum. Manila, Marty, 1892. 162p. C

FP4. VEREA, F. G. Guide for the American in the Philippines. Tr. from the Spanish by F. C. Fisher. Manila, Chofré, 1899. 289p. Y

FP5. PHILIPPINE ISLANDS. DEPT. OF COMMERCE AND POLICE. The Philippines, the land of palm and pine, an official handbook. Manila, GPO, 1912. 214p. Y

FP6. PHILIPPINE ISLANDS. INDEPENDENCE COMMISSION. Beautiful Philippines; a handbook of general information. Manila, 1923. 239p. Y

FP7. The Philippines; visitors handbook. Manila, Board of travel and tourist industry, 195? 72p. C

FP8. CALTEX (PHILIPPINES) INC. Philippines touring guide. 40th ed. Manila, 1951. 320p. C

FP9. AMERICAN ASSOCIATION OF THE PHILIPPINES. Introducing Manila. Manila, 1952. 39p. Y

FP10. ABRAHAMSEN, HELEN MARY. The Philippine Islands, a guide. Palo Alto, Cal., Pacific Books, 1954. 96p. C, Y

FP11. AMERICAN ASSOCIATION OF THE PHILIPPINES, MANILA. Introducing Manila. Rev. ed. Manila, 1959. vi, 57p. C

FP12. JESUS, DOMINGO D. DE. Cadastral handbook of City of Manila. Manila, Azucena, 1959–60. 13v. in 21. C

FP13. U. S. DEPT. OF DEFENSE. ARMED FORCES INFORMATION AND EDUCATION DIVISION. A pocket guide to the Philippines. Washington, 1961. 206p. (DOD pamp. 2–3A) C, Y

FP14. ALUIT, ALFONSO J. The Galleon guide to Manila and the Philippines. Manila, Galleon, 1968. 178p. Y

FT — THAILAND

FT1. ANTONIO, J. Guide to Bangkok and Siam compiled by J. Antonio, revised by W. W. Fegen. Bangkok, Siam Observer Pr., 1904. 104p. Y

FT2. SEIDENFADEN, ERIK. Guide to Bangkok, with notes on Siam. Bangkok, Royal State Railway, 1927. 320p. Y

FT3. SEIDENFADEN, ERIK. Guide to Nakon Patom. 2d ed. Bangkok, Royal State Railways of Siam, 1929. 46p. C, Y

FT4. Siam guidebook to the chief monuments of Bangkok, Bang Pa-In, Ayudhya and Lopburi. Bangkok, 1930. 43p. C

FT5. SEIDENFADEN, ERIK. Guide to Petchaburi. Bangkok, Royal State Railways of Siam, 1931. 54p. C

FT6. SEIDENFADEN, ERIK. Guide to Bangkok, with notes on Siam. 3d ed. Bangkok, Royal State Railways of Siam, 1932. 324p. Y

FT7. KORWONG, KIM. A new guide to Bangkok, compiled by Kim Korwong and Jaivid Rangthong. 2d. ed. Bangkok, Hatha Dhip, 1950. 290p. C, Y [Cornell entry: Kim Korwong]

FT8. TRI AMATYAKUL. The Thai guidebook: Ayudhya. Bangkok, National Institute of Culture, 1957. 74p. C

FT9. CHAWIT RANGTHONG. A week in Bangkok. Bangkok, Hatha Dhip, 1958. 288p. C

FT10. TRI AMATYAKUL. Cholburi. Bangkok, National Institute of Culture, 1958. 49p. C

FT11. WELLS, MARGARETTA B. Guide to Bangkok. Bangkok, Police Printing Pr., 1958. 100p. C, Y

FT12. WELLS, MARGARETTA B. Guide to Bangkok. Bangkok, Christian Bookstore, 1959. 128p. Y
FT13. SCHMIDT, KURT O. Thailand (Siam) mit Stadtführer Bangkok. Buchenhain vor München, Volk und Heimat, 1960. 94p. (Mai's Weltführer, nr. 1) C
FT14. Thai tourist guide. Bangkok, 1961. 97p. C
FT15. Travel tips to Bangkok. Bangkok, Thai Promotion and Publications Co., 1961. 56p. C
FT16. Bangkok bulletin. Bangkok, 1962. 106p. C
FT17. WELLS, MARGARETTA B. Guide to Chiang Mai. Bangkok, Kramol Tiranasar, 1962. 88p. C, Y
FT18. MALAYSIAN AIRWAYS. Bangkok, London, Warner Publicity, 1964. 40p. C
FT19. WELLS, MARGARETTA B. Guide to Chiang Mai. Rev. ed. Bangkok, Christian Bookstore, 1964. 107p. C
FT20. HUDSON, ROY. Handbook to Chiengmai. Chiengmai, 1965. 139p. C
FT21. THONGQIN SUNSAWAL. Panorama of Thailand; a guide to places of interest, particularly Bangkok. Bangkok, Sammitr, 1965. 115p. C
FT22. Bangkok guide and street directory with sectional maps. Bangkok, Royal Thai Survey Dept., 1966. 245p. C

FV — VIETNAM

FV1. MADROLLE, CLAUDIUS. Tonkin du sud, Hanoi. Les annamites, Hanoi, Pays de So'n-nam. Paris, Comité de l'Asie française, 1907. lxxiv, 96, xvip. C, Y
FV2. EBERHARDT, PHILIPPE. Guide de l'Annam. Paris, Librairie Maritime et Coloniale, 1914. 172p. C, Y
FV3. VIETNAM. NHA QUOC-GIA DU-LICH. Banmethuot. Saigon, National Tourist Office, 195? 12p. C
FV4. VIETNAM. NHA QUOC-GIA DU-LICH. Dalat. Saigon, National Tourist Office, 195? 24p. C
FV5. VIETNAM. OFFICE NATIONAL DU TOURISME. Vietnam as a tourist center. Saigon, 1953. 65p. C
FV6. Guide touristique, 1956-57. Saigon, 1956. 206p. C
FV7. ROTARY CLUB, SAIGON. Guide touristique. Saigon, 1956. 206p. C
FV8. Sai-gon-cho-lon chi-nan. Guide de Saigon-Cholon. Guide to Saigon-Cholon. Saigon, Sao-Mai, 1956. 323p. C
FV9. VIETNAM. NHA QUOC-GIA DU-LICH. Hue co-do. Saigon, 1957. 61p. C
FV10. VIETNAM. NHA QUOC-GIA DU-LICH. Saigon, capital of Vietnam. Saigon, National Tourist Office, 1957. 34p. C
FV11. VIETNAM. DAI-SU-QUAN. U.S. A guide to Viet-Nam. Washington, Embassy of Vietnam, 1960. 42p. C
FV12. U.S. OFFICE OF ARMED FORCES INFORMATION AND EDUCATION. A pocket guide to Viet-Nam. Washington, GPO, 1962. 130p. C
FV13. VIETNAM. NHA QUOC-GIA DU-LICH. Saigon. Saigon, Vietnam National Tourist Office, 1967. 19p. C
FV14. VIETNAM. NHA QUOC-GIA DU-LICH. Vietnam. Saigon, Vietnam National Tourist Office, 1967. 24p. C

G—SOCIAL SCIENCE

GA—GENERAL

GA1. U.S. DEPT. OF STATE. EXTERNAL RESEARCH DIVISION. Southeast Asia. Washington. v.1– C, Y
[Beginning in 1954 Apr. issue lists studies in progress; Oct. issue lists completed studies.]

GA2. South Asia social science abstracts. Calcutta, 1952–58. 7v. annual. C, Y
[Absorbed by: Southern Asia social science bibliography.]
[Cornell entry: UNESCO. Research Center on Social and Economic development in Southern Asia.]

GA3. Southern Asia social science bibliography, with annotations and abstracts. Calcutta, Research Centre on the Social Implications of Industrialization in Southern Asia, 1960– annual. C, Y
[Cornell entry: UNESCO. Research Center on Social and Economic development in Southern Asia.]

GI—INDONESIA

GI 1. Literatuur-overzicht voor de taal-, land- en volkenkunde en geschiedenis van Nederlandsch-Indië voor het jaar 1936–, The Hague, 1937– C, Y
[Cornell entry: Instituut voor Taal-, Land- en Volkenkunde.]

GI 2. SJAHRIAL-PAMUNTJAK, RUSINA. A regional bibliography of social science publications: Indonesia. Djakarta, National Bibliographic Centre, Ministry of Education and Culture, 1955. 65p. C, Y
[Cornell entry: Indonesia. Kantor Bibliografi Nasional.]

GI 3. BHATTA, J. N. Social science bibliography on Indonesia with special emphasis on demographic and geographic materials. Djakarta, 1965. 221p. (Dinas Geografi Direktorat Topografi, Departemen Angkat Darat, Publication no. 13) C

GI 4. MAKAGIANSAR, M. Research di Indonesia, 1945–65. Djakarta, Departemen Urusan Research National Republik Indonesia, 1965. 4v. C

GM—MALAYSIA

GM1. COTTER, CONRAD P. Reading list of English language materials in the social sciences on British Borneo, with critical annotations. Honolulu, 1960. 88ℓ C, Y

GP—PHILIPPINES

GP1. QUEZON, PHILIPPINES. UNIVERSITY OF THE PHILIPPINES. SOCIAL SCIENCE RESEARCH CENTER. An annotated bibliography of Philippine social sciences. Quezon City, 1956–60. 3v. C, Y
[Cornell entry: Lopez, Cecilio.]

GP2. QUEZON, PHILIPPINES. ATENEO DE MANILA. INSTITUTE OF PHILIPPINE CULTURE. Research projects of the Institute of Philippine Culture, Ateneo Language Center and Bikol area survey, January 1, 1950 to Sept. 30, 1960. Manila, 1960. 6ℓ C

GT—THAILAND

GT1. Directory of social sciences in Thailand. Bangkok, Faculty of Political Science, Chulalongkorn Univ., 1963– annual. C, Y
[Cornell entry: Amyot, Jacques]

GT2.   BROUGHTON, JERALD D. A literature survey of environmental factors in Thailand. Vicksburg, 1965. 336, 6p. (In U.S. Waterways Experiment Station, Vicksburg, Miss. Mobility environmental research study. Vicksburg, 1965. Report 1- Technical report no. 3-681) Y
GT3.   AMARA RAKSASATAYA. Thailand: social science materials in Thai and western languages. Bangkok, National Institute of Development Administration, 1966. 378p. Y

GV—VIETNAM

GV1.   Muc-luc phan-tich tap-chi khoa-hoc xa-hoi Viet-nam. Index to Vietnamese social science periodicals. Saigon, 1958/60- C
GV2.   Bibliography of social sciences published in Vietnam. Thu-tich khao ve Khoa-hoc xa-hoi tai Viet-nam, 1947-1959. Saigon, 1960. 2pts. in 1v. C

H — LAW AND POLITICAL SCIENCE

HA — GENERAL

HA1. CAMPBELL, FRANCIS BANBURY FITZGERALD. Index-catalogue of Indian official publications in the Library, British Museum. London, Library Supply, 1900. 193, 314, 72p. Y

HA2. Overseas official publications, quarterly bulletin of official publications received by the Royal empire society and issued in the Overseas British Empire or relating thereto. London, 1927-32. 5v. Y

HA3. ROYAL COMMONWEALTH SOCIETY. LIBRARY. List of publications on the constitutional relations of the British Empire, 1926-1932, compiled by Evans Lewin. London, 1933. vii, 71p. Y

HA4. GREAT BRITAIN. COLONIAL OFFICE. An annotated bibliography on land tenure in the British and British protected territories in Southeast Asia and the Pacific. London, GPO, 1952. 164p.
(Gt. Brit. Colonial Office. Colonial research studies, no. 6) C, Y

HA5. INTERNATIONAL ASSOCIATION OF LEGAL SCIENCE. Catalogue des sources de documentation juridique dans le monde. A register of legal documentation in the world. Paris, UNESCO, 1953. 362p.
(Documentation dans les sciences sociales) Y

HA6. Legal bibliography of the British Commonwealth of nations. London, Sweet & Maxwell, 1955- C, Y
[Vol. 7 The British Commonwealth, excluding the United Kingdom, Australia, New Zealand, Canada, India and Pakistan. 2nd. ed. compiled by Leslie F. Maxwell, 1964. 459p.]

HA7. INTERNATIONAL ASSOCIATION OF LEGAL SCIENCE. Catalogue des sources de documentation juridique dans le monde. 2nd. ed. Paris, UNESCO, 1957. 423p. C, Y

HA8. HART, DONN V. Selected abstracts in development administration: field reports of directed social change. Syracuse, Maxwell Graduate School of Citizenship and Public Affairs, Syracuse Univ., 1962. 199, 63p. (Syracuse Univ. Maxwell Graduate School of Citizenship and Public Affairs. Publication no. 3) C, Y

HB — BURMA

HB1. BURMA. The Burma legislative manual. Rangoon. v.1- Y
HB2. BURMA. ACCOUNTS DEPT. Manual of appointments and allowances in Burma. Rangoon. v.1- Y
HB3. BURMA. GOVERNMENT BOOK DEPOT. Monthly list of publications. Rangoon, GPO. v.1- monthly. Y
HB4. BURMA (UNION) FOREIGN OFFICE. List of representatives of foreign states and international organizations in the Union of Burma. Rangoon. v.1- C
HB5. BURMA (UNION) INSTITUTE OF PUBLIC ADMINISTRATION, RANGOON. LIBRARY. A selective bibliography on public administration in Burma. Rangoon, 1961. ii, 15ℓ C

HC — CAMBODIA

HC1. CAMBODIA. MINISTÈRE DES AFFAIRES ÉTRANGÈRES. Annuaire diplomatique et consulaire, Ministère des affaires étrangères du gouvernement royal du Cambodge, Missions diplomatiques et consulaires du Cambodge à l'étranger. Phnom-Penh. v.1- C

HH—INDOCHINA

HH1. PETITJEAN, HIPPOLYTE CONSTANT. Répertoire chronologique et alphabétique des lois, décrets, ordonnances, etc., promulgués ou appliqués en Indochine depuis l'occupation de la Cochin-chine (1861) jusqu'au 31 décembre 1917. Saigon, 1918. 913p. C, Y
[The list actually goes back to 1776.]
[Cornell entry: Indochina, French. Laws, statutes, etc. (Indexes)]

HH2. BODIN DE GALEMBERT, JACQUES DE. Les administrations et les services publics indochinois. 2d. ed., revue et augm. par E. Erard. Hanoi, Le-van-tan, 1931. 1023p. Y

HH3. INDOCHINA, FRENCH. LAWS, STATUES, ETC. (INDEXES). Répertoire chronologique et alphabétique des lois, décrets, arrêtés ministériels promulgués en Indochine du 1. janvier 1926 au 1. janvier 1935 par Raoul Nicolas. Hanoi, Extrême-Orient, 1935. 565p. C

HI—INDONESIA

HI 1. DUTCH EAST INDIES. Regeeringsalmanak voor Nederlandsch-Indië. Batavia, GPO. v.1- C, Y
[Issued in two sections: 1. Gedeelte Grondgebied en bevolking, inrichting van het bestuur van Nederlandsch-Indië en bijlagen; 2. Gedeelte, Kalendar en personalia.]

HI 2. DUTCH EAST INDIES. Staatsblad van Nederlandsch-Indië. Batavia, GPO, 1816-1938. 63v. in 96. C, Y

HI 3. BERG, LODEWIJK WILLEM CHRISTIAAN VAN DEN. De inlandsche rangen en titels op Java en Madoera. Batavia, GPO, 1887. C, Y

HI 4. INDONESIA. DEPARTEMEN PENERANGAN. Arsip dokumentasi. Djakarta. v.1- C, Y
[Cornell entry: Indonesia. Kementerian Penerangan.]

HI 5. BERG, LODEWIJK WILLEM CHRISTIAAN VAN DEN. De inlandsche rangen en titels op Java en Madoera. 2. herz. druk. The Hague, Nijhoff, 1902. 129p. Y

HI 6. NETHERLANDS (KINGDOM, 1815-) COMMISSIE VOOR HET ADATRECHT. Adatrechtbundels bezorgd door de Commissie voor het adatrecht. The Hague, 1910-55. 45v. C, Y

HI 7. ADATRECHTSTICHTING TE LEIDEN. Literatuurlijst voor het adatrecht van Indonesië. The Hague, Nijhoff, 1927. 192p. C, Y

HI 8. ADATRECHTSTICHTING TE LEIDEN. Literatuurlijst voor het adatrecht van Indonesië. 2. druk. The Hague, Nijhoff, 1927. 452p. C, Y

HI 9. Literatuuropgave voor het adatrecht. The Hague, 1927-35. 20v. Y
[Replaced by Aanvullende literatuurlijst voor het Adatrecht van Indonesië.]

HI 10. Bibliografie van in Nederland verschenen officiële en semi-officiële uitgaven. The Hague, GPO, 1929- C, Y
[Cornell entry: Hague. Koninklijke Bibliotheek.]
[Title varies: 1929-52, Nederlandse overheidsuitgaven.]

HI 11. LABBERTON, DIRK VAN HINLOPPEN. Dictionnaire de termes de droit coutumier indonésien, avec six cartes hors textes. The Hague, Nijhoff, 1934. 732p. C, Y

HI 12. ADATRECHTBUNDEL. Aanvullende literatuurlijst voor het Adatrecht van Indonesië, 1927- 1 Sept. 1937. Overdruk uit Adatrechtbundel XL. The Hague, Nijhoff, 1938. 159p. Y

HI 13. INDONESIA. KEMENTERIAN PENDIDIKAN, PENGADJARAN DAN KEBUDAJAAN. Daftar boekoe2 dan Karengan2 tentang hoekoem adat Indonesia, 1927-1 Djanoeari 1942. Djakarta, Ditjetak oleh Balai Poestaka, 1947. 112p. C

HI 14. Ensiklopedi politik, oleh Tatang Sastrawiria dan Haksan Wirasatisna. Djakarta, Perpustakaan Perguruan Kem. P. P. dan K., 1955. 412p. C

HI 15. INDONESIA. DEPARTEMEN PENERANGAN. List of publications issued by the Department of Information, Republic of Indonesia. Djakarta, 1960. 14p. (Its special issue, 61) C

HI 16. INDONESIA. DEPARTEMEN PENERANGAN. List of publications issued by the Department of Information, Republic of Indonesia. Djakarta, 1960. 7p. (Its special issue, 62) C

HI 17. INDONESIA. LEMBAGA ADMINISTRASI NEGARA. Almanak organisasi negara Republik Indonesia. Djakarta, 1960- annual. C, Y
[Cornell entry: Djakarta. Lembaga Administrasi Negara.]

HI 18. INDONESIA. DEPARTEMEN PENERANGAN. Katalogus penerbitan Departemen Penerangan semendjak tahun 1950-1961. Djakarta, 1961. 28p. C

HI 19. INDONESIA. LAWS, STATUTES, ETC. Almanak lembaga2 negara dan Kepartaian. Djakarta, Departemen Penerangan, 1962. 499p. C, Y
[Cornell entry: Indonesia. Departemen Penerangan]

HI 20. SALAYAN, ABDUL WAHID. Ensiklopedia hukum. Padang, Minbor, 1963- C, Y

HI 21. SURJO UNTORO, S. Ensiklopedia sosialisme. Surabaja, Ksatrya, 1963. 102p. C, Y
[Cornell entry: Surjountoro, S]
[PL 480 Indo-70]

HI 22. Insurgency and counterinsurgency in Indonesia. n.p. 1964. 10ℓ Y

HM—MALAYSIA

HM1. GREAT BRITAIN. COLONIAL OFFICE. Straits Settlements; reference list of original correspondence of the Secretary of State, 1838-1928. London, n.d. 155-171c 8ℓ Y
[Photocopy of lists in the Public Record Office.]

HM2. STRAITS SETTLEMENTS. Blue book for the year. Singapore, GPO. v.1- annual. C, Y

HM3. MALAYA (FED.) PARLIAMENT. HOUSE OF REPRESENTATIVES. Votes and proceedings. Kuala Lumpur, 1959/60- C

HM4. MALAYA (FED.) ELECTION COMMISSION. Report on the Parliamentary and State elections, 1959. Kuala Lumpur, GPO, 1960. v, 57p. C, Y

HM5. TILMAN, ROBERT O. A guide to British library holdings of government publications relating to Malaysia in the field of the social sciences by Robert O. Tilman and Peter L. Burns. n.p. 1964. 67ℓ C, Y

HP—PHILIPPINES

HP1. QUEZON, PHILIPPINES. ATENEO DE MANILA. COLLEGE OF LAW. Catalog. Manila, 19?? Y

HP2. PHILIPPINE ISLANDS. BUREAU OF CIVIL SERVICE. Manual of information relative to the Philippine civil service showing the positions, classified and unclassified, the methods governing examinations and certifications for appointment, the regulations for rating examination papers, specimen examination questions and conditions of appointment and service. Manila, 1901- C, Y

HP3. PHILIPPINE ISLANDS. Handbook on the executive departments of the government of the Philippine Islands. Manila, GPO, 1912. 174p. Y

HP4. MANILA. NATIONAL LIBRARY. LEGISLATIVE REFERENCE DIVISION. Checklist of publications of the government of the Philippine Islands September 1, 1900, to December 31, 1917, compiled by Emma Osterman Elmer. Manila, GPO, 1918. 288p. Y

HP5. CARNEGIE ENDOWMENT FOR INTERNATIONAL PEACE. LIBRARY. Philippine independence. Select list of books and articles on independence of the Philippine Islands, published since 1930. Washington, 1939. 7ℓ (Its select bibliographies no. 9) Y

HP6. ANDAYA, ARACELI. An annotated bibliography on Philippine public administration. Manila, 1953. iii, 53ℓ C

HP7. BIBLIOGRAPHICAL SOCIETY OF THE PHILIPPINES. Checklist of Philippine government documents, 1950. Washington, Library of Congress, 1953. 62p. C

HP8. TAYONA, AGAPITO G. Organization charts of Philippine government. Quezon, Institute of Public Administration, Univ. of the Philippines, 1953. 16 charts. C

HP9. JACOBINI, H. B. Governmental services in the Philippines. Manila, Institute of Public Administration, Univ. of the Philippines, 1956. 640p. (Quezon, Philippines. Univ. of the Philippines. Institute of Public Administration. Studies in public administration, no. 3) C, Y
[Cornell entry: Jacobini (H.B.) and Associates.]

HP10. MORENO, FEDERICO B. Official gazette desk book. Quezon City, Index Pub. House, 1956– C, Y
[Cornell entry: Philippines (Rep.) Official gazette (Indexes)]
[Annual index of the official gazette of the Philippines.]

HP11. QUEZON, PHILIPPINES. UNIVERSITY OF THE PHILIPPINES. INSTITUTE OF PUBLIC ADMINISTRATION. LIBRARY. Ramon Magsaysay, a bibliography. Manila, 1957. 185p. C, Y

HP12. PHILIPPINES (REP.) BUREAU OF PUBLIC LIBRARIES. Philippine government publications. Manila, 1958– monthly or bimonthly. C

HP13. QUEZON, PHILIPPINES. UNIVERSITY OF THE PHILIPPINES. INSTITUTE OF PUBLIC ADMINISTRATION. LIBRARY. List of Philippine Government publications, 1945–1958, compiled by Andrea C. Ponce and Jacinta C. Yatco. Manila, 1959–60. 2pts. C, Y

HP14. PHILIPPINES (REP.) COMMISSION ON ELECTIONS. Canvass of votes cast 1946–61. Manila. 2 reels of microfilm. C, Y

HP15. REBADAVIA, CONSOLACION B. Checklist of Philippine government documents, 1917–1949. Quezon City, University of the Philippines Library, 1960. 817p. C, Y
[Cornell entry: Bibliographical Society of the Philippines.]

HP16. MORENO FEDERICO B. Philippine legal bibliography. Manila, Sancas, 1960. 1v. C

HP17. MORENO, FEDERICO B. Philippine legal bibliography. 2d ed. Manila, 1962. 139ℓ C

HP18. PHILIPPINES (REP.) BUREAU OF PUBLIC LIBRARIES. Manuel L. Quezon: a bio-bibliography. Manila, 1962. 170ℓ C

HP19. FELICIANO, MYRNA. Checklist of legal periodicals available in the Law Library. Quezon City, 1963. 22ℓ (Quezon, Philippines. University of the Philippines. Library. Research guide, no. 4) C, Y

HP20. CORDERO, FELICIDAD V. An annotated bibliography on community development in the Philippines from 1946–1959. Diliman, Rizal, 1965–

(Quezon, Philippines. University of the Philippines. Community Development Research Council. Special research project, no. 4) C, Y

HP21. HART, DONN V. An annotated bibliography on Barrio Councils. Manila, Presidential Assistant on Community Development, 1965. 50p. C, Y

HP22. QUEZON, PHILIPPINES. UNIVERSITY OF THE PHILIPPINES. INSTITUTE OF PLANNING. An annotated bibliography of Philippine planning. Manila, 1968. 203ℓ Y

HT — THAILAND

HT1. U.S. OPERATIONS MISSION TO THAILAND. PUBLIC ADMINISTRATION DIVISION. Organizational directory of the Government of Thailand. n.p. v.1– C, Y

HT2. BANGKOK, THAILAND. HO SAMUT HAENG CHAT. List of Thai government publications covering the years 1954–1956. Bangkok, 1958. 31p. C

HT3. BANGKOK, THAILAND. THAMMASAT MAHAWITTHAYALAI. KHANA RATTHAPRASASANASAT. List of Thai government publications by Research Division, Institute of Public Administration, Thammasat University. Bangkok, 1958. 43ℓ C

HT4. Thailand official yearbook. Bangkok, GPO, 1964– annual. Y

HT5. THROMBLEY, WOODWORTH GILBERT. Thai government and its setting, a selective annotated bibliography. Bangkok, National Institute of Development Administration, 1968. 93, 513p. C

HV — VIETNAM

HV1. CUA, HUYN-TINH-PAULUS. Sach quan che; des titres civils et militaires français avec leur traduction en quoc-ngu; les six ministères de l'Annam et leur composition, organisation civile et militaire. Saigon, Ban in Nha Nu'oc, 1888. 94p. Y

HV2. SAIGON. HOC-VIEN QUOC-GIA HANH-CHANH THU-VIEN. Ban tong-ke phan-loai sach thu-vien. Classified catalog of books in the library. Saigon, 1957. 150ℓ C

HV3. SAIGON. HOC-VIEN QUOC-GIA HANH-CHANH. Viet Nam government organization manual, 1957–58. Saigon, National Institute of Administration, Research Division, 1958. 275p.
Supplement. Saigon, 1960. 174ℓ C, Y

HV4. NGUYEN THE ANH. Bibliographie critique sur les relations entre le Vietnam et l'Occident (ouvrages et articles en langues occidentales). Paris, Maisonneuve et Larose, 1967. 310p. Y

I—ECONOMICS

IA—GENERAL

IA1. Economic survey of Asia and the Far East. Bangkok, United Nations, ECAFE, 1948- annual. C, Y
[Cornell entry: United Nations. ECAFE.]

IA2. HAWAII. UNIVERSITY. INDUSTRIAL RELATIONS CENTER. Selected bibliographies on labor and industrial relations in Burma, Indonesia, Korea, Malaya, Singapore and Thailand. Honolulu, 1962. ii, 64p. C, Y

IA3. HARVARD UNIVERSITY. GRADUATE SCHOOL OF BUSINESS ADMINISTRATION. Bibliography, cases and other materials for the teaching of business administration in developing countries: South and Southeast Asia. Boston, 1968. 408p. C, Y

IH—INDOCHINA

IH1. INDOCHINA, FRENCH. DIRECTION DES SERVICES ÉCONOMIQUES. Répertoire des sociétés anonymes indochinoises. Hanoi, d'Extrême-Orient, 1944. 235p. Y

II—INDONESIA

II 1. KONINKLIJKE VEREENIGING JAVA MOTOR CLUB. Naamlijst, residentiesgewijze en alfabetisch, van de ondernemingen, huurlanden en particuliere landerijen voorkomende op de kaart van Java en Madoera. Weltevreden, 1926. 77p. Y

II 2. SCHLEIFFER, HEDWIG. Bibliography on the economic and political development of Indonesia by Hedwig Schleiffer and Douglas S. Paauw. Cambridge, Massachusetts Institute of Technology, Center for International Studies. 1953-55. 6v. C, Y

II 3. HICKS, GEORGE L. The Indonesian economy 1950-1965, a bibliography by George L. Hicks and Geoffrey McNicoll. New Haven, Yale University, 1967. 248p. (Yale Univ. Graduate School. Southeast Asia Studies. Bibliography series, no. 9) C, Y

II 4. HICKS, GEORGE L. The Indonesian economy, 1950-1967, a bibliography by George L. Hicks and Geoffrey McNicoll. New Haven, Yale University, 1968. 211p. (Yale Univ. Graduate School. Southeast Asia Studies. Bibliography series, no. 10) C, Y

IM—MALAYSIA

IM1. MALAYA (FED.) REGISTRAR OF SOCIETIES. Societies in the Federation of Malaya; application for registration as registered or exempted societies. Kuala Lumpur. v.1- C, Y

IM2. BURKILL, ISAAC HENRY. A dictionary of the economic products of the Malay peninsula. London, 1935. 2v. C, Y

IP—PHILIPPINES

IP1. QUEZON, PHILIPPINES. UNIVERSITY OF THE PHILIPPINES. Asian Labor Education Center. Major labor federations in the Philippines. Quezon City, Research and Publications Section, Asian Labor Education Center, Univ. of the Philippines, 1963. 70p. Y

IP2.   PHILIPPINES (REP.) PROGRAM IMPLEMENTATION AGENCY. The Philippine economic atlas. Manila, 1965. 163p. C, Y
[Cornell entry: Philippines (Rep.) Office of the President. Program Implementation Agency.]

See also FP12

J—HISTORY

JA—GENERAL

JA1.   CENTRE D'ÉTUDE DES RELATIONS INTERNATIONALES. Chronologie de l'Asie du Sud et du Sud-Est. Paris. v.1- quarterly. C, Y
[Cornell entry: Centre d'Étude des relations internationales, Paris. Section Asie du Sud-Est.]

JA2.   VROMANS, A. G. List of books on prisoners of war and internment camps in the Far East during the Second World War. Amsterdam, 1953. 24p. Y

JA3.   LONDON. UNIVERSITY. SCHOOL OF ORIENTAL AND AFRICAN STUDIES. Historical writing on the peoples of Asia. London, Oxford Univ. Pr., 1961-62. 4v. C, Y
[V.1 Historians of South East Asia by D. G. E. Hall. 342p.]

JA4.   HAY, STEPHEN N. Southeast Asian history; a bibliographic guide edited by Stephen N. Hay and Margaret H. Case. New York, Praeger, 1962. 138p. (Books that matter) C, Y

JA5.   LONDON. UNIVERSITY. SCHOOL OF ORIENTAL AND AFRICAN STUDIES. Handbook of oriental history. London, Offices of the Royal Historical Society, 1963. 265p. (Royal Historical Society London Guides and handbooks, no. 6) C, Y

JA6.   SAUVAGET, JEAN. Introduction to the history of the Muslim East; a bibliographical guide. Based on the 2d ed. as recast by Claude Cahen. Berkeley, Univ. of Cal. Pr., 1965. 252p. C, Y

JA7.   PLUVIER, JAN MEINHARD. A handbook and chart of South-East Asian history. Kuala Lumpur, Oxford Univ. Pr., 1967. 58p. C, Y

JB—BURMA

JB1.   THAN HTUN. A bibliographical essay on the Burmese sources for the history of the Konbaung period, 1752-1885. Rangoon, 19?? 20ℓ
[Appendices: I. A selected bibliography of Burmese historical records in the National Library, 12p. II. An annotated bibliography of Burmese sources 1750-1900, 26p.] C

JB2.   BLACKMORE, THAUNG. A few observations on Burmese historical literature and native and foreign scholarship. n.p. 195? 17ℓ C

JB3.   THAN HTUN. Luce's contribution to Burmese history. Rangoon, 1959. 117-122p. C

JB4.   YI YI, DAW. A bibliographical essay on the Burmese sources for the history of the Konbaung period, 1752-1885. Rangoon, 1961. 26p. C

JH—INDOCHINA

JH1.   GREAT BRITAIN. CENTRAL OFFICE OF INFORMATION. Cambodia, Laos and Vietnam; chronology of events, 1945-1966. London, 196? 117ℓ C

JI—INDONESIA

JI 1.   TIELE, PIETER ANTON. Mémoire bibliographique sur les journaux des navigateurs néerlandais réimprimés dan les collections de de Bry et de Hulsius, et dans les collections hollandaises du XVII siècle, et sur les anciennes éditions hollandaises des journaux de navigateurs étrangers. Amsterdam, Muller, 1867. 372p. C, Y

JI 2.   HOOYKAAS, J. C. Repertorium op de koloniale literatuur of systematische inhoudsopgaaf van het geen voorkomt over de kolonien (beoosten de Kaap) in mengelwerken en tijdschriften, van 1595 tot 1865 uitgegeven in Nederland en zijne overzeesche bezittingen. Amsterdam, van Kampen, 1877-80. 2v. C, Y
[Cornell entry: title]

JI 3.   FEITH, P. R. Catalogus der verzameling van boeken en prenten betrekking hebbende op de stad Batavia, bijeengebracht door en eigendom. Batavia, 1937. 54p. C

JI 4.   LEMBAGA KEBUDAJAAN INDONESIA. Catalogus der praehistorische verzameling. Bandoeng, Nix, 1941. 400p.

JI 5.   COOLHAAS, WILLEM PHILIPPUS. A critical survey of studies on Dutch colonial history. The Hague, Nijhoff, 1960. 154p. (Koninklijk Instituut voor Taal-, Land- en Volkenkunde, bibliographical series, 4) C, Y

JI 6.   INDONESIA. DEPARTEMEN PENERANGAN. Chronologie de l'histoire Indonésienne. Djakarta, 1960. 83p. C, Y

JI 7.   INDONESIA. DEPARTEMEN PENERANGAN. A chronology of Indonesian history. Djakarta, 1960. 83p. C, Y

JI 8.   WASEDA DAIGAKU, TOKYO. OKUMA KÌNEN SHAKAI KAGAKU KENKYŪJO. List of collected materials concerning the Japanese military administration in Indonesia. Tokyo, Waseda Univ., Ohkuma Institute of Social Sciences, 1960. 93p. Y

JI 9.   Gids van in Nederland aanwezige bronnen betreffende de geschiedenis van Nederlands-Indië/Indonesië, 1816-1942. Leiden, Koninklijk Instituut voor Taal-, Land- en Volkenkunde, 1968-   C

JM—MALAYSIA

JM1.   TREGONNING, KENNEDY GORDON. Malaysian historical sources. Singapore, Dept. of History, Univ. of Singapore, 1962. 130p. C, Y

JP—PHILIPPINES

JP1.   Biblioteca histórica filipina: historias, crónicas, anales, memorias, relaciones, cartas, papeles sueltos y demas documentos históricos, todós inéditos y desconocidos, sobre la conquista militar, civilización cristiana, gobierno y administración de este archipiélago, escogidos en los archivos de sus conventos religiosos y establecimientos oficiales del estado y de los pueblos. Manila, Eco de Filipinas, 1892- 3v. C, Y

JP2.   U.S. LIBRARY OF CONGRESS. DIVISION OF BIBLIOGRAPHY. List of works relating to the American occupation of the Philippine Islands, 1898-1903, with some additions to 1905. Washington, 1905. 100p. C, Y

JP3.   ROBERTSON, JAMES ALEXANDER. Bibliography of early Spanish Japanese relations, compiled from manuscripts and books in the Philippine library, Manila. Yokohama, Kelly and Walsh, 1915. 170p. (In Asiatic society of Japan. Transactions. vol. XLIII pt. 1) C, Y

JP4.   U.S. LIBRARY OF CONGRESS. DIVISION OF BIBLIOGRAPHY. Philippine Islands, with special reference to the question of independence; a bibliographical list of recent writings compiled by Anne L. Baden. Washington, 1931. 25p. C, Y

JP5.   U.S. ARMY. FORCES IN THE PACIFIC. The Philippines during the Japanese regime, 1942-1945; an annotated list of the literature published in or about the Philippines during the Japanese occupation. Prepared by Office of the Chief of Counterintelligence, Philippine research and information section, GHQ., AFPAC. Manila, 1945. 44p. C, Y

JP6.	WU, CHING-HUNG. A chronological table of important events relating to the Chinese in the Philippines during the Spanish period. n.p. 195? 12-57p. Y
JP7.	WU, CHING-HUNG. A study of references to the Philippines in Chinese sources from earliest times to the Ming dynasty. Quezon City, 1953. 260, 34ℓ C, Y [MA thesis, Univ. of the Philippines.]
JP8.	PEÑA CÁMARA, JOSÉ MARÍA DE LA. A list of Spanish residencias in the Archives of the Indies, 1516-1775; administrative judicial reviews of colonial officials in the American Indies, Philippine and Canary Islands. Washington, Library of Congress, Reference Dept., 1955. 109p. C, Y
JP9.	WU, CHING-HUNG. References on the Chinese in the Philippines during the Spanish period found in Blair and Robertson, The Philippine Islands. Singapore, 1959. 90p. Y [Reprinted from the Bulletin of Institute of Southeast Asia, Nanyang Univ., Singapore.]

JV — VIETNAM

JV1.	TRAN-VAN-GIAP. Les chapitres bibliographiques de Le-qui-Don et de Phan-huy-Chu. Saigon, Testelin, 1938. 217p. C
JV2.	JUMPER, ROY. Bibliography on the political and administrative history of Vietnam, 1802-1962, selected and annotated. Saigon, Michigan State University, Vietnam Advisory Group, 1962. 179ℓ C, Y
JV3.	JUMPER, ROY. Bibliography on the political and administrative history of Vietnam, 1802-1962, selected and annotated. Saigon, Michigan State Univ., Vietnam Advisory Group, 1964. 115p. Y [Agency for International Development contract ICA c1126.]
JV4.	PHAN GIA BEN. La recherche historique en République Démocratique du Vietnam, 1953-1963. Hanoi, Editions Scientifiques, 1965. 99p. Y

K—ANTHROPOLOGY

KA—GENERAL

KA1. TIELE, PIETER ANTON. Nederlandsche bibliographie van land- en volkenkunde. Amsterdam, Muller, 1884. 288p. (Bijdragen tot eene Nederlandsche Bibliographie, uitgegeven door het Frederik Muller-Fonds, I) C, Y

KA2. FEGAN, ETHEL SOPHIA. Bibliography of Alfred Cort Haddon. Hilo, Hawaii, 1942. 49ℓ C, Y

KA3. EMBREE, JOHN FEE. Selected bibliography of peoples and cultures of mainland Southeast Asia. New Haven, 1948. 85ℓ (Yale Univ. Southeast Asia Studies. Bibliography Series) Y

KA4. EMBREE, JOHN FEE. Bibliography of the peoples and cultures of mainland Southeast Asia by John F. Embree and Lillian Ota Dotson. New Haven, Yale Univ. Southeast Asia Studies, 1950. 821p. C, Y

KA5. YALE UNIVERSITY. GRADUATE SCHOOL. SOUTHEAST ASIA STUDIES. Ethnic groups of northern Southeast Asia. New Haven, 1950. 175p. (Its cultural report series) C, Y

KA6. EMBREE, JOHN FEE. A selected bibliography on Southeast Asia compiled with an introduction by John F. Embree; rev. and expanded by Bruno Lasker. 2d ed. New York, American Institute of Pacific Relations, 1952. 27ℓ C, Y

KA7. CALIFORNIA. UNIVERSITY. UNIVERSITY AT LOS ANGELES. DEPARTMENT OF ANTHROPOLOGY AND SOCIOLOGY. LAOS PAPERS. An annotated bibliography on the peoples of Laos and northern Thailand; selected sources in English, French and Japanese published since 1945. Los Angeles, 1961. 6ℓ (Laos project paper, no. 5) C, Y

KA8. LeBAR, FRANK M. Ethnic groups of mainland Southeast Asia. New Haven, HRAF, 1964. 288p. C, Y

KH—INDOCHINA

KH1. JANSE, OLOV ROBERT THURE. The peoples of French Indochina. Washington, Smithsonian Institution, 1944. iv, 28p. (Smithsonian institution. War Background studies, no. 19) C, Y

KI—INDONESIA

KI 1. LEMBAGA KEBUDAJAAN INDONESIA. MUSEUM. Catalogus der ethnologische afdeeling van het Museum van het Bataviaasch Genootschap van Kunsten en Wetenschappen. 2. druk. Batavia, Bruining, 1877. 186p. Y

KI 2. LEMBAGA KEBUDAJAAN INDONESIA. MUSEUM. Supplement der catalogus der ethnologische verzameling van het Bataviaasch Genootschap van Kunsten en Wetenschappen door J. A. van der Chijs. 4. druk. Batavia, Albrecht & Rusche, 1894. 195p. C

KI 3. LUMMEL, HENDRIK JAN VAN. Literatuurstudie van Halmahera en Morotai, bewerkt door H. J. van Lummel en L. Van Vuuren. Batavia, Javasche Boekhandel & Drukkerij, 1918. 126p. (Vereeniging tot Bevordering van het Bibliotheekwezen in Nederlandsch-Indië. Mededeelingen, 1) Y

KI 4. ALKEMA, B. Beknopt handboek der volkenkunde van Nederlandsch-Indië door B. Alkema en T. J. Bezemer. Haarlem, Tjeenk Willink, 1927. 583p. Y

KI 5. KLEIWEG DE ZWAAN, JOHANNES PIETER. Anthropologische bibliographie van den Indischen archipel en van Nederlandsch West-Indië, supplement by A. J. van Bork-Feltkamp. Leiden, Brill, 1940. 130p. (Mededeelingen van de Afdeeling volkenkunde van het Koloniaal Instituut, Extra serie, no. 3) C, Y

KI 6. KENNEDY, RAYMOND. Bibliography of Indonesian peoples and cultures. New Haven, Yale Univ. Pr., 1945. 212p. (Yale anthropological studies, v.4) C, Y

KI 7. KENNEDY, RAYMOND. Bibliography of Indonesian peoples and cultures. Rev. ed. New Haven, HRAF, 1955. 2v. (Behavior science bibliographies) C, Y

KI 8. SUZUKI, PETER. Critical survey of studies on the anthropology of Nias, Mentawei and Enggano. The Hague, Nijhoff, 1958. 87p. (Koninklijk Instituut voor Taal-, Land- en Volkenkunde, Bibliographical series, 3) C, Y

KI 9. JASPAN, MERVYN AUBREY. Social stratification and social mobility in Indonesia, a trend report and annotated bibliography. Djakarta, Seri Ilmu dan Masjarakat, Gunung Agung, 1959. 76p. C, Y

KI 10. JASPAN, MERVYN AUBREY. Social stratification and social mobility in Indonesia, a trend report and annotated bibliography. 2d enl. ed. Djakarta, Gunung Agung, 1961. 95p. (Science and society series no. 1) C, Y

KI 11. KENNEDY, RAYMOND. Bibliography of Indonesian peoples and cultures. 2d. rev. ed. Rev. and edited by Thomas W. Maretzki and H. Th. Fischer. New Haven, HRAF, 1962. 207p. (Behavior science bibliographies) C, Y

KI 12. AUSTRALIAN NATIONAL UNIVERSITY, CANBERRA. DEPT. OF ANTHROPOLOGY AND SOCIOLOGY. An ethnographic bibliography of New Guinea. Canberra, Australian National Univ. Pr., 1968. 3v. in 1. Y

See also PI 40, PI 48, PI 49

KM— MALAYSIA

KM1. SKEAT, WALTER WILLIAM. Pagan races of the Malay Peninsula by Walter William Skeat and Charles Otto Blagden. London, Macmillan, 1906. 2v. C, Y

KM2. COTTER, CONRAD P. Bibliography of English language sources on human ecology, Eastern Malaysia and Brunei, compiled by Conrad P. Cotter with the assistance of Shiro Saito. Honolulu, Dept. of Asian Studies, Univ. of Hawaii, 1965. 2v. C, Y

KP— PHILIPPINES

KP1. FOX, ROBERT B. A selected bibliography of the peoples of Mountain Province, Northern Luzon, Philippines. Chicago, Univ. of Chicago, Dept. of Anthropology, 1956. 14ℓ C

KP2. MANUEL, E. ARSENIO. The Beyer Collection of original sources in Philippine ethnography. Manila, 1958. 46−66p. Y

KP3. ANTONIO, CELIA M. A preliminary bibliography of Philippine cultural minorities by Celia M. Antonio and Allen L. Tan. Quezon City, Commission on National Integration, Rep. of the Philippines, 1967. 34p. C, Y

KP4. CONKLIN, HAROLD C. Ifugao bibliography. New Haven, Yale Univ., Southeast Asia Studies, 1968. vi, 75p. (Yale Univ. Southeast Asia Studies. Bibliography series, no. 11) C, Y

KP5. SAITO, SHIRO. Preliminary bibliography of Philippine ethnography. Loyola Heights, Institute of Philippine Culture, Ateneo de Manila, 1968. 388p. Y

KV—VIETNAM

KV1.   VIETNAM. UY-HOI QUOC-GIA UNESCO. Thu-muc chu-qiui ve-van-hoa Viet-Nam. Bibliographie commentée sur la culture vietnamienne. Commented bibliography on Vietnamese culture. Saigon, 1966. 226p. C

L—EDUCATION (INCLUDING THESES)

LA—GENERAL

LA1. UTRECHT. RIJKSUNIVERSITEIT. BIBLIOTHEEK. Catalogus van Academische geschriften in Nederland en Nederlandsch-Indië verschenen. Utrecht, 1924–49. 22v. C, Y

LA2. JANERT, KLAUS LUDWIG. Verzeichnis indienkundlicher Hochschulschriften: Deutschland, Österreich, Schweiz. Wiesbaden, Harrassowitz, 1961. ix, 80p. Y

LA3. NEFF, KENNETH LEE. Selected bibliography on education in Southeast Asia. Washington, Dept. of Health, Education and Welfare, 1963. iii, 16p. (U.S. Office of Education. Studies in comparative education) C, Y

LA4. STUCKI, CURTIS W. American doctoral dissertations on Asia, 1933–1962, including appendix of master's theses at Cornell University. Ithaca, Southeast Asia Program, Cornell Univ., 1963. 204p. (Cornell Univ. Southeast Asia Program. Data paper no. 50) C, Y

LA5. HART, DONN V. An annotated bibliography of theses and dissertations on Asia accepted at Syracuse University, 1907–1963. Syracuse, Syracuse Univ. Library, 1964. xii, 46p. C, Y

LA6. BLOOMFIELD, BARRY CAMBRAY. Theses on Asia accepted by universities in the United Kingdom and Ireland, 1877–1964. London, Cass, 1967. 127p. C, Y

LA7. STUCKI, CURTIS W. American doctoral dissertations on Asia, 1933–June 1966, including appendix of master's theses at Cornell University, 1933–June 1968. Ithaca, 1968. 304p. (Cornell Univ. Southeast Asia Program. Data paper, no. 71) C, Y

LA8. THE, LIAN. Treasures and trivia: doctoral dissertations on Southeast Asia accepted by universities in the United States, compiled by Lian The and Paul W. van der Veur. Athens, Ohio, 1968. 141p. (Ohio. Univ. Center for International Studies. Papers in International Studies. Southeast Asia Series, no. 1) C, Y

LB—BURMA

LB1. NEFF, KENNETH LEE. Burma education data. Washington, Dept. of Health, Education and Welfare, 1965. 14p. C, Y

LI—INDONESIA

LI 1. INDOLOGISCHE STUDENTENCORPS, DELFT. Almanak, 1897– annual. C, Y
[Supersedes Indologische Vereniging, Delft. Almanak.]
[Cornell entry: Almanak van het Indologisch Studentencorps.]

LI 2. INDONESIA. DEPARTEMEN PERGURUAN TINGGI DAN ILMU PENGETAHUAN. Perguruan tinggi di Indonesia. Djakarta. v.1– Y

LI 3. INDONESIA. DJAWATAN PENDIDIKAN KEDJURUAN. Almanak. Djakarta, 1960– annual. Y

LI 4. THEE, TJOEN GIAP. Pedoman sekolah2 di Indonesia. Djakarta, Kinta, 1962. 177p. C, Y

LI 5. RASJIDI, CHALID. Bagaimana memilih sekolah. Petundjuk praktis bagi tamatan sr, slp, sla, orangtua, murid dan umum untuk memilih djenis sekolah landjutan dengan tepat, disertai lampiran daftar persamaan

LI 6.   idjazah, disusun oleh Chalid Rasjidi dan Munir Sjahdana. Djakarta, Djambatan, 1963. 125p. C, Y
[Cornell entry: Chalid Rasjidi]
PUDJIADI, R. Penerbitan2 staf pengadjar Institut Keguruan dan Ilmu Pendidikan, Bandung 1954-1964, disusun oleh R. Pudjiadi dan Ratna Wilis Dahar. Bandung, 1964. 35𝑙 C, Y

LI 7.   GERUNGAN, W. A. Kemana melandjutkan sekolah. Bandung, Eresco, 1965. 2v. Y

LM — MALAYSIA-SINGAPORE

LM1.   SINGAPORE. MINISTRY OF EDUCATION. Lists of schools. Singapore. v.1- C

LM2.   SARAWAK. INFORMATION SERVICE. A guide to education in Sarawak. Kuala Belait, Brunei Pr., 1961. 55p. C, Y
[Cornell entry: Sarawak. Perkhidmatan Penerangan.]

LM3.   WANG, HSIU CHIN (CHEN). Education in Malaysia; a bibliography. Singapore, Univ. of Singapore Library, 1964. 35p. C, Y
[Cornell entry: Singapore (City) University. Library. Reference Dept.]

LM4.   The educational directory of Malaysia and Singapore. Kuala Lumpur, 1965- C, Y

LM5.   YIP, WENG KEE. Educational institutions in Singapore. Singapore, The Vocational Guidance Steering Committee, 1965. 127p. C, Y

LM6.   JACKSON, JAMES C. Recent higher degree theses on social, political and economic aspects of Southeast Asia presented in the Universities of the United Kingdom and in the Universities of Malaya and Singapore. Hull, Eng., Univ. of Hull, Dept. of Geography, 1966. 1v. (Univ. of Hull. Dept. of Geography. Miscellaneous series, no. 6) C, Y

See also   BP3

LP — PHILIPPINES

LP1.   MANILA. UNIVERSITY OF SANTO TOMAS. General index of academic works. Manila, Office of the Secretary General. v.1- C, Y
[Title varies: 1956- Index of the published works of the faculty members.]

LP2.   Compilation of graduate theses prepared in the Philippines 1913-1960. Manila. nos. 1-11. C

LP3.   QUEZON, PHILIPPINES. UNIVERSITY OF THE PHILIPPINES. Research works and other publications of the faculties. Quezon City, 1957/59- C, Y

LP4.   QUEZON, PHILIPPINES. UNIVERSITY OF THE PHILIPPINES. SOCIAL SCIENCE RESEARCH CENTER. List of graduates with graduate degrees and titles of their theses. Quezon City, 1957. 108p. C, Y

LP5.   PHILIPPINES (REP.) BUREAU OF PUBLIC SCHOOLS. Catalogue of publications of the Bureau of Public Schools. Manila, 1962. 139p. C

LP6.   QUEZON, PHILIPPINES. UNIVERSITY OF THE PHILIPPINES. GRADUATE SCHOOL OF ARTS AND SCIENCES. Theses abstracts, 1947/54- Quezon City, 1962- C, Y

LP7.   ONORATO, MICHAEL PAUL. The Philippines; a list of doctoral dissertations in American universities in the fields of economics, history, political science and sociology (1916-1964). Rev. ed. New York, New York State Univ., Foreign Area Materials Center, 1964. 4p. C, Y

LT — THAILAND

LT1.   BANGKOK, THAILAND. CHULALONGKON MAHAWITTHAYALAI. Hand-

         book Chulalongkorn University. Bangkok, Chatra Pr., 1955. 216p. C
LT2.   FRANZEN, CARL GUSTAVE FREDERICK. Thailand; a guide to the academic placement of students from the Kingdom of Thailand in United States educational institutions, 1959. n.p. Committee on Foreign Students of the American Association of Collegiate Registrars and Admissions Officers, 1959. xi, 84p. (World education series) C, Y

LV — VIETNAM

LV1.   ANDREATTA, LOUIS. Education in Vietnam; a selected bibliography. New York, American Friends of Vietnam, 1961. 6p. C

M—GEOGRAPHY AND GAZETTEERS

MA—GENERAL

MA1. HAMILTON, WALTER. The East Indian gazetteer; containing particular descriptions of the empires, kingdoms, principalities, provinces, cities, towns, districts, fortresses, harbours, rivers, lakes, etc. of Hindostan, and the adjacent countries, India beyond the Ganges, and the Eastern archipelago; together with sketches of the manners, customs, institutions, agriculture, commerce, manufactures, revenues, population, castes, religion, history, etc. of their various inhabitants. London, Dove, 1815. 862p. C, Y

MA2. HAMILTON, WALTER. A geographical, statistical and historical description of Hindostan, and the adjacent countries. London, 1820. 2v. C, Y

MA3. HAMILTON, WALTER. East-India gazetteer; containing particular descriptions of Hindostan, and the adjacent countries, India beyond the Ganges, and the Eastern Archipelago. 2d. ed. London, 1828. 2v. Y

MA4. DANIEL, HAWTHORNE. Islands of the East Indies, with six maps by Lucien G. Picard. New York, Putnam, 1944. 266p. C, Y

MA5. PELZER, KARL JOSEF. Selected bibliography on the geography of Southeast Asia. New Haven, Yale University, Southeast Asia Studies, 1949-56. 3v. (Behavior science bibliographies) C, Y

MA6. U.S. BOARD ON GEOGRAPHIC NAMES. Indian Ocean gazetteer. Washington, GPO, 1957. 54p. (Its Gazetteer no. 32) C, Y
[Cornell entry: U.S. Office of Geography.]

MA7. STERNSTEIN, LARRY. An annotated bibliography of material concerning Southeast Asia from Petermanns Geographische Mitteilungen (1885-1966) by Larry Sternstein and Carl Springer. Bangkok, The Siam Society, 1967. 389p. C

MB—BURMA

MB1. SPEARMAN, HORACE RALPH. The British Burma gazetteer. Rangoon, GPO, 1879-80. 2v. Y

MB2. SCOTT, JAMES GEORGE. Gazetteer of Upper Burma and the Shan States. Rangoon, GPO, 1900-01. 5v. C, Y

MB3. Imperial gazetteer of India. Provincial series. Burma. Calcutta, 1908. 2v. Y

MB4. BURMA. Burma gazetteer, volume A, descriptive. Rangoon, GPO, 1910-12. 7v. Y

MB5. Burma gazetteer, volume B. Census of India, 1911, Burma. Rangoon, 1912-13. 7v. Y

MB6. U.S. BOARD ON GEOGRAPHIC NAMES. Burma gazetteer. Washington, GPO, 1955. 175p. (Its Gazetteer no. 9) C, Y
[Cornell entry: U.S. Office of Geography]

MB7. U.S. BOARD ON GEOGRAPHIC NAMES. Burma gazetteer. 2d. ed. Washington, GPO, 1966. 725p. (Its Gazetteer no. 96) C, Y
[Cornell entry: U.S. Office of Geography]

MC—CAMBODIA

MC1. U.S. BOARD ON GEOGRAPHIC NAMES. Cambodia gazetteer. Washington, GPO, 1963. 199p. (Its Gazetteer no. 74) C, Y
[Cornell entry: U.S. Office of Geography]

MH — INDOCHINA

MH1. U.S. ARMY MAP SERVICE. Gazetteer to AMS 1:250,000 maps of Indochina (Series L509) 1958. Washington, 1959. 305p. C, Y

MI — INDONESIA

MI 1. VETH, PIETER JOHANNES. Aardrijkskundig en statistisch woordenboek van Nederlandsch Indië, bewerkt naar de jongste en beste berigten. Amsterdam, van Kampen, 1869. 3v. C, Y
[Cornell entry: title]

MI 2. KAN, C. M. Proeve eener geographische bibliographie van Nederlandsch Oost-Indië voor de jaren 1865–1880. Utrecht, Beijers, 1881. 128p. Y

MI 3. BEUS, G. DE. Plaatselijk woordenboek van Java en Madoera, bevattende alphabetische naamlijst van de voornaamste plaatsen en van alle landbouwondernemingen op Java en Madoera, met gegevens betreffende den post-, telegraaf- en telefoondienst, ligging ten opzichte van spoor- en tramwegen, logeergelegenheden, vervoermiddelen. Amsterdam, de Bussy, 1912. 607p. C

MI 4. DUTCH EAST INDIES. ALGEMENE SECRETARIE. Residentie Semarang. Afstandswijzer van het wegennet met kaart. Batavia, 1914. 171p. Y

MI 5. DUTCH EAST INDIES. ALGEMENE SECRETARIE. Residentie Lampongsche Districten. Afstandswijzer met kaart. Batavia, 1915. 39p. Y

MI 6. DUMONT, CHARLES FRANÇOIS HENRI. Aardrijkskundig woordenboek van Nederlandsch Oost-Indië. Rotterdam, Nijgh & van Ditmar, 1917. 654p. C, Y

MI 7. WIERINGA, B. Beknopt aardrijkskundig woordenboek van Nederlandsch-Indië; met toestemming van den heer chef van den post-, telegraaf- en telefoondienst mede uit officieele gegevens. 3 verm. druk. Haarlem, Visser, 1917. 373p. C

MI 8. DUTCH EAST INDIES. ALGEMENE SECRETARIE. Residentie Palembang. Afstandswijzer met kaart. Batavia, 1921. 19p. Y

MI 9. WIERINGA, B. Aardrijkskundig woordenboek van Nederlandsch-Indië. 3 verm. druk. Haarlem, Visser, 1921. 502p. C

MI 10. NEDERLANDSCH AARDRIJKSKUNDIG GENOOTSCHAP, AMSTERDAM. Lijst van de voornaamste aardrijkskundige namen in den Nederlandsch-Indischen Archipel. 2 herz. uitg. Weltevreden, GPO, 1923. 361p. C, Y
[Cornell entry: Dutch East Indies.]

MI 11. SCHOEL, W. F. Alphabetisch register van de administratieve- (bestuurs-) en adatrechtelijke indeeling van Nederlandsch-Indië. Batavia, GPO, 1931. 2v. C, Y
[Cornell entry: Dutch East Indies. Kantoor voor de Volkstelling 1930]

MI 12. DUTCH EAST INDIES. TOPOGRAPHISCHE DIENST. Alphabetische lijst der namen, voorkomende op de kaart van Java, Madoera en Bali. Batavia, 1932. 15p. C

MI 13. U.S. BOARD ON GEOGRAPHIC NAMES. Gazetteer to maps of Java, Madura and Bali, map series AMS T251, scale 1:250,000. 2d. ed. Washington, Army Map Service, 1944. vi, 88p. C, Y

MI 14. U.S. BOARD ON GEOGRAPHIC NAMES. Gazetteer to maps of Lesser Sunda islands scale 1:250,000. Washington, U.S. Army, 1944. iii, 62p. C, Y

MI 15. U.S. BOARD ON GEOGRAPHIC NAMES. Gazetteer to maps of Molukken Islands, scale 1:100,000 map series AMS T662. 2d. ed. Washington, Army Map Service, 1944. v, 83p. C

MI 16.   U.S. BOARD ON GEOGRAPHIC NAMES. Indonesia gazetteer. Washington, GPO, 1955. 2v. (Its Gazetteer no. 13) C, Y
[Cornell entry: U.S. Office of Geography]

MI 17.   INDONESIA. DJAWATAN HIDROGRAFI. Daftar2 ilmu pelajaran; dilengkapi dengan keterangan2 singkat den tjara penggunaanuja. Djakarta, 1962. 1v. C, Y
[Cornell entry: Indonesia. Angkatan Laut. Djawatan Hidrografi.]

MI 18.   U.S. BOARD ON GEOGRAPHIC NAMES. Indonesia gazetteer. 2d. ed. Washington, GPO, 1968. 901p. (Its Gazetteer no. 13) C, Y
[Cornell entry: U.S. Office of Geography]

See also FI 42, PH50

ML— LAOS

ML1.   U.S. BOARD ON GEOGRAPHIC NAMES. Laos gazetteer. Washington, GPO, 1962. 214p. (Its Gazetteer no. 69) C, Y
[Cornell entry: U.S. Office of Geography]

MM— MALAYSIA— SINGAPORE

MM1.   U.S. BOARD ON GEOGRAPHIC NAMES. British Borneo, Singapore and Malaya gazetteer. Washington, GPO, 1955. 463p. (Its Gazetteer no. 10) C, Y
[Cornell entry: U.S. Office of Geography]

MM2.   MALAYA (FED.) SURVEY DEPT. Street directory and guide to Kuala Lumpur with sectional maps. Kuala Lumpur, 1957. 52p. C, Y

MM3.   RAJA SINGAM, S. DURAI. Malayan place names. 4th ed. Singapore, Liang Khoo, 1962. 253p. Y
[Earlier editions have title: Port Weld to Kuantan.]

See also FM17, FM18, FM22

MP— PHILIPPINES

MP1.   U.S. BUREAU OF INSULAR AFFAIRS. Pronouncing gazetteer and geographical dictionary of the Philippine Islands. Washington, GPO, 1902. 39, 933p. C, Y

MP2.   U.S. BOARD ON GEOGRAPHIC NAMES. Gazetteer to maps of the Philippine Islands, map series AMS S401, scale 1:500,000. 2d. ed. Washington, 1944. 239p. C, Y

MP3.   U.S. COAST AND GEODETIC SURVEY. Gazetteer of the Philippine Islands. Washington, 1945. 350p. C, Y

MP4.   PHILIPPINES (REP.) BUREAU OF COAST AND GEODETIC SURVEY. Geographical data of the Philippines. Rev. ed. Manila, 1962. 220 C

MP5.   HUKE, ROBERT E. Bibliography of Philippine geography, 1940-1963; a selected list. Hanover, N.H., 1964. 84p. (Geography publications at Dartmouth, no. 1) C, Y

MT— THAILAND

MT1.   PERMANENT COMMITTEE ON GEOGRAPHICAL NAMES FOR BRITISH OFFICIAL USE. Glossaries. London, 1942-54. 8v. C
v.6 - Thai

MT2.   THAILAND. LEGATION U.S. Gazetteer to maps of Thailand compiled under the supervision of the United States Board on Geographic Names. Washington, U.S. Army, 1944. 971p. C, Y

MT3. U.S. BOARD ON GEOGRAPHIC NAMES. Thailand gazetteer. Washington, GPO, 1966. 675p. (Its Gazetteer no. 97) C, Y
[Cornell entry: U.S. Office of Geography]

MV — VIETNAM

MV1. U.S. BOARD ON GEOGRAPHIC NAMES. South Vietnam and the South China Sea gazetteer. Washington, GPO, 1961. 248p. (Its Gazetteer no. 58) C, Y
[Cornell entry: U.S. Office of Geography]

MV2. U.S. BOARD ON GEOGRAPHIC NAMES. North Vietnam gazetteer. Washington, GPO, 1964. 311p. (Its Gazetteer no. 79) C, Y
[Cornell entry: U.S. Office of Geography]

N—ATLASES AND MAP BIBLIOGRAPHIES

NA—GENERAL ATLASES TO THE REGION

NA1.   Atlas semesta dunia. Djakarta, Djambatan, 1952. 256p. C, Y

NA2.   SELLMAN, ROGER RAYMOND. An outline atlas of Eastern history. London, Arnold, 1954. 63p. C, Y

NA3.   ROOLVINK, ROELOF. Historical atlas of the Muslim peoples. Amsterdam, Djambatan, 1957. 40p. C, Y

NA4.   ROMEIN, JAN ERIK. Atlas nasional seluruh dunia untuk sekolah landjutan. Djakarta, Ganaco, 1960. iv, 72p. C

NA5.   DJAMBATAN UITGEVERSBEDRIJF, N.V., AMSTERDAM. Atlas of Southeast Asia, with an introduction by D. G. E. Hall. London, Macmillan, 1964. 84p. C, Y

NA6.   Atlas of physical, economic and social resources of the Lower Mekong Basin. Atlas des ressources physiques, économiques et sociales du Bassin Inférieur du Mekong. Prepared under the direction of the United States Agency for International Development, Bureau for East Asia, by the Engineer Agency for Resources Inventories and the Tennessee Valley Authority for the Committee for Coordination of Investigations of the Lower Mekong Basin (Cambodia, Laos, Republic of Viet-Nam and Thailand), United Nations Economic Commission for Asia and the Far East. New York, 1968. x, 257p. Y

NB—BURMA

NB1.   BURMA. COMMISSIONER OF SETTLEMENTS AND LAND RECORDS. Atlas of the Province of Burma. Rangoon, 1923. 73ℓ C

NB2.   BARTHOLOMEW, JOHN. The Oxford school atlas for India, Pakistan, Burma and Ceylon. 20th ed. London, Oxford Univ. Pr., 1958. 63p. C

<u>See also</u> BD1

NH—INDOCHINA

NH1.   LUNET DE LAJONQUIÈRE, ETIENNE EDMOND. Atlas archéologique de l'Indo-Chine, monuments du Champa et du Cambodge. Paris, Impr. nationale, 1901. 24p. (Publications de l'École française d'Extrême-Orient) C, Y

NH2.   PAVIE, AUGUSTE JEAN MARIE. Mission Pavie Indo-Chine: Atlas. Ouvrage pub. sous les auspices du Ministère des affaires étrangères, du Ministère des colonies, et du Ministère de l'instruction publique et des beaux-arts. Paris, Challamel, 1903. 54p. C, Y

NH3.   CHABERT, OSTLÂND DE. Atlas général de l'Indochine française par Chabert et L. Gallois. Hanoi, Ideo, 1909. 169p. C

NH4.   GALLOIS, LUCIEN LOUIS JOSEPH. Atlas général de l'Indochine français. Hanoi, Extrême-Orient, 1909. vip. 63 double maps. C

NH5.   INDOCHINA, FRENCH. SERVICE GÉOGRAPHIQUE. Atlas de l'Indochine. Hanoi, 1928. 51 col. maps. Y

NI—INDONESIA

NI 1.   DERFELDEN VAN HINDERSTEIN, GIJSBERT FRANCO. Algemeene kaart van Nederlandsch Oostindie. The Hague. 1842. 1v. Y

NI 2.   MELVILL VAN CARNBEE, PIETER. Algemeene atlas van Nederlandsch-Indië. 2de. uitgave. Gouda, 1870. 1v. Y

NI 3.   PIJNAPPEL, J. Atlas van Nederlandsche bezittingen in Oost-Indie. Nieuw bewerkte uitgave. Amsterdam, 1872. 1v. Y

NI 4.   GELDER, WILLEM VAN. Schoolatlas van Nederlandsch Oost-Indië. 4. herz. druk. Groningen, Wolters, 1895. 4p. 6 double col. maps. Y

NI 5.   DUTCH EAST INDIES. DIENST VAN DEN MIJNBOUW. Geologische kaart van Java, schaal 1:100,000. Batavia, 19?? v. C, Y

NI 6.   DUTCH EAST INDIES. DIENST VAN DEN MIJNBOUW. Geologische kaart van Java, schaal 1:100,000. Toelichting bijblad. Batavia, 19?? v. C, Y

NI 7.   GELDER, WILLEM VAN. Atlas ketjil Hindia-Nederland, dengan kitab peta. Tjet. 3. The Hague, De Swart, 1902. 28p. C

NI 8.   NETHERLANDS (KINGDOM, 1815–) DEPARTEMENT VAN ZAKEN OVER-ZEE. Atlas van Nederlandsch Oost-Indië, bij het Topographisch Bureau te Batavia samengesteld in de jaren 1897–1904. The Hague, 1907. 2, 16 (i.e. 20) col. maps. C, Y
[Cornell entry: Stemfoort, J. W.]

NI 9.   DORNSEIFFEN, ISAÄC. Atlas van Nederlandsch Oost- en West-Indië. 5. druk. Amsterdam, Seyffardt, 1908. 26 maps. Y

NI 10.   GELDER, WILLEM VAN. School atlas van Nederlandsch Oost-Indië. 11 herz. en verm. druk. Groningen, Wolters, 1911. 4p. 12 col. maps. C

NI 11.   GELDER, WILLEM VAN. School atlas van Nederlandsch Oost-Indië. 15 herziene en verm. druk. Groningen, Wolters, 1918. 5p. 12 col. maps. C

NI 12.   BUSSY, J. H. DE., PUBLISHER, AMSTERDAM. Atlas van Nederlandsch Oost-Indië voor kantoor, school en huis. Amsterdam, 1919. 30p. Y

NI 13.   DUTCH EAST INDIES. KANTOOR VOOR DE VOLKSLECTUUR. Nederlandsch-Indië platen atlas met korten beschrijvenden tekst. Weltevreden, Kolff, 1926. 176p. Y

NI 14.   DUTCH EAST INDIES. DIENST VAN DEN MIJNBOUW. Geologische kaart van Sumatra, schaal 1:200,000. Blad 1- Batavia, 1931- C, Y

NI 15.   DUTCH EAST INDIES. DIENST VAN DEN MIJNBOUW. Geologische kaart van Sumatra, schaal 1:200,000. Toelichting bijblad, 1- Batavia, 1931- C, Y

NI 16.   DUTCH EAST INDIES. DEPARTEMENT VAN ECONOMISCHE ZAKEN. Landbouwstatistiekkaart van Java en Madoera op schaal 1:150,000 (in 26 bladen). Batavia, 1934. 2p. 26 double maps. Y

NI 17.   GELDER, WILLEM VAN. Atlas van Nederlandsch-Indië, door W. van Gelder en C. Lekkerkerker. Groningen, Wolters, 1937. 16p. C

NI 18.   NEDERLANDS AARDRIJKSKUNDIG GENOOTSCHAP, AMSTERDAM. Atlas van tropisch Nederland, uitgegeven door het Koninklijk nederlandsch aardrijkskundig genootschap in samenwerking met den Topografischen dienst in Nederlandsch-Indië. Batavia, Reproductiebedrijf van den Topografischen dienst in Ned.-Indië, 1938. 5p. 31 (i.e. 37) maps. C, Y
[Cornell entry: Nederlandsch aardrijkskundig . . .]

NI 19.   ZENDING DER NEDERLANDSE HERVORMDE KERK. Atlas van de terreinen der Protestantsche zending in Nederlandsch Oost- en West-Indië. 2. druk. Oegstgeest, Zendingsbureau der Samenwerkende Zendingscorporaties, 1939. 19p. 18 col. maps. C, Y
[Cornell entry: Zendingsbureau, Oegstgeest.]

NI 20.   LEKKERKERKER, CORNELIS. Atlas Indonesia, untuk sekolah rendah. Jakarta, Wolters, 1940. 16 charts. C

NI 21.   INDONESIA. KEMENTERIAN PENDIDIKAN, PENGADJARAN DAN KEBUDAJAAN. Atlas, Indonesia dan dunia untuk sekolah rakjat. Djakarta, Djambatan, 1951. 48p. C

NI 22.   TEEUW, ANDRIES. Dialect-atlas van/of Lombok Indonesia. Djakarta, Biro Reproduksi Djawatan Topografi, 1951. 1v. C, Y

NI 23.   SASTROAMIDJOJO, ACHMAD SENO. Atlas gambar-gambar termasuk bilangan buku fungsi makanan. Djakarta, Wolters, 1953. 92p. C

NI 24.   SOEKARNO, C. S. Atlas Indonesia, untuk madrasah permulaan, kelas V-VI-VII. Djakarta, Penerbitan dan Balai Buku Indonesia, 1953. 56p. Y

NI 25.   YAMIN, MUHAMMAD. Atlas sedjarah, jaitu risalah berisi 83 peta melukiskan perdjalanan sedjarah Indonésia dan sedjarah dunia untuk dipergunakan dipelbagai perguruan. Djakarta, Djambatan, 1956. 88p. C, Y
[PL 480 Indo-5609]

NI 26.   SOEKARNO, C. S. Atlas Indonesia untuk sekolah rakjat kelas IV-V-VI. Djakarta, Ichtiar, 1958. 52p. C, Y
[PL 480 Indo-5509]

NI 27.   PROP, G. Atlas van Nederland, de West, Ned. Nieuw Guinea en Indonesië voor de lagere school. 66. druk. Zutphen, Thieme, 1959. 16p. 34 col. maps. C

NI 28.   Nusantara; atlas Indonesia untuk sekolah dan umum. Bandung, Kilat Madju, 196? 1v. C

See also   BC1

NM—MALAYSIA

NM1.   Collins-Longmans world atlas for Malaya. 2d. ed. Glasgow, Collins, 1955. 24p. C

NP—PHILIPPINES

NP1.   PISON, DOMINGO M. DE. Atlas geográfico de la isla de Luzón y adyacentes. Manila, Chofré, 189? 4p. 33 col. maps. Y

NP2.   ALGUÉ, JOSÉ. Atlas of the Philippine Islands. Washington, GPO, 1900. 24p. 30 maps. (U.S. Coast and Geodetic Survey. Special publication no. 3) C, Y
[Published also as Senate doc. 138, 56th Cong. 1st sess.]
[Cornell entry: Manila. Observatorio.]

NP3.   PHILIPPINES (COMMONWEALTH) DEPT. OF AGRICULTURE AND COMMERCE. Atlas of Philippine statistics. Manila, GPO, 1939. 43p. C

NP4.   JESUS, DOMINGO D. DE. Manila at your fingertips. Corrected to 1955. 2d. ed. Manila, Great Eastern, 1954. 94p. C, Y

NP5.   JESUS, DOMINGO D. DE. Suburbs of Manila; map directory. Manila, Great Eastern, 1955. 114p. C, Y

NP6.   HENDRY, ROBERT S. Atlas of the Philippines. Manila, Phil-Asian, 1959. 228p. C, Y

NP7.   PHILIPPINES (REP.) DIV. OF AGRICULTURAL ECONOMICS. Philippine agricultural atlas, 1957. Quezon City, 1960. 108p. C

NP8.   PHILIPPINES (REP.) PROGRAM IMPLEMENTATION AGENCY. The Philippine economic atlas. Manila, 1965. 163p. C, Y

NP9.   KENNEDY, THOMAS FILLANS. A descriptive atlas of the Pacific Islands, New Zealand, Australia, Polynesia, Melanesia, Micronesia, Philippines. Rev. ed. New York, Praeger, 1968. 64p. Y

NT—THAILAND

NT1.   SHELL COMPANY OF THAILAND, LTD. Road atlas of Thailand. Bangkok, 195? 56p. C

NV — VIETNAM

NV1. Hong-duc ban do. Hung te pan t'u. Saigon, Bo Quoc-gia Giao-duc, 1962. 276p. (Vietnam. Vien Khao Co. Tu sach, 3) Y

NV2. U.S. CONGRESS. HOUSE OF REPRESENTATIVES. Vietnam and Asian continent maps; including indexes and economic and topographic maps. Washington, GPO, 1967. 2p. C, Y

NZ — BIBLIOGRAPHIES AND CATALOGS OF MAPS

NZ1. LEMBAGA KEBUDAJAAN INDONESIA. Alphabetische lijst van land-, zee-, rivier-, wind-, storm- en andere Kaarten, toebehoorende aan het Bataviaasch Genootschap van Kunsten en Wetenschappen. Batavia, Bruining en Wijt, 1873. 12p. Y

NZ2. KAN, C. M. Proeve eener geographische bibliographie van Nederlandsch Oost-Indië voor de jaren 1865–1880. Utrecht, Beijer, 1881. 128p. C, Y

NZ3. INSTITUUT VOOR TAAL-, LAND- EN VOLKENJUNDE, THE HAGUE. Catalogus der land- en zeekaarten toebehoorende aan het Koninklijk instituut voor de taal-, land- en volkenkunde van Nederlandsch-Indië. The Hague, Nijhoff, 1898. 85p. C, Y

NZ4. INSTITUUT VOOR DE TAAL-, LAND- EN VOLKENKUNDE VAN NEDERLANDSCH-INDIË, THE HAGUE. Catalogus der land- en zeekaarten, van en uitgegeven door het Koninklijk Instituut voor de Taal-, Land- en Volkenkunde van Nederlandsch-Indië, samengesteld door W. C. Muller. The Hague, Nijhoff, 1913. 150p. C, Y

NZ4a. NEWBERRY LIBRARY, CHICAGO. EDWARD E. AYER COLLECTION. List of manuscript maps in the Edward E. Ayer collection compiled by Clara A. Smith. Chicago, 1927. 101p. Y

NZ5. INDOCHINA, FRENCH. SERVICE GÉOGRAPHIQUE. Catalogue des plans et cartes. Hanoi, 1936. 15p. C

NZ6. DUTCH EAST INDIES. TOPOGRAFISCHE DIENST. Voorloopige catalogus; opgave van kaarten, legenda, verslagen, enz., verkrijgbaar bij den beheerder van het kaarten magazijn van den Topografischen dienst te Batavia C. Batavia, 1946. 21p. C

NZ7. DUTCH EAST INDIES. TOPOGRAFISCHE DIENST. Catalogus; opgave van legenda, kaarten, verslagen. Batavia, 1947. vi, 27p. C

NZ8. NETHERLANDS (KINGDOM 1815–) DEPARTEMENT VAN MARINE. Catalogus van Nederlandse zeekarten en boekwerken uitg. door de Afdeling Hydrografie van het Ministerie van Marine. Catalogue of charts and books published by the Hydrographic Department of the Royal Netherlands Navy. The Hague, Van Cleef, 1950. xiv, 43p. C

NZ9. VINDEL, FRANCISCO. Mapas de América en los libros españoles de los siglos XVI al XVIII (1503–1798) con 241 facsímiles. Madrid, 1955. 378p.
Apendice a los de América. Adicion de los de Filipinos. Madrid. 1959. 129p. C, Y

NZ10. QUIRINO, CARLOS. Philippine cartography, 1320–1899. Manila, Carmelo & Bauermann, 1959. 140p. C, Y

O—LANGUAGE AND LITERATURE

OA—GENERAL

OA1. DEUTSCHE MORGENLÄNDISCHE GESSELSCHAFT. Wissenschaftlicher Jahresbericht über die morgenländischen Studien, 1859–1881. Leipzig, Brockhaus, 1868–85. 5v. C, Y

OA2. Litteraturblatt für orientalische Philologie. n.p. 1883–88. 4v. in 3. Y

OA3. SENNY, JACQUELINE. Contributions à l'appréciation des valeurs culturelles de l'Orient: traductions françaises de littératures orientales. Bruxelles, Commission Belge de Bibliographie, 1958. 299p. (Bibliographia belgica, 37) C

OA4. Bibliografiia IUgo-Vostochnoi Azii; dorevoliutsionnaia i sovetskaia literatura na russkom iazyke, original'naiai perevodnaia. Moscow, Izd-vo Vostochnoi Lit-ry, 1960. 255p. C, Y

OA5. HOLLYMAN, K. J. A checklist of Oceanic languages (Melanesia, Micronesia, New Guinea, Polynesia). Auckland, Linguistic Society of New Zealand, 1960. 32p. (Te Reo monographs). C, Y

OA6. SHORTO, HARRY LEONARD. Bibliographies of Mon-Khmer and Tai linguistics. London, Oxford Univ. Pr., 1963. x, 87p. (London oriental bibliographies, v.2) C, Y

OB—BURMA

OB1. BURMA. SUPERINTENDENT, GOVERNMENT PRINTING. Tables for the transliteration of Burmese into English, with list showing the names in English and Burmese, of the divisions, districts, subdivisions, townships, and circles of Burma; also of the post offices, and other places of interest. Rangoon, GPO, 1898. xviiip. Y

OB2. BURMA. SUPERINTENDENT, GOVERNMENT PRINTING. Tables for the transliteration of Burmese into English, with list showing the names in English and Burmese, of the divisions, districts, subdivisions, townships, and villages containing more than 100 houses in Burma. Rangoon, 1907. 185p. Y

OB3. SOUTHEAST ASIA INSTITUTE. Selected list of materials for the study of the languages of Burma. New York, 1946. 4ℓ (Its language series, no. 2) Y

OB4. BURMA (UNION) LINGUISTIC SURVEY. Preparatory stage or [i.e. of] linguistic census. Rangoon, GPO, 1950. xiii, 67p. C
[Published in 1917 by The Linguistic Survey of Burma.]

OH—INDOCHINA

OH1. SAVINA, FRANÇOIS MARIE. Guide linguistique de l'Indochine Française. Hongkong, Société des missions-étrangères, 1939. 2v. C, Y

OH2. U.S. ARMY MAP SERVICE. Glossary of Indochinese terms. Washington, 1945. 1, 34ℓ C, Y

OH3. BARQUISSAU, RAPHAËL. L'Asie française et ses écrivains (Indochine-Inde) avec une bibliographie indochinoise. Paris, Vigneau, 1947. 246p. C

OH4. BARUCH, JACQUES. Bibliographie des traductions françaises des littératures du Viêt-Nam et du Cambodge. Brussels, Thanh-Long, 1968. 63ℓ (Études orientales, no. 3) Y

OL— LAOS

OL1. U.S. INFORMATION SERVICE, VIENTIANE. Publications in Lao language, unofficial. Vientiane, 1960. 4p. C

OM— MALAYSIA AND INDONESIA

OM1. INDONESIA. LEMBAGA PERS DAN PENDAPAT UMUM, DJAKARTA. Petundjuk pers. Djakarta. v.1- annual. C, Y
[Cornell entry: Djakarta. Lembaga . . .]

OM2. WERNDLY, GEORGE HENRY. Maleische spraakkunst, uit de eige schriften der Maleiers opgemaakt; met eene voorreden, behelzende eene inleiding tot dit werk; en een dubbeld aanhangsel van twee boekzalen van boeken, in deze tale zo van Europeërs, als van Maleiers geschreven. Amsterdam, Bewindhebberen, 1736. 357p. C, Y

OM3. HOLLE, KAREL FREDERIK. Tabel van oud- en nieuw- Indische alphabetten. Bijdrage tot de palaeographie van Nederlandsch-Indië. Batavia, Bruining, 1882. 1v. Y

OM4. LEMBAGA KEBUDAJAAN INDONESIA. PERPUSTAKAAN. Javaansche bibliographie, gegrond op de boekwerken in die taal, aanwezig in de boekerij van het Bataviaasch Genootschap van Kunsten en Wetenschappen. Batavia, Drukkerij Ruygrok, 1920-21. 2v. C

OM5. SENSTIUS, MAURICE WILLIAM. A survey of aids for the study and teaching of the Malay language. Ann Arbor, Univ. of Michigan Pr., 1943. 2, 64p. C, Y

OM6. SOUTHEAST ASIA INSTITUTE. Selected list of materials for the study of the Malay language. New York, 1946. 4ℓ (Its Language series, no. 1) Y

OM7. VOORHOEVE, PETRUS. Critical survey of studies on the languages of Sumatra. The Hague, Nijhoff, 1955. 55p. (Koninklijk Instituut voor Taal-, Land- en Volkenkunde. Bibliographical series 1) C, Y

OM8. BROWN, CHARLES CUTHBERT. A guide to English-Malay translation. London, Longmans, Green, 1956. vi, 89p. C, Y

OM9. ECHOLS, JOHN M. Indonesian writing in translation. Ithaca, Cornell Univ., Modern Indonesia Project, 1956. 178p. (Cornell University. Modern Indonesia Project. Translation series) C, Y

OM10. CENSE, ANTON ABRAHAM. Critical survey of studies on the languages of Borneo by A. A. Cense and E. M. Uhlenbeck. The Hague, Nijhoff, 1958. 82p. (Koninklijk Instituut voor Taal-, Land- en Volkenkunde. Bibliographical series 2) C, Y

OM11. SINGAPORE. TEACHERS TRAINING COLLEGE. LIBRARY. A list of books for students of Malay literature. Singapore, 1959. 15p. C

OM12. TEEUW, ANDRIES. A critical survey of studies on Malay and Bahasa Indonesia. The Hague, Nijhoff, 1961. 176p. (Koninklijk Instituut voor Taal-, Land- en Volkenkunde. Bibliographical series 5) C, Y

OM13. Dua zaman, Hiasan dalam: Rosdin. Kuala Lumpur, Pustaka Antara, 1963. 191p. C, Y
[Cornell entry: Pustaka Antara, Kuala Lumpur.]

OM14. UHLENBECK, EUGENIUS MARIUS. A critical survey of studies on the languages of Java and Madura. The Hague, Nijhoff, 1964. 207p. (Koninklijk Instituut voor Taal-, Land- en Volkenkunde. Bibliographical series 7) C, Y

OM15.   ANDRONOV, MIKHAIL SERGEEVICH. Materials for a bibliography of Dravidian linguistics. Kuala Lumpur, Dept. of Indian Studies, Univ. of Malaya, 1966. 52p. (International Association of Tamil Research series) Y

OM16.   INDONESIA. LEMBAGA BAHASA DAN KESUSASTERAAN. Daftar pustaka bahasa dan Kesusastraan Indonesia, termasuk bahasa2 dan Kesusastraan Nusantara. Djakarta, 1966. 116p. C

OM17.   KAHLER, HANS. Wörterverzeichnis des Omong Djakarta. Berlin, Reimer, 1966. 351p. (Veröffentlichungen des Seminars für Indonesische und Südseesprachen der Universität Hamburg, Bd.5) C, Y

OM18.   THANI NAYAGAM, XAVIER S. A reference guide to Tamil studies: books. Kuala Lumpur, Univ. of Malaya Pr., 1966. 122p. C, Y

See also   PH72

OP — PHILIPPINES

OP1.   YABES, LEOPOLDO Y. A brief survey of Iloko literature from the beginnings to its present development, with a bibliography of works pertaining to the Iloko people and their language. Manila, The Author, 1936. 155p. Y
[Bibliography pp. 75–155.]

OP2.   BLAKE, FRANK RINGGOLD. Selected list of materials for the study of the Tagalog language. New York, Southeast Asia Institute, 1947. 13ℓ (Language series, no. 4) C

OP3.   NEWBERRY LIBRARY, CHICAGO. Checklist of Philippine linguistics in the Newberry Library compiled by Doris Varner Welsh. Chicago, Newberry Library, 1950. 176p. C, Y

OP4.   BERNARDO, GABRIEL A. A bibliography of the old Philippine syllabaries; a paper presented at the joint meeting of the fourth Far-Eastern Prehistory Congress and Anthropology Division of the eighth Pacific Science Congress, held at Quezon City, Philippines, Nov. 16–28, 1953. Quezon City, Univ. of the Philippines Library, 1953. 52p. Y

OP5.   SUMMER INSTITUTE OF LINGUISTICS. Kalagan alphabet. Manila, 1955. 1v. Y

OP6.   YABES, LEOPOLDO Y. Philippine literature in English 1898–1957, a bibliographical survey. pp. 343–434 In Philippine social sciences and humanities review v. 22, Dec. 1957. C, Y

OP7.   SUMMER INSTITUTE OF LINGUISTICS. Twenty-fifth anniversary bibliography. Glendale, Cal., 1960. 52p. C

OP8.   MOREY, VIRGINIA. Cebuana reference materials. Manila, Summer Institute of Linguistics, Philippines, 1961. 223p. C

OP9.   FLORENTINO, ALBERTO S. Midcentury guide to Philippine literature in English. Manila, Filipiniana, 1963. 96p. C, Y

OP10.   MANUEL, E. ARSENIO. Philippine folklore bibliography; a preliminary survey. Quezon City, 1965. 125p. (Philippine Folklore Society. Paper no. 1) C, Y

OT — THAILAND

OT1.   BANGKOK. NATIONAL LIBRARY. Sixteen tables of Thai alphabets current in Siam by O. Franfurter. Bangkok, 1914. 1v. C, Y
[Cornell entry: Bangkok, Thailand. Ho samut haeng chat.]

OT2.   U.S. ARMY LANGUAGE SCHOOL, MONTEREY, CALIF. Thai; information booklet for graduates of the Thai Language Department. Presidio of Monterey, 1960. 16ℓ C, Y

OV — VIETNAM

OV1.   U.S. ARMY LANGUAGE SCHOOL, MONTEREY, CALIF. Vietnamese; information booklet for graduates of the Vietnamese Language Department. Presidio of Monterey, 1961. 29ℓ   C, Y

P—DICTIONARIES

PB—BURMESE DICTIONARIES

Burmese-English

PB1. English idioms with Burmese equivalents. Rangoon, Nu Yin Pr., n.d. 171p. C

PB2. HOUGH, G. H. An English and Burman vocabulary, preceded by a concise grammar. Serampore, 1825. 424p. Y

PB3. SLOAN, W. H. A practical method with the Burmese language. Rangoon, American Mission Pr., 1876. 232p. Y

PB4. BURMA. EDUCATION DEPT. SCHOOL TEXTBOOK COMMITTEE. Revised Burmese orthographical vocabulary drawn up by the School Textbook Committee as the standard of Burmese spelling in the province. Rangoon, 1890. 98p. Y

PB5. JUDSON, ADONIRAM. Burmese-English dictionary. Rev. and enl. by Robert C. Stevenson. Rangoon, GPO, 1893. 1188, 6p. C

PB6. JUDSON, ADONIRAM. Judson's pocket dictionary. Rev. ed. Rangoon, Baptist Board of Publications, 19?? 671p. C

PB7. HTUN NYEIN, U. The student's English-Burmese dictionary by Tun Nyein. Rangoon, GPO, 1906. 820p. Y

PB8. JUDSON, ADONIRAM. School dictionary, Burmese and English. Rangoon, American Baptist Mission Pr., 1910. 643p. C, Y

PB9. JUDSON, ADONIRAM. The Judson Burmese-English dictionary. Rev. and enl. by Robert C. Stevenson. Rangoon, American Baptist Mission Pr., 1921. 1123p. C, Y

PB10. JUDSON, ADONIRAM. English and Burmese dictionary. 8th ed. Rangoon, American Baptist Mission Pr., 1922. 928p. Y

PB11. STEWART, JOHN ALEXANDER. A Burmese-English dictionary compiled by J. A. Stewart and C. W. Dunn. London, Published under the auspices of the University of Rangoon by Luzac, 1940-63. 4v. C, Y

PB12. Lu-du myan-ma-loun:boun:qabei'dan by U: San Hta: The Burmese spelling dictionary for millions. Rangoon, 1947. 251p. Y

PB13. AMERICAN BAPTIST FOREIGN MISSION SOCIETY. 1200 common Burmese words and their meanings; a vocabulary for beginners. n.p. 1949. 1v. Y

PB14. AGARWAL, R. C. S. The basic English-Burmese dictionary giving more than 40,000 senses of over 20,000 words in basic English. Mandalay, International Book Depot, 1955. 1294p. Y

PB15. KHIN, U. Burmese English dictionary compiled by U Khin and Glen San Lwin. Washington, 1956. 2v. C, Y

PB16. HTUN: NYEIN:, U. The student's English-Burmese dictionary by U Tun Nyein, with supplement by U Tun Aung Gyaw, and also supplement of economic usages. 4th ed. Rangoon, A.B.M.S.U. Central Concos, 1957. 991, 130, 74p. Y

PB17. U.S. ARMY LANGUAGE SCHOOL, MONTEREY, CALIFORNIA. Burmese: consolidated vocabulary, basic course; phonemic/Burmese-English, alphabetic. Presidio of Monterey, 1959. 295p. C, Y

Burmese-Pali

PB18. BA, MAUN. A dictionary of the Pali language, specially adapted for the use of Burmese students by Maung Ba and Maung Tha Din. Rangoon, American Baptist Mission Pr., 1914. 326p. Y

PB19.   Myan-ma qabi' dan can compiled by Ashin Oi ba-tha. Burmese to Burmese and Pali dictionary. Rangoon, 1948. 1v. Y

PC — CAMBODIAN DICTIONARIES

Polyglot

PC1.   SUNG, LIANG. Lexique khmero-franco-chinois. Phnom Penh, 1959. 219p. C

Cambodian-French

PC2.   AYMONIER, ETIENNE FRANÇOIS. Dictionnaire khmêr-français. Saigon, 1878. 436p. Y

PC3.   MOURA, JEAN. Vocabulaire français-cambodgien et cambodgien-français contenont une règle pour la prononciation, les locutions en usage pour parler au roi, aux bonzes, aux mandarins, la numération, la division du temps, les poids, les mesures, les monnoies et quelques exercices de traduction. Paris, Challamel, 1878. 235p. C

PC4.   BERNARD, JEAN BAPTISTE. Dictionnaire cambodgien-français. Hongkong, Société des missions étrangèrs, 1902. 386p. Y

PC5.   TANDART, S. Dictionnaire français-cambodgien. Hongkong, Société des missions étrangèrs, 1910–11. 2v. C, Y

PC6.   GUESDON, JOSEPH. Dictionnaire cambodgien-français. Paris, Les Petits-fils de Plon et Nourrit, 1930. 2v. (At head of title: Ministère de l'instruction publique et des beaux-arts. Commission archéologique de l'Indochine.) C, Y

PC7.   RAY-BUC. Dictionnaire khmero-français. Phnom Penh, Man-Hue, 1957– C

PC8.   Dictionnaire cambodgien. 4th ed. Phnom Penh, Editions de l'Institute bouddhique, 1962. 2v. C

PC9.   TEP YOK. Dictionnaire français-khmer par Tep Yok et Thao-Kun. Phnom Penh, Librairie Boutneang, 1962–64. 2v. C

PH — INDONESIAN-MALAY DICTIONARIES

Polyglot

PH1.   MARSDEN, WILLIAM. Dictionnaire malai, hollandais et français par C. P. J. Elout, tr. du Dictionnaire malai et anglais de Mr. W. Marsden. Haarlem, Enschedé, 1825. 604p. C, Y

PH2.   THOMSON, T. A vocabulary of the English, Bugis and Malay languages, containing about 2000 words. Singapore, Mission Pr., 1833. 64p. Y

PH3.   LEGGE, JAMES. A lexilogus of the English, Malay and Chinese languages, comprehending the vernacular idioms of the last of the Hok-keen and Canton dialects. Malacca, Anglo-Chinese College Pr., 1841. 111p. Y

PH4.   THOMAS, J. W. Niasch-Maleisch-Nederlandsch woordenboek, door J. W. Thomas en E. A. Taylor Weber. Batavia, GPO, 1887. 186p. Y

PH5.   BADINGS, A. H. L. Neues Wörterbuch der deutschen, malaischen und holländischen Sprache. Amsterdam, Elsevier, 1894. 415p. Y

PH6.   KAHLO, GERHARD. Kleines vergleichendes malayo-polynesisches Wörterbuch. Leipzig, Harrassowitz, 1941. 78p. C, Y

PH7.   DUTCH EAST INDIES. LEGER. Zakwoordenboek Nederlandsch-Maleisch-Engelsch. Melbourne, Koninklijk Nederlandsch Indisch Leger, 1945. 220p. C

PH8. HELSLOOT, N. Malay, English, Dutch pocket vocabulary of 20,000 words. Melbourne, Cheshire, 1946. 142p. C

PH9. LIE, JOEK KOY. A classified dictionary of Chinese-Malay-Dutch-English with Chinese pronounciation. Batavia, Kuo Min, 1948. 293p. C
[Cornell entry: Li, Yü-K'ai]

PH10. OSMENA, JOHAN. Kamus umum tiga bahasa: Inggeris-Indonesia-Belanda; Indonesia-Belanda-Inggeris; Belanda-Indonesia-Inggeris. Surabaja, Asiatic Pr., 195? 340p. C

PH11. BONS, L. Kamus Indonesia-Belanda-Inggeris. Edjaan bahasa Inggeris menurut bunjinja. Djakarta, van Dorp, 1951. 174p. C, Y

PH12. AHMADY, S. Kamus praktis Inggeris-Indonesia-Belanda. Surabaja, Marhaen, 1952. 116p. C

PH12a. ANWIR, BOGINDA SJARIFOEL. Kamus istilah tehnik; bahasa Indonesia, bahasa Inggeris, bahasa Belanda. Djakarta, Stam, 1952. 416p. C
[Cornell entry: Anwir, Baginda Sjariful]

PH13. BONS, L. Kamus Belanda-Indonesia-Inggeris; edjaan bahasa Inggeris menurut bunjinja, Nederlands-Indonesisch-Engels woordenboek met phonetische spelling van het Engels en gegevens betreffende de vorming van Indonesische werkwoorden. 4. druk. Djakarta, Kolff, 1956. 307p. C

PH14. RALIBY, OSMAN. Kamus internasional. Djakarta, Bulan Bintang, 1956. 449p. C

PH15. BONS, L. Kamus Indonesia-Inggeris-Belanda; edjaan bahasa Inggeris menurut bunjinja. Djakarta, Kolff, 1957. 378p. C

PH16. Hamid's kamus bahasa Melayu-Inggeris-China, dengan bunyi Melayu dan China. Malay-English-Chinese dictionary with pronounciation by M. A. Karim and C. A. Meng. Kuala Lumpur, Andul Hamid, 1958. 178p. C

PH17. ANWIR, BOGINDA SJARIFOEL. Kamus tehnik 4 bahasa: Belanda, Inggeris, Djerman, Indonesia. Djakarta, Technipress, 196? 265p. C
[Cornell entry: Anwir, Baginda Sjariful]

PH18. DOBLE, MARION. Kapauku-Malayan-Dutch-English dictionary. The Hague, Nijhoff, 1960. 156p. C, Y

PH19. ABDULLAH BIN NUH. Kamus Indonesia-Arab-Inggeris oleh Abd. bin Nuh & Oemar Bakry. Tjet. 2. Djakarta, Mutiara, 1961. 363p. C

PH20. ABDULLAH BIN NUH. Kamus baru; dalam bahasa: asing/Eropah-Indonesia-Arab sekitar hubungan2 diplomatic-politik-economic d.ℓ.ℓ. Tjet.2. Djakarta, Pustaka Islam, 1961. 215p. C, Y

PH21. BROOKS, ROBERT JONES. Kamus Melayu-Tionghoa-Inggeris setandar yang terbaharu. Newest standard Malay-Chinese-English dictionary. Hongkong, Educational Book, 1961. 14, 1366, 139p. C

PH22. YEH, SHAO-CH'ING. A dictionary of antonyms, English, Malay, Chinese. Singapore, Malay-Chinese-English Pub. House, 1961. 129p. C

PH23. ASPILLERA, PARALUMAN S. A common vocabulary for Malay, Pilipino and Bahasa Indonesia. Manila, St. Anthony Book Service, 1964. xii, 98ℓ. C, Y

Indonesian

PH24. IKEN, D. Kitab arti logat melajoe, oleh D. Iken dan E. Harahap. Tjet. 4. Weltevreden, N.V. Boekhandel Visser, 1923. 426p. C, Y
[Cornell entry: title]

PH25. HARAHAP, ELISA SUTAN. Kamoes Indonesia. Tjet. 7. Djakarta, Gunseikanboe Kanri Insatu Kodjo, 1942. 427p. C

PH26. HARAHAP, ELISA SUTAN. Kamoes Indonesia ketjik. Tjet. 2. Djakarta, Angin, 1946. 309p. C

PH27. LEMBAGA BAHASA INDONESIA, MEDAN. Kamoes istilah bahasa Indonesia. Disoesoen menoeroet Kepoetoesan Lembaga Bahasa Indonesia di Medan dan Djakarta. Tjet. 2. Bukittinggi, Pentjetak Pertjetakan Peroesahaan N.R.I., 1946. 79p. C

PH28. HARAHAP, ELISA SUTAN. Kamoes Indonesia. Tjet. 8. Djakarta, Gunseikanbu Kanri Insatu Kodjo, 1948. 493p. Y

PH29. ZAIN, SUTAN MOHAMMAD. Kamus moderen bahasa Indonésia. Djakarta, Jajasan Dharma, 195? 1090p. C

PH30. HARAHAP, ELISA SUTAN. Kamus Indonesia ketjik. 3d. ed. Bandung, Kolff, 1950. 328p. C

PH31. NASUTION, AMIR TAAT. Kamus kata2 politik. Tjet. 5. Medan, Pustaka Andalas, 1950. 122p. C

PH32. POERWADARMINTA, WELFRIDUS JOSEPH SABARYA. Logat ketjil bahasa Indonesia. Tjet. 2. Djakarta, Wolters, 1950. 138p. C, Y
[Cornell entry: Purwadarminta, . . .]

PH33. SAMAH, A. Kamus harian kata-kata sulit bahasa Indonesia. Medan, Pustaka Andalas, 1950. 144p. C

PH34. GAZALI GELAR SUTAN MAHARADJA. Kamus dagang. Medan, Madju, 1951. 56p. C

PH35. HARAHAP, ELISA SUTAN. Kamus Indonesia besar. 9th. ed. Bandung, Kolff, 1951. 452p. C

PH36. POERWADARMINTA, WELFRIDUS JOSEPH SABARYA. Kamus umum bahasa Indonesia. Djakarta, Balai Pustaka, 1952. 903p. C, Y
[Cornell entry: Purwadarminta, . . .]

PH37. ADINEGORO, DJAMALUDIN. Kamus pengetahuan umum. Tjet. 2. Djakarta, Bulan Bintang, 1953. 111p. C, Y

PH38. KUSBINI. Kamus musik. Jogja, U.P. Indonesia, 1953. 103p. C

PH39. DJAKARTA. UNIVERSITAS INDONESIA. LEMBAGA BAHASA DAN BUDAJA. Kamus istilah kedokteran, asing-Indonesia. Djakarta, Perpustakaan Perguruan Kementerian P. P. dan K., 1954. 145p. C

PH40. WEST-JAVA (PROVINCE) KANTOR URUSAN AGAMA. Kamus kerdja. Werksencyclopaedia. Bandung, 1954— C

PH41. ARIEF, M. ISA. Kamus hukum dagang. Djakarta, Pustaka Islam, 1955. 72p. C

PH42. IBNU RASJID. Kamus S. R. Medan, Amsal, 1955. 469p. C

PH43. KUSNODIPRODJO. Kamus singkat dari singkatan-kata dalam-negeri dan luar-negeri, dengan terdjemahan dan pendjelasannja. Tjet. 2. Djakarta, Seno, 1955. 497p. C

PH44. SCHMIDGALL TELLINGS, ALUZIUS EDUARD. Kasip; kamus singkatan Indonesia pertama. Djakarta, Suluh Indonesia, 1955. 417p. C, Y

PH45. DJAKARTA. UNIVERSITAS INDONESIA. LEMBAGA BAHASA DAN BUDAJA. Intisari tatanama kimia anorganik dan kimia organik, beserta kamus istilah kimia. Djakarta, Balai Pustaka, 1956. 99p. C

PH46. DJAKARTA. UNIVERSITAS INDONESIA. LEMBAGA BAHASA DAN BUDAJA. Kamus istilah pelajaran, asing-Indonesia. Djakarta, Perpustakaan Perguruan Kementerian P. P. dan K., 1956. 60p. C

PH47. DJAKARTA. UNIVERSITAS INDONESIA. LEMBAGA BAHASA DAN BUDAJA. Kamus istilah teknik, asing-Indonesia. Djakarta, 1956. 120p. C

PH48. DJAKARTA. UNIVERSITAS INDONESIA. LEMBAGA BAHASA DAN BUDAJA. Kamus istilah seksi kehewanan, asing-Indonesia. Djakarta, Balai Pustaka, 1956. 24p. C

PH49. NASUTION, AMIR TAAT. Kamus politik. Tjet. 13. Djakarta, Pustaka Dewata, 1956. 138p. C

PH50. BAHAR, S. M. Kamus ilmu bumi Indonesia. Bandung, Triguna, 1957. 255p. C

PH51. DJAKARTA. UNIVERSITAS INDONESIA. LEMBAGA BAHASA DAN BUDAJA. Kamus istilah keradjinan wanito, asing-Indonesia. Djakarta, Balai Pustaka, 1957. 70p. C

PH52. MUHAMMAD SHAH BIN YUSUF, H. Kamus 'am bahasa Melayu. Malacca, Pustaka Rakyat, 1957. 692p. C

PH53. DJAKARTA. UNIVERSITAS INDONESIA. LEMBAGA BAHASA DAN BUDAJA. Kamus istilah hukum, asing-Indonesia. Djakarta, Dinas Penerbitan Balai Pustaka, 1958. 52p. C

PH54. DJAKARTA. UNIVERSITAS INDONESIA. LEMBAGA BAHASA DAN BUDAJA. Kamus istilah pendidikan, pengadjaran dan ilmu djiwa; asing-Indonesia. Djakarta, Balai Pustaka, 1958. 190p. C

PH55. Kamus sederhana bahasa Indonesia. Djakarta, 1958. 372p. C

PH56. AHMAD BIN ISMAIL. Kamus istilah bahasa. Penang, Sinaran, 1959. 35p. C

PH57. SA'AD BIN HAJI MUDA. Kamus hewan, mengan dongi nama2 hewan dalam bahasa Melayu. Singapore, Persatuan Persuratan Pemuda Pemudi Melayu, 1959. 146p. (Siri Perpustakaan 4PM bilangan 1) C

PH58. DJAKARTA. UNIVERSITAS INDONESIA. LEMBAGA BAHASA DAN BUDAJA. Kamus istilah ekonomi-keuangan asing-Indonesia. Djakarta, 196? 121p. C

PH59. SA'AD SHUKRY BIN MUDA. Kamus adat Istiadat Melayu. n.p. Peterchong, 196? 157p. Y

PH60. SALEH SUBEDJO, MOH. Kamus rakjat populer. Surabaja, Marfiah, 196? 217p. C

PH61. INDONESIA. LEMBAGA BAHASA DAN KESUSASTERAAN. Kamus istilah pertanian, kehutanan dan perikanan, asing-Indonesia. Djakarta, 1960. 106p. C

PH62. MALAYA (FED.) DEWAN BAHASA DAN PUSTAKA. Istilah jawatan dan jabatan; kementerian, jabatan, pejabat dan bahagian2-nya. Kuala Lumpur, 1960. 87p. (Its siri istilah DBP bil. 1) C

PH63. WINSTEDT, RICHARD OLOF. Kamus bahasa Mĕlayu. Singapore, Marican, 1960. 338p. C

PH64. ZAIN, SUTAN MUHAMMAD. Kamus moderen bahasa Indonesia. Djakarta, Grafika, 1960. 896p. C, Y

PH65. MALAYA (FED.) DEWAN BAHASA DAN PUSTAKA. Istilah jawatan dan jabatan; kementerian, jabatan, pejabat dan bahagian2-nya. Chet. 2. Kuala Lumpur, 1961. 175p. (Its siri istilah DBP bil. 1) C

PH66. POERWADARMINTA, WELFRIDUS JOSEPH SABARYA. Kamus umum bahasa Indonesia. Tjet. 3. Djakarta, Dinas Penerbitan Balai Pustaka, 1961. 1122p. C, Y
[Cornell entry: Purwadarminta, . . .]

PH67. SURJO UNTORO, S. Kamus indoktrinasi dan socialisme Indonesia. Surabaja, Marfiah, 1961. 84p. C

PH68. HABEYB. Kamus populer. Tjet. 8. Jogjakarta, Dian, 1962. 350p. C, Y
[Cornell entry: title]

PH69. Kamus politik; himpunan. Tjet. 8. Surabaja, Ksatrya, 1962. 345p. C

PH70. NASUTION, AMIR TA'AT. Kamus politik. Tjet. 15. Djakarta, Pustaka Dewata, 1962. 188p. C, Y

PH71. ADINDA, A. M. Kamus politik. Tjet. 9. Surabaja, Ksatrya, 1963. 358p. C, Y

PH72. INDONESIA. LEMBAGA BAHASA DAN KESUSASTERAAN. Kamus ilmu bahasa dan Kesusasteraan. Djakarta, 1965. ii, 46*l* C
PH72a. POERWADARMINTA, WELFRIDUS JOSEPH SABARYA. Kamus umum bahasa Indonesia. Tjet. 4. Djakarta, Balai Pustaka, 1966– C
[Cornell entry: Purwadarminta, . . .]

Arabic

PH73. FADLULLAH, MUHAMMED. Kamoes Arab-Melajoe by Muh. Fadlullah and B. Th. Brondgeest. Weltevreden, Balai Poestaka, 1925–27. 1027p. C

Chinese

PH74. LIE, JOEK KOY. Kamus ketjil bahasa Indonesia-Tionghoa. Tjet. 2. Batavia, Kuo Min, 1949– C
[Cornell entry: Li, Yü-k'ai]
PH75. WÊN, HSI-T'AO. Kamus besar Tionghoa-Indonesia. Djakarta, Sastera Nan Pei, 1951. 2v. C
PH76. PAO, SSU-CHING. Indonesian-Chinese dictionary. Singapore, Nan Chian Pr., 1952. 332p. C
PH77. PAO, SSU-CHING. Kamus Tionghoa-Indonesia. n.p. 1952. 493p. C
PH78. PAO, SSU-CHING. Kamus Tionghoa-Indonesia. n.p. 1952. 576p. C
PH79. LIE, JOEK KOY. Kamus baharu bahasa Indonesia-Tionghoa. Djakarta, Toko Buku "Kuo Min," 1957. 486, 158p. C, Y
[Cornell entry: Li, Yü-k'ai]
PH80. LIE, JOEK KOY. Kamus baharu bahasa Tionghoa-Indonesia. Tjet. 9. Djakarta, Toko Buku "Kuo Min," 1957. 332, 203p. C
[Cornell entry: Li, Yü-k'ai]
PH81. LIE, JOEK KOY. Kamus baharu bahasa Indonesia-Tionghoa. Djakarta, Penerbit Tjahaja Agung, 1958. 1v. C
[Cornell entry: Li, Yü-k'ai]
PH82. Kamus baharu Melayu-Tionghoa, Tionghoa-Melayu. Hong Kong, English Lang. Pub., 1960. 1027p. C
PH83. Kamus Indonesia-Tionghoa, disusun oleh Shan Nu. Djakarta, Jajasan Kebudajaan Sadar, 1963. 550p. Y
PH84. Kamus istilah ilmu pasti, alam & kimia: Indonesia-Tionghoa, Tionghoa-Indonesia. Djakarta, Jajasan Kebudajaan Sadar, 1964. 133p. C

Dutch

PH85. ROORDA VAN EYSINGA, PHILIPPUS PIETER. Nederduitsch en Maleisch woordenboek. Batavia, GPO, 1824. 497c. C
PH86. MARSDEN, WILLIAM. Dictionnaire hollandais et malai, suivi d'un Dictionnaire français et malai, par C. P. J. Elout, d'après le Dictionnaire anglais et malai de Mr. W. Marsden. Haarlem, Enschedé, 1826. 432p. Y
PH87. ROORDA VAN EYSINGA, PHILIPPUS PIETER. Algemeen Nederduitsch-Maleisch woordenboek, in de hof-, volks- en lage taal. Met aanduiding der woorden, welke uit oostersche en westersche talen ontleend zijn; voorafgegaan van een beschouwing over de Maleijers, hunne geschiedenis, taal en hare verwantschap met indische en andere talen; verrijkt met aahalingen uit geschriften en vertalingen van volzinnen; gevolgd door een alphabetisch register van voorname plaatsen en personen. The Hague, Van Cleef, 1855. 1087p. C

PH88.   ROORDA VAN EYSINGA, W. A. P.   Maleisch en Nederduitsch woorden
        boek, ook ten dienste van hen, die geen Arabisch karakter verstaan.
        Nieuwediep, Hoogvorst, 1856. 173p. Y
PH89.   PIJNAPPEL, JAN. Maleisch-nederduitsch woordenboek, naar het werk
        van W. Marsden en andere bronnen bewerkt door J. Pijnappel. Haarlem,
        Enschedé, 1863. 275p. Y
PH90.   CLERCQ, FREDERIK SIGISMUND ALEXANDER DE.   Het Maleisch der
        Molukken. Lijst der meest voorkomende vreemde en van het gewone
        Maleisch verschillende woorden, zooals die gebruikt worden in de resi-
        dentiën Manado, Ternate, Ambon met Banda en Timor Koepang, benevens
        eenige proeven van aldaar verwaardigde pantoens, prozastukken en ge-
        dichten. Batavia, Bruining, 1876. 96p. C, Y
PH91.   WALL, HERMANN THEODOR FRIEDRICH KARL EMIL WILHELM
        AUGUST CASIMIR VAN DE. Maleisch-Nederlandsch woordenboek. Op
        last van het gouvernement van Nederlandsch-Indië samengesteld door
        wijlen H. von de Wall, en, met weglating van al het overtollige, uitge-
        geven door H. N. van der Tuuk. Batavia, GPO, 1877-84. 3v. C, Y
PH92.   ROORDA VAN EYSINGA, PHILIPPUS PIETER. Algemeen Hollandsch-
        Maleisch woordenboek. Herzien en vermeerderd door G. J. Grashuis.
        Leiden, Kolff, 1878. 1005p. C, Y
PH93.   BADINGS, A. H. L. Nieuw hollandsch-maleisch, maleisch-hollandsch
        woordenboek. 4. druk. Schoonhoven, van Nooten, 1884. 394p. Y
PH94.   PIJNAPPEL, JAN. Maleisch-hollandsch woordenboek. 3. verm. druk.
        Haarlem, Enschedé, 1884. 343p. C, Y
PH95.   MAYER, LEENDERT THEODORUS. Practisch maleisch-hollandsch,
        hollandsch-maleisch handwoordenboek, benevens een "Kort begrip der
        maleische woordvorming en spraaklr." Amsterdam, Scheltema & Hol-
        kema, 1895. 608p. Y
PH96.   Alphabetisch register van Maleische woorden en uitdrukkingen. Bandung,
        Kleijne, 19?? 415p. C
PH97.   Kamoes Belanda-Indonesia. Surabaja, Pendidikan Oemoen, 19?? 149p.
        C
PH98.   Van Goor's miniatuur Maleisch woordenboek; Maleisch-Nederlandsch en
        Nederlandsch-Maleisch, door A. A. Fokker. Gouda, van Goor, 19?? 804p.
        C
PH99.   BADINGS, A. H. L. Nieuw Hollandsch-Maleisch, Maleisch-Hollandsch
        woordenboek, zoo gemakkelijk mogelijk ingericht ten dienste van Neder-
        landers, die zich in Indië wenschen te vestigen. 7. druk. Zwolle, Tjeenk
        Willink, 1901. 480p. C
PH100. KLINKERT, HILLEBRANDUS CORNELIUS. Nieuw nederlandsch-maleisch
        woordenboek. 2. verm. en verb. druk. Leiden, Brill, 1901. 868p. Y
PH101. KLINKERT, HILLEBRANDUS CORNELIUS. Nieuw maleisch-nederlandsch
        woordenboek met arabisch karakter. 2. verb. en verm. druk. Leiden,
        Brill, 1902. 904p. Y
PH102. OPHUIJSEN, CH. A. VAN. Kitab logat Melajoe. Woordenlijst voor de spel-
        ling der Maleische taal met Latijnsch karakter. 2. druk. Batavia, GPO,
        1903. 94p. C
PH103. MAYER, LEENDERT THEODORUS. Practisch Maleisch-Hollandsch en
        Hollandsch-Maleisch handwoordenboek, benevens kort begrip der Maleische
        woordvorming en spraakleer. 5. druk. Semarang, van Dorp, 1906. 622p.
        C
PH104. HALKEMA, H. Maleisch-Hollandsch en Hollandsch-Maleisch handwoorden-
        boek met een toelichting voor het gebruik van de Maleische woorden als
        zinsdeel. Batavia, Kolff, 1909. 614p. Y

PH105. OPHUIJSEN, CH. A. VAN. Kitab logat Melajoe. Woordenlijst voor de spelling der Maleische taal met Latijnsch karakter. 4. druk. Batavia, Kolff, 1911. 91p. Y

PH106. KLINKERT, HILLEBRANDUS CORNELIUS. Nieuw maleisch-nederlandsch zakwoordenboek, ten behoeve van hen, die het maleisch met Latijnsch karakter beoefenen. 2. uitg. Leiden, Brill, 1918. 462p. C, Y

PH107. RONKEL, PHILIPPUS SAMUEL VAN. Maleisch woordenboek; Maleisch-Nederlandsch, Nederlandsch-Maleisch, in de officieele Maleische spelling. Gouda, van Goor, 1918. 306p. Y

PH108. OPHUIJSEN, CH. A. VAN. Kitab logat Melajoe; woordenlijst voor de spelling der Maleische taal met Latijnsch karakter. 7. druk. Weltevreden, Papyrus, 1921. xvi, 89p. Y

PH109. KLINKERT, HILLEBRANDUS CORNELIUS. Nieuw Nederlandsch-Maleisch woordenboek. 3. druk. Leiden, Brill, 1926. 682p. Y

PH110. ADINEGORO, DJAMALUDIN. Kamoes kemadjoean (Modern zakwoordenboek) oleh Adi Negoro. Gouda, van Goor, 1928. 151p. C, Y

PH111. OPHUIJSEN, CH. A. VAN. Kitab logat Melajoe; woordenlijst voor de spelling der Maleische taal met Latijnsch karakter. 8. druk. 87p. Weltevreden, GPO, 1929. C

PH112. KLINKERT, HILLEBRANDUS CORNELIUS. Nieuw maleisch-nederlandsch woordenboek met arabisch karakter, naar de beste en laatste bronnen bewerkt. 4. druk. Leiden, Brill, 1930. 1047p. C, Y

PH113. Hollandsch-Maleisch en Maleisch-Hollandsch zakwoordenboek. 7. herz. druk. Batavia, Kolff, 1932. 124p. C

PH114. JAVA (JAPANESE MILITARY ADMINISTRATION 1942-45) KOMISI BAHASA INDONESIA. Kamoes istilah. Djakarta, Poestaka Rakjat, 1945. 2v. C

PH115. RONKEL, PHILIPUS SAMUEL VAN. Maleis woordenboek; Maleis-Nederlands, Nederlands-Maleis in de officiële Maleise spelling, met supplement samengesteld door A. L. N. Kramer. 5. druk. The Hague, van Goor, 1946-47. 313, 56p. C, Y

PH116. KRAMER, A. L. N. Maleis-Nederlandse en Nederlands-Maleise woordenlijst. The Hague, van Goor, 1947. 56p.

PH117. DUTCH EAST INDIES. DEPARTEMENT VAN ONDERWIJS EN EEREDIENST. Lijst van termen, Nederlands-Bahasa Indonesia. Batavia, 1947. 72p. C

PH118. PERNIS, H. D. VAN. Aanvullende lijst van Maleise woorden en uitdrukkingen. Djakarta, Netherlands Forces Intelligence Service, 1947. 1v. C

PH119. EGGES POST, A. Indonesische woordenlijst met beknopte spraakkunst. The Hague, van Goor, 1948. 205p. C, Y

PH120. ENNEN, H. Ennen's Indonesisch zakwoordenboek, Indonesisch-Nederlands en Nederlands-Indonesisch. The Hague, van Goor, 1948. 101p. Y

PH121. KRAMER, A. L. N. Kamoes Indonésia; Indonesisch-Nederlands en Nederlands-Indonesisch. The Hague, van Goor, 1948. 428p. C, Y

PH122. BOER, D. W. N. DE. De indonesische aanvulling van het maleise woordenboek in het bijzonder de "Kata 'Istilah" vaktechnische termen en uitdrukkingen. Leiden, Brill, 1949. xiv, 68p. C, Y

PH123. ALISJAHBANA, SUTAN TAKDIR. Istilah rumahtangga. Djakarta, Pustaka Rakjat, 1950. 2v. C

PH124. Istilah rumahtangga. Djakarta, Pustaka Rakjat, 1950. 2v. C

PH125. KRAMER, A. L. N. Apakah Indonésianja? Hoe zeg je 't in Indonesisch? Tjétakan jang ketiga jang diperbaiki dan ditambahi. 3. druk. The Hague, van Goor, 1950. 288p. C, Y

PH126. PERNIS, H. D. VAN. Woordenboek bahasa Indonesia-Nederlands. Groningen, Wolters, 1950. 317p. C, Y

PH127. POERWADARMINTA, WELFRIDUS JOSEPH SABARYA. Indonesisch-Nederlands woordenboek, samengesteld door W. J. S. Poerwadarminta en A. Teeuw. Groningen, Wolters, 1950. 369p. C, Y
[Cornell entry: Purwadarminta, . . .]

PH128. PANGGABÉAN, K. Kata2-dagang, Belanda-Indonesia, Indonesia-Belanda. Djakarta, van Dorp, 1951. 58p. C

PH129. ARNOWO, DUL. Kamus marhaen; berisi pendjelasan kata2 jang sering dipergunakan didalam rapat2, pidato radio, surat kabar, madjallah dan lain2. Tjet. 5. Surabaja, Toko Alwan, 1952. 165p. C

PH130. ANWIR, BOGINDA SJARIFOEL. Kamus istilah tehnik bahasa Belanda-bahasa Indonesia. Tjet. 2. Djakarta, Stam, 1952. 463p. C
[Cornell entry: Anwir, Baginda Sjariful.]

PH131. POERWADARMINTA, WELFRIDUS JOSEPH SABARYA. Indonesisch-Nederlands woordenboek, samengesteld door W. J. S. Poerwadarminta en A. Teeuw. 2. bijgewerkte druk. Groningen, Wolters, 1952. 383p. C, Y
[Cornell entry: Purwadarminta, . . .]

PH132. Van Goor's Indonesisch-Nederlands zakwoordenboek, Nederlands-Indonesisch en Indonesisch-Nederlands. 2. druk. The Hague, van Goor, 1953. 573p.

PH133. TAIR, M. A. Kamus Belanda; Belanda-Indonesia, Indonesia-Belanda oleh M. A. Tair dan H. van der Tas. Djakarta, Timun Mas, 1957. 687p. Y

PH134. ANWIR BOGINDA SJARIFOEL. Kamus istilah tehnik, bahasa Belanda-bahasa Indonesia. Tjet. 3. Djakarta, Technipress, 1960. 236p. C, Y
[Cornell entry: Anwir Baginda Sjariful.]

PH135. DJAKARTA. UNIVERSITAS INDONESIA. LEMBAGA BAHASA DAN BUDAJA. Kamus istilah pertanian, kehutanan dan perikanan asing-Indonesia. Djakarta, 1960. 106p. C

PH136. TAS, H. VAN DER. Kamus hukum, Belanda-Indonesia. Tjet. 2. Djakarta, Timun Mas, 1961. 390p. C, Y

PH137. KRAMER, A. L. N. Kamus Belanda, Nederlands-Indonesisch en Indonesisch-Nederlands. 5. druk. The Hague, van Goor, 1966. 600p. C, Y

English

PH138. SAMAH, A. Sovereign vocabulary, Indonesian-English and English-Indonesian. Medan, Pustaka Indonesia, n.d. 272p. C

PH139. HOWISON, JAMES. A dictionary of the Malay tongue, as spoken in the Peninsula of Malacca, the islands of Sumatra, Java, Borneo, Pulo Pinang &c. in two parts, English and Malay, and Malay and English. London, Sewell, 1801. 2v. C, Y

PH140. MARSDEN, WILLIAM. A dictionary of the Malayan language, in two parts, Malayan and English, and English and Malayan. London, Cox and Baylis, 1812. 589p. C, Y

PH141. CRAWFURD, JOHN. A grammar and dictionary of the Malay language, with a preliminary dissertation. London, Smith, Elder, 1852. 2v. Y

PH142. KEASBERRY, BENJAMIN PEACH. A vocabulary of the English and Malay languages. 3d. ed. Singapore, 1854. x, 99p. Y

PH143. WILKINSON, RICHARD JAMES. An abridged Malay-English dictionary romanised. Kuala Lumpur, GPO, 1908. 248p. Y

PH144. SHELLABEAR, WILLIAM GIRDLESTONE. Malay-English vocabulary; containing over 7,000 Malay words or phrases with their English equivalents together with an appendix of household, nautical and medical terms, etc. 2d. ed., rev. and enl. Singapore, Methodist Pub. House, 1912. 157p. C, Y

PH145. SHELLABEAR, WILLIAM GIRDLESTONE. An English-Malay dictionary. Singapore, Methodist Pub. House, 1916. 573p. Y

PH146. SWETTENHAM, FRANK ATHELSTANE. Vocabulary of the English and Malay languages. Shanghai, Kelly & Walsh, 1922-27. 2v. in 1. C, Y

PH147. WILKINSON, RICHARD JAMES. A Malay-English dictionary (romanised). Mytilene, Greece, Salavopoulos and Kinderlis, 1932. 2v. C, Y

PH148. WILKINSON, RICHARD JAMES. Malay-English dictionary romanised. Tokyo, 1943. 657p. C

PH149. HAMILTON, ARTHUR WEDDERBURN HARTWIG. Easy Malay vocabulary, covering the Dutch East Indies and Malaya. 5th. ed. Sydney, Australasian Pub. Co., 1944. 192p. Y

PH150. U.S. ARMY. FORCES IN THE FAR EAST. A Malay dictionary: Malay-English, English-Malay. Sydney, 1944. 285p. C, Y
["Based primarily on a translation of van Rondel's Malay-Dutch dictionary, amplified and amended to meet the specific need of United States forces."]

PH151. HENDERSHOT, VERNON EDWARDS. A dictionary of standard Malay by Vernon E. Hendershot and W. G. Shellabear. Mountain View, Calif., Pacific Pr., 1945. 235p. C, Y

PH152. Pocket vocabulary, English-Malay, Malay-English. New York, NKPM, 1945. 46p. C

PH153. WINSTEDT, RICHARD OLOF. Dictionary of colloquial Malay (Malay-English and English-Malay). London, Kegan Paul, Trench, Trubner, 1945. 175p. C, Y

PH154. KEASBERRY, BENJAMIN PEACH. A vocabulary of the English and Malay languages. Enl. and rev. ed. Singapore, 1946. 30p. Y

PH155. WILKINSON, RICHARD JAMES. An abridged Malay-English dictionary (romanised). 7th. ed., rev. and enl. by A. E. Coope. London, Macmillan, 1948. 269p. Y

PH156. LATHIEF, A. K. The Indonesian-English dictionary of terminology, defined in English. Medan, Gedung Pustaka, 1949. 207p. C

PH157. WINSTEDT, RICHARD OLOF. An English-Malay dictionary (roman characters). 3d. ed. Singapore, Kelly and Walsh, 1949. 524p. C, Y
["Based on Mr. R. J. Wilkinson's Malay-English dictionary."]

PH158. Kathay's kamus moderen bahasa Melayu-Inggeris. A modern unabridged Malay-English dictionary. Singapore, Pustaka Kathay, 195? 448p. C

PH159. SAMAH, A. Everyday Indonesian English dictionary. Medan, Pustaka Andalas, 1950-51. 2v. in 1. C

PH160. NUH, MUHAMMAD. Ksatrya vocabulary kamus Inggeris Indonesia dan Indonesia Inggeris. Medan, Pustaka Madju, 1951. 224p. C

PH161. Van Goor's Pandu bahasa; Indonesia-Inggeris dan Inggeris-Indonesia, tersusun oleh Ach. Sulaiman. The Hague, van Goor, 1951. viii, 96p. C

PH162. DILMY, NJONJA. Kamus bahasa Inggeris Indonesia dan Indonesia-Inggeris. Bogor, Oranje, 1952. 151p. C

PH163. SHAMSUDDIN BIN M. JOONOOS. Concise English-Malay dictionary. 2d. ed. rev. Penang, Shah, 1952. 105p. C, Y

PH164. Van Goor's kamus Inggeris ketjil. Inggeris-bahasa Indonesia; bahasa Indonesia-Inggeris, oleh A. L. N. Kramer. The Hague, van Goor, 1952. 359p. C, Y

PH165. WINSTEDT, RICHARD OLOF. Practical modern-English-Malay dictionary. Singapore, Kelly and Walsh, 1952. 387p. C

PH166. WOJOWASITO, A. Kamus bahasa Inggeris-Indonesia. Tjet. 2. Amsterdam, Versluys, 1952. 282p. C

PH167. WITTERMANS-PINO, ELIZABETH. Kamus Inggeris by E. Pino and T. Wittermans. Djakarta, Wolters, 1953. 2v. C, Y
[Cornell entry: Pino, E.]

PH168. WINSTEDT, RICHARD OLOF. Unabridged English-Malay dictionary. Singapore, Marican, 1955. 398p. C

PH169. WINSTEDT, RICHARD OLOF. An unabridged Malay-English dictionary. Singapore, Kelly and Walsh, 1955. 359p. C, Y

PH170. WITTERMANS-PINO, ELIZABETH. Kamus Inggeris by E. Pino and T. Wittermans. 2d. ed. Djakarta, Wolters, 1955. 2v. Y

PH171. HAMILTON, ARTHUR WEDDERBURN HARTWIG. Easy Malay vocabulary new and improved covering Malaya and Indonesia. 6th. ed. Singapore, Moore, 1956. 192p. Y

PH172. FORBES, D. C. Dictionary of English and Roman Malay. Kamus bahasa Inggeris Melayu. Rev. ed. Singapore, Marican, 1957. 297p. Y

PH173. SULAIMAN BIN AHMAD. Easy Malay-English dictionary. 2nd. ed. Singapore, Marican, 1957. 155p. C

PH174. WINSTEDT, RICHARD OLOF. Unabridged Malay-English dictionary. 2d. ed. Singapore, Marican, 1957. 370p. C

PH175. ZAIN, SUTAN MUHAMMAD. English dictionary: English-Indonesian. Djakarta, Wolters, 1957. 556p. C

PH176. WOJOWASITO, S. Kamus bahasa Indonesia-Inggeris. Tjet. 2. Amsterdam, Versluys, 1958. 269p. C

PH177. WINSTEDT, RICHARD OLOF. A practical modern Malay-English dictionary. 3d. ed. Singapore, Marican, 1959. 203, 225p. C, Y

PH178. WOJOWASITO, S. Kamus bahasa Inggeris-Indonesia. Tjet. 5. Edisi populer. Djakarta, Versluys, 1959. 268p. Y

PH179. WOJOWASITO, S. Kamus umum Inggeris-Indonesia. Djakarta, Versluys, 1959. 451p. C, Y

PH180. KWEE, OEN GOAN. Kamus Inggeris-Indonesia; memuat 8,500 pendjelasan, daftar irregular verbs dan pemakaian mudah, praktis. Djakarta, Sunrise, 196? 121p. C, Y

PH181. ECHOLS, JOHN M. An Indonesian-English dictionary by John M. Echols and Hassan Shadily. Ithaca, Cornell Univ. Pr., 1961. 384p. C, Y

PH182. WITTERMANS-PINO, ELIZABETH. Kamus Inggeris, oleh E. Pino dan T. Wittermans. Tjet. 3, tanpa perubahan. Djakarta, Pradnajaparamita, 1961. 2v. C, Y
[Cornell entry: Pino, E.]

PH183. FORBES, D. C. Dictionary of English and Roman Malay. Kamus bahasa Inggeris Melayu. 3d. rev. ed. Singapore, Marican, 1962. 293p. C

PH184. Kamus senang; English-Malay dictionary, disusun oleh Maimoon Binti Abdullah. Singapore, Kader, 1962. 250p. C

PH185. LA DAGE, JOHN HOFFMAN. Kamus istilah pelajaran. Dictionary of nautical terms. Djakarta, 1962. 218p. C, Y

PH186. MALAYA (FED.) DEWAN BAHASA DAN PUSTAKA. Istilah pertadbiran; termasok kata2 dan rangkaikata yang lazim di-gunakan dalam surat-menyurat, Inggeris-Melayu-Inggeris. Kuala Lumpur, 1962. 196p. (Its Siri istilah DBP Bil. 2) C

PH187. WINSTEDT, RICHARD OLOF. A practical modern English-Malay dictionary with an appendix. 5th. ed. Singapore, Marican 1962. 421p. Y

PH188. ECHOLS, JOHN M. An Indonesian-English dictionary. 2d. ed. Ithaca, Cornell Univ. Pr., 1963. 431p. C, Y

PH189. Kathay's unabridged new Crown dictionary of national language by S. Santoso and Y. K. Lee (Lee Yu Kai) rev. and supplemented by Kathay's

Malay Editorial Board. 5th. ed. Singapore, Kathay Pr., 1963. 32, 288, 83, 42p. C, Y

PH190. Collins Malay gem dictionary: Malay-English, English-Malay, compiled by Abdul Rahman bin Yusop. London, Collins, 1964. 702p. C

PH191. Kamus istilah pengetahuan alam, Inggeris Indonesia. Scientific dictionary, English-Indonesian. Bandung, Dept. of Chemistry, FKIP, 1964. 28ℓ C

PH192. MALAYSIA. DEWAN BAHASA DAN PUSTAKA. Istilah jawatan dan jabatan (kementerian, Jabatan, Pejabat dan bahagian2-nya). Kuala Lumpur, 1964. 232p. (Its Siri istilah, bil. 1) Y

PH193. NUH, MOHAMMAD. Ksatrya dictionary. Kamus Inggeris-Indonesia. Tjet. 2. Djakarta, Perpustakaan Kesatria, 1964. 311p. C, Y

PH194. SCHMIDGALL TELLINGS, ALUZIUS EDUARD. Indonesian-English supplemental word-list to existing dictionaries. Djakarta, Lembaga Administrasi Negara, 1964. 222ℓ C, Y

PH195. WILKINSON, RICHARD JAMES. An abridged Malay-English, English-Malay dictionary. Pocket ed. London, Macmillan, 1964. 307, 162p. C

PH196. WOJOWASITO, S. Kamus bahasa Indonesia-Inggeris (Indonesian-English dictionary) oleh S. Wojowasito dan W. J. S. Poerwadarminta. Tjet. 4. Djakarta, Tiara, 1964. 270p. C, Y

PH197. MALAYSIA. DEWAN BAHASA DAN PUSTAKA. Istilah Ekonomi: Inggeris-Melayu-Inggeris. Kuala Lumpur, Kementerian Pelajaran Malaysia, 1965. 151p. C, Y
[Cornell entry: title]
[Cornell series note: (Malaya (Fed.) Dewan Bahasa dan Pustaka. Siri istilah DBP, Bil. 3)]

PH198. WINSTEDT, RICHARD OLOF. An unabridged Malay-English dictionary. 6th. ed. enl. Kuala Lumpur, Marican, 1965. 390p. Y

PH199. MAIMOON BINTI ABDULLAH. Kamus mudah 2d. i.e. 3d. rev. ed. Singapore, Kader, 1966. 3v. C

PH200. WINSTEDT, RICHARD OLOF. Unabridged English-Malay dictionary. 4th. ed. enl. Kuala Lumpur, Marican, 1966. 437p. C

PH201. ZAINAL ABIDIN BIN SAFARWAN. Advanced Malay-English dictionary. Kuala Lumpur, Marican, 1966. 367p. C

Esperanto

PH202. MUSLIMIN, K. A. Kamus Esperanto oleh Kamsta [pseud.] Djakarta, Eldonistino, 19?? 31p. C

French

PH203. BOZE, P. Dictionnaire français et malais, contenant des dialogues familiers. Hongkong, De Souza, 1871. 119p. Y

PH204. RICHARD, LÉONCE. Kitab pada meniata-kan. Dictionnaire de la langue commerciale de l'archipel d'Asia (dite malaise) telle qu'elle se parle à Sumatra, Singapour. Bordeaux, Féret, 1873. 124, 153p. C, Y

PH205. FAVRE, PIERRE ETIENNE LAZARE. Dictionnaire malais-français. Vienne, Impériale et Royale, 1875. 2v. C, Y

PH206. FAVRE, PIERRE ETIENNE LAZARE. Dictionnaire français-malais. Vienne, Impériale et Royale, 1880. 2v. C, Y

PH207. ERRINGTON DE LA CROIX, JOHN. Vocabulaire français-malais et malais-français. Paris, Leroux, 1889. 252p. Y

PH208. BRISSAUD, LOUIS DESIRE. Petit recueil malais-français à l'usage des élèves de premier et de seconde année. Paris, Leroux, 1891. 72p. C, Y

PH209. TUGAULT, ALFRED. Dictionnaire malais-français. Paris, Leroux, 1898. 527p. Y

PH210. ERRINGTON DE LA CROIX, JOHN. Vocabulaire français-malais et malais-français. Paris, Leroux, 1910. 260p.

PH210a. SOEMARGONO, F. Kamus dasar: Perantjis-Indonesia. Dari G. Gougenheim, Dictionnaire Fondamental de la langue française, Didier, 1958, oleh Farida Soemargono dan Pierre Labrousse. Bandung, Ananta, 1969. 277p. C, Y

German

PH211. KAHLO, GERHARD. Malayisch-Deutsches und Deutsch-Malayisches Wörterbuch. Berlin, Akademie-Verlag, 1950. 422p. C, Y

PH212. SITUMORANG, F. Kamus bahasa Djerman, Djerman-Indonesia dan Indonesia-Djerman. Tjet. 2. Medan, Medanse Drukkerij, 1952. 310p. C

PH213. KAHLO, GERHARD. Moderne indonesische Ausdrücke; Nachtrag zum malayschen Wörterbuch. Berlin, Akademie-Verlag, 1956. 215p. C, Y

PH214. AËTIUS, BROTHER. Kamus Djerman-Indonesia. Tjet. 3. Djakarta, Erlangga, 1962. 140p. C, Y

PH215. KAROW, OTTO. Indonesisch-Deutsches Wörterbuch. Kamus bahasa Indonesia-Djerman, verfaszt von Otto Karow und Irene Hilgers-Hesse. Wiesbaden, Harrossawitz, 1962. 483p. C, Y

PH216. KAHLO, GERHARD. Indonesisch-deutsches Wörterbuch von Gerhard Kahlo und Rosemarie Bärwinkel. Leipzig, Verlag Enzyklopädie, 1963. 510p. C, Y

PH217. RAHAJOEKOESOEMAH, DATJE. Kamus bahasa Djerman; diperiksa kembali oleh Makmoer Soerjonagoro. Bandung, Sumur Bandung, 1963– C, Y
[Cornell entry: Datje Rahajukusumah.]

PH218. KAHLO, GERHARD. Deutsch-indonesisches Wörterbuch, von Gerhard Kahlo und Rosemarie Simon-Bärwinkel. Leipzig, Verlag Enzyklopädie, 1967. 400p. Y

Italian

PH219. ITALY. AMBASCIATA. INDONESIA. Kamus Italia; Italia-Indonesia, Indonesia-Italia. Dizionario italo-indonesiano. Djakarta, Noordhoff-Kolff, 1957. 144p. C

Japanese

PH220. POERWADARMINTA, WELFRIDUS JOSEPH SABARYA. Kamoes harian Nippon-Indonesia, Indonesia-Nippon. Djakarta, Toko Boekoe Pendidikan, 1942. 158p. C
[Cornell entry: Purwadarminta, . . .]

PH221. POERWADARMINTA, WELFRIDUS JOSEPH SABARYA. Kamoes harian Nippon-Indonesia, Indonesia-Nippon. Tjet. 2. Djakarta, Pendidikan, 1942. 191p. C
[Cornell entry: Purwadarminta, . . .]

PH222. Indone djoeten. n.p. 1943. 249p. C

PH223. JAVA (JAPANESE MILITARY ADMINISTRATION, 1942–45) BUNKYOKYOKU. Kamoes bahasa Nippon-Indonesia. Djakarta, Djawa Gunseikaubu, 1943. 950p. C

PH224. Kamoes bahasa Melajoe (Indonesia)-Nippon jang lengkap, compiled by Tjoi Kakumei. Tokyo, Kobunkan, 1943. 1774p. Y

PH225. Kamoes bahasa Nippon-Indonesia. Disoesoen oleh Syo Sunda Minseibu. Denpasar, Bali Sinbun Sya, 1944. 111p. C

PH226. RATA, A. WAHID. Kamoes dan peladjaran bahasa Nippon. Medan, Boekhandel Deli, 1944. 101p. C

PH227. POERWADARMINTA, WELFRIDUS JOSEPH SABARYA. Logat Nippon. Djakarta, Gunseikanbu Kokumin Toshokyohu, 1945. 304p. C
[Cornell entry: Purwadarminta, . . .]

PH228. ADINEGORO, DJAMALUDIN. Kamoes bahasa Indonesia-Nippon dan Nippon-Indonesia. Medan, 1947. 197p. C

PH229. SASTRANEGARA, RD. M. Kamus Djepang-Indonesia. Djakarta, Jos, 1962. 75p. C, Y

Russian

PH230. KORIGODSKY, R. N. Kamus Bahasia Indonesia-Rusia. Terlampir adalah ichtisar singkat tatabahasa Indonesia disusun verbit Kamus-kamus Bahasa Asing dan Nasional. n.p. 1961. 1171p. C, Y

PH231. LORDKIPANIDZE, ALEKSANDR GRIGOR'EVICH. Kamus peladjaran Rusia-Indonesia, disusun oleh A. G. Lordkipanidze dan A. P. Pavlenko. Moscow, Badan Penerbit Kamus Asing dan Nasional Negara, 1963. 707p. C, Y
[Cornell entry: title]

PH232. TESELKIN, AVENIR STEPANOVICH. Kamus peladjaran Indonesia-Rusia; 7,000 kata. Moscow, Sovjetskaja Ensiklopedia, 1964. 577p. C

PI — OTHER LANGUAGES OF MALAYSIA AND INDONESIA

Javanese

PI 1. CORNETS DE GROOT, ADRIAAN DAVID. Javaansche spraakkunst . . . op nieuw uitgegeven en voorzien van een nieuw woordenboek door T. Roorda. Amsterdam, Müller, 1843. 2v. Y

PI 2. GERICKE, JOHANN FRIEDRICH CARL. Javaansch-Nederduitsch woordenboek. Amsterdam, Müller, 1847. 796p. Y

PI 3. FAVRE, PIERRE ETIENNE LAZARE. Dictionnaire javanais-français. Vienne, Impériale et Royale, 1870. 544p. C, Y

PI 4. WINTER, CAREL FRIEDRICH. Kawi-Javaansch woordenboek, ten behoeve van degenen, die Javaansche gedichten wenschen te lezen. Batavia, GPO, 1880. 576p. C, Y

PI 5. JANSZ, PIETER. Practisch Nederlandsch-Javaansch woordenboek met Latijnsche karakters. 5. verb. en weder verm. uitg. Semarang, van Dorp, 1898. 324p. Y

PI 6. Kamus kemadjuan anak2 sekolah rakjat Indonesia. Djawa-Indonesia oleh R. Md. 'A. Dirdja Supraba. Tjet. 2. Jogjakarta, Toko Buku S. M. Diwarno, 19?? v. C

PI 7. GERICKE, JOHANN FRIEDRICH CARL. Javaansch-Nederlandsch handwoordenboek van J. F. C. Gericke en T. Roorda, verm. en verb. door A. C. Vreede met medewerking van J. G. H. Gunning. Amsterdam, Müller, 1901. 2v. C, Y

PI 8. BEZEMER, TAMMO JACOB. Javaansch-Hollandsche woordenlijst behoorende bij de oefeningen ter vertaling uit en in het Javaansch. 2. verb. druk. Zwolle, Tjeenk Willink, 1907. 51p. C

PI 9. JANSZ, PIETER. Practish Javaansch-Nederlandsch woordenboek met Latijnsche karakters. 2. verb. en veel verm. uitg. Semarang, van Dorp, 1913. 1204p. C

PI 10.   EGNER, D. W. English Javanese vocabulary. Amsterdam, Hollandsch-Amerikaansche plantage, 19?? 100p. Y

PI 11.   JANSZ, PIETER. Nederlandsch-Javaansch woordenboek. 5 weder verm. druk. Semarang, van Dorp, 1920. 441p. C, Y

PI 12.   SASRASAGANDA, RADEN. Baoesastra Mlajoe-Djawa. Tjap-tjapan kang2. Weltevreden, Balé Poestaka, 1922. 563p. C

PI 13.   BEZEMER, TAMMO JACOB. Javaansch-Hollandsche en Hollandsch-Javaansche woordenlijst behoorende bij de oefeningen ter vertaling uit en in het Javaansch. 7. verb. druk. Zwolle, Tjeenk Willink, 1931. 97p. Y

PI 14.   JANSZ, PIETER. Practisch Javaansch-Nederlandsch woordenboek met Latijnsche karakters. 3. verb. en veel verm. uitg. Semarang, van Dorp, 1932. 1216p. C, Y

PI 15.   POERWADARMINTA, WELFRIDUS JOSEPH SABARYA. Baoesastra Walandi-Djawi of Nederlands-Javaans woordenboek. Amsterdam, Versluys, 1936. 215p. C, Y
[Cornell entry: Purwadarminta, . . .]

PI 16.   PIGEAUD, THEODOR. Javaans-Nederlands handwoordenboek. Groningen, Wolters, 1938. 624p. C, Y

PI 17.   POERWADARMINTA, WELFRIDUS JOSEPH SABARYA. Baoesastra Djawa. Batavia, Wolters, 1939. 670p. C, Y
[Cornell entry: Purwadarminta, . . .]

PI 18.   POERWADARMINTA, WELFRIDUS JOSEPH SABARYA. Katerangan tegesing temboeng2 Baoesastra tjilik. Batavia, Wolters, 1940. 281p. C, Y
[Cornell entry: Purwadarminta, . . .]

PI 19.   POERWADARMINTA, WELFRIDUS JOSEPH SABARYA. Kawi-Djarwa. Djakarta, Balé Poestaka, 1943. 48p. C, Y
[Cornell entry: Purwadarminta, . . .]

PI 20.   POERWADARMINTA, WELFRIDUS JOSEPH SABARYA. Baoesastra Indonesia Djawi. Tjap-tjapan kaping 3. Djakarta, Balé Poestaka, 1945. 203p. C, Y
[Cornell entry: Purwadarminta, . . .]

PI 21.   PIGEAUD, THEODOR. Nederlands-Javaans en Javaans-Nederlands zakwoordenboekje; voorafgegaan door een kort begrip van de Javaanse spraakkunst. Groningen, Wolters, 1948. 200p. C, Y

PI 22.   PIGEAUD, THEODOR. Nederlands-Javaans handwoordenboek. Jakarta, Wolters, 1948. 664p. C

PI 23.   POEWADARMINTA, WELFRIDUS JOSEPH SABARYA. Baoesastra Djawi-Indonesia. Djakarta, Balé Poestaka, 1948. 243p. C
[Cornell entry: Purwadarminta, . . .]

Sundanese

PI 24.   RIGG, JONATHAN. A dictionary of the Sunda language of Java. Batavia, Lange, 1862. 537p. (Verhandelingen van het Bataviaasch Genootschap van Kunsten en Wetenschappen, deel 29) C, Y

PI 24a. COOLSMA, SIERK. Soendaneesch-Hollandsch woordenboek. Leiden, Sijthoff, 1884. 422p. C, Y

PI 25.   COOLSMA, SIERK. Hollandsch-Soendaneesch woordenboek. Leiden, Sijthoff, 1910. 730p. Y

PI 26.   Visser's Soendaasch zakwoordenboekje, met eenige samenspraken uit het dagelijksche leven. Ten dienste van Nederlanders die zich in Indië komen vestigen. Weltevreden, Visser, 1928. 210p. Y

PI 27. COOLSMA, SIERK. Soendaneesch-Hollandsch woordenboek. 3. druk. Leiden, Sijthoff, 1930. 729p. C, Y

PI 28. LEZER, LEO ANDRIES. Lezer's Soendasch woordenboek; Soendasch-Nederlandsch, Nederlandsch-Soendasch. Bandung, Boekenverzendhuis L. A. Lezer, 1931. 350p. C, Y

PI 29. SATJADIBRATA, R. Kamoes Soenda-Melajoe. Djakarta, Gunseikanbu Kokumin Tosyokyoku (Balai Poestaka), 1944. 379p. C, Y

PI 30. SATJADIBRATA, RADEN. Kamoes leutik Soenda-Indonesia. Djakarta, Gunseikanbu Kokumin Tosyokyoku, 1945. 102p. C, Y

PI 31. SATJADIBRATA, RADEN. Kamoes basa Soenda katoet ketjap2 asing hoe geus ilahar. Djakarta, Bale Poestaka, 1948. 446p. C

PI 32. SATJADIBRATA, RADEN. Kamus Indonesia-Sunda. Djakarta, Pustaka Rakjat, 1950. 304p. C

PI 33. SATJADIBRATA, RADEN. Kamus basa Sunda katut ketjap2 asing nu geus ilahar. Tjit. 2. Djakarta, 1954. 476p. C

PI 34. SATJADIBRATA, RADEN. Kamus leutik Indonesia-Sunda djeung Sunda-Indonesia. Tjit. 3. Djakarta, Bale Poestaka, 1956. 199p. C

OTHER LANGUAGES OF MALAYSIA AND INDONESIA—ARRANGED ALPHABETICALLY BY LANGUAGE

PI 35. DJAJADININGRAT, HOESEIN. Atjehsch-Nederlandsch woordenboek met Nederlandsch-Atjehsch register door G. W. J. Drewes. Batavia, GPO, 1934. 2v. Y

PI 36. ANANDA KUSAMA, I GUSTI. Kamus Bali-Indonesia, Indonesia-Bali. Denpasar, Pustaka Balima, 1956. 2v. C

PI 37. ADRIANI, NICOLAUS. Bare'e-Nederlandsch woordenboek met Nederlandsch-Bare'e register. Leiden, Brill, 1928. 1074p. Y

PI 38. JOUSTRA, M. Karo-bataksch woordenboek. Leiden, Brill, 1907. 244p. C, Y

PI 39. NEUMANN, JOSHUA H. Karo-Bataks—Nederlands woordenboek. Djakarta, Lembaga Kebudajaan Indonesia, 1951. 343p. C

PI 40. MATTHES, BENJAMIN FREDERIK. Boegineesch-Hollandsch woordenboek, met Hollandsch-Boeginesche woordenlijst, en verklaring van een tot opheldering Ethnographischen atlas. The Hague, Nijhoff, 1874. 1180p. Supplement. The Hague, Nijhoff, 1889. 150p. C, Y

PI 41. MAGER, JOHN FREDERICK. Gedaged-English dictionary. Columbus, Ohio, Board of Foreign Missions of the American Lutheran Church, 1952. 353p. C, Y

PI 42. ANTONISSEN, A. Kadazan-English and English-Kadazan dictionary. Canberra, GPO, 1958. 273p. C, Y

PI 43. JOUSTRA, M. Nederlandsch-Karosche woordenlijst. Tweede, verm. druk. Leiden, Doesburgh, 1922. 103p. (Uitgaven van het Bataksch Instituut, no. 20) C, Y

PI 44. JUYNBOLL, HENDRIK HERMAN. Oudjavaansch-Nederlandsche woordenlijst. Leiden, Brill, 1923. 685p. C, Y

PI 45. ARNDT, PAUL. Li'onesisch-deutsches Wörterbuch. Ende, Flores, Arnoldus-Druckerei, 1933. 555p. C, Y

PI 46. KILIAAN, H. N. Madoereesch-Nederlandsch woordenboek. Leiden, Brill, 1904-05. 2v. C

PI 47. PENNINGA, P. Practisch Madurees-Nederlands woordenboek van P. Penninga en H. Hendriks. 2e. verm. druk. Semarang, van Dorp, 195? 2v. C, Y

PI 48. MATTHES, BENJAMIN FREDERIK. Makassaarsch-Hollandsch woordenboek, met Hollandsch-Makassaarsche wordenlijst, opgave van Makas-

PI 49. saarsche plantennamen, en verklaring van een tot opheldering bijgevoegden Ethnographischen atlas. Amsterdam, Müller, 1859. 943p. Y
PI 49. MATTHES, BENJAMIN FREDERIK. Makassaarsch-Hollandsch woordenboek, met Hollandsch-Makassaarsche wordenlijst, en verklaring van een tot opheldering bijgevoegden Ethnographischen atlas. 2. druk. The Hague, Nijhoff, 1885. 1170p. C, Y
PI 50. DAOED, RADJA MEDAN. Menangkabausch-Maleische zamenspraken. The Hague, Nijhoff, 1872. xxxv, 58p. C
PI 51. PAMUNTJAK, MUHAMMAD THAIB SUTAN. Kamoes bahasa Minangkabau-bahasa Melajoe-Riau. Batavia, Balai Poestaka, 1935. 271p. C, Y
PI 52. ANAK MINANG, pseud. Logat ketjik Indonesia-Minang. Bukittinggi, Indah, 1960. 42p. C
PI 53. ARNDT, PAUL. Wörterbuch der Ngadhasprache. Fribourg, Posieux, 1961. 646p. (Anthropos Institute. Studia, v. 15) C, Y
PI 54. STELLER, K. G. F. Sangirees-Nederlands woordenboek met Nederlands-Sangirees register door K. G. F. Steller en W. E. Aebersold. The Hague, Nijhoff, 1959. 622p. C, Y
PI 55. HOWELL, WILLIAM. A Sea Dyak dictionary, in alphabetical parts, with examples and quotations showing the use and meaning of words by William Howell and D. J. S. Bailey. Singapore, American Mission Press, 1900. 186, 21p. C
PI 56. SCOTT, NORMAN CARSON. A dictionary of Sea Dayak. London, School of Oriental and African Studies, 1956. 218p. C, Y

PL—LAO DICTIONARIES

<u>English</u>

PL1. COLLINS, D. G. An English Laos dictionary. 3d. ed. Chiengmai, Mission Pr., 1915. 291p. C, Y

<u>French</u>

PL2. ESTRADE. Dictionnaire et guide franco-laotiens. Prononciation en français avec signes conventionnels; transcription de tous les termes en caractères laotiens; manuel de conversation. Toulouse, Berthoumieu, 1895. 325p. C
PL3. CHEMINAUD, GUY. Nouveau dictionnaire français-laotien, contenant plus de 5,500 mots, appayés par les locutions familières. Tulle, France, Crouffon, 1906. 198p. Y
PL4. GUIGNARD, TH. Dictionnaire laotien-français. Hong Kong, Nazareth, 1912. 959p. C, Y
PL5. REINHORN, MARC. Dictionnaire laotien-français. Ed. 1956. n.p. Centre Militaire d'Information et de Specialisation pour l'Outre-mer, Section de Documentation, 1956. 5v. C, Y

PP—THE LANGUAGES OF THE PHILIPPINES

<u>Polyglot Dictionaries</u>

PP1. JUANMARTI, JACINTO. Diccionario moro-maguindanao-español. Manila, Amigos del país, 1892. 1v. C, Y
PP2. COWIE, ANDSON. English-Sulu-Malay vocabulary with useful sentences, tables, etc. London, May, 1893. 288p. C, Y
PP3. CALDERÓN, SOFRONIO G. Pocket dictionary English-Spanish-Tagalog. Manila, Soriano, 1914. 343p. Y
PP4. CALDERÓN, SOFRONIO G. Pocket dictionary English-Espanish-Tagalog. 3d. ed. Manila, Santos y Bernat, 1930. 428p. C

PP5. GALLAS, VICENTE. English-Visayan-Spanish dictionary. Cebu, Barba, 1937. 461p. C

PP6. ENRÍQUEZ, PABLO JACOBO. Pocket dictionary English-Tagalog-Ilocano vocabulary containing 8,000 words most commonly used by students of the elementary and secondary schools by P. Jacobo Enríquez and J. Ben Quimba. Manila, Philippine Book Co., 1949, 190p. Y

PP7. ENRÍQUEZ, PABLO JACOBO. Pocket dictionary English-Tagalog-Spanish vocabulary containing 8,000 words most commonly used by students of the elementary and secondary schools. Manila, Philippine Book Co., 1949. 224p. (National language books, 7) Y

PP8. ENRÍQUEZ, PABLO JACOBO. Pocket dictionary English-Tagalog-Visayan (Cebuano-Ilongo) vocabulary containing 8,000 words most commonly used by students of the elementary and secondary schools by P. Jacobo Enríquez, Jose A. Bautista and Francis J. Jamolangue. Manila, Philippine Book Co., 1949. 249p. C, Y

PP9. ENRÍQUEZ, PABLO JACOBO. Pocket dictionary English-Tagalog-Spanish-Pangasinan vocabulary. Manila, Philippine Book Co., 1952. 249p. C

PP10. GUZMAN, MARIA ODULIO DE. Pocket dictionary English-Tagalog-Spanish and Tagalog-English vocabulary. Quezon City, Pressman, 1963. 229p. C

PP11. MANALILI, BIENVENIDO M. Pocket dictionary English-Tagalog-Pampango vocabulary containing more than 15,000 words of common usage. A helpful guide to students in the elementary, secondary and collegiate courses as well as to laymen by Bienvenido M. Manalili and J. P. Tamayo. Quezon City, Pressman, 1964. 215p. C, Y

PP12. HERMOSISIMA, TOMÁS V. Dictionary, Bisayan-English-Tagalog, standarized spelling. Manila, Ayuda, 1966. 648p. C, Y

Bisaya

PP13. KAUFMANN, JOHN. Visayan-English dictionary. Kapulúñgan binisayá-iniglís. Iloilo, La Editorial, n.d. 1045p. C, Y

PP14. FELIX DE LA ENCARNACIÓN, JUAN. Diccionario bisaya-español. 3d. ed. Manila, Amigos del país, 1885. 2v. in 1. C, Y

PP15. SÁNCHEZ DE LA ROSA, ANTONIO. Diccionario hispano-bisaya para las Provincias de Sámar y Leyte. Manila, Chofré, 1895. 2v. Y

PP15a. MAXFIELD, CHARLES L. English-Visayan dictionary and grammatical notes. Iloilo, Philippine Baptist Mission Pr., 1913. 162p. Y

PP16. The Subanu, studies of a sub-Visayan mountain folk of Mindanao. Washington, Carnegie Institution, 1913. 236p. (Carnegie Institution of Washington. Publication no. 184) C, Y
[pt. III vocabulary]

PP17. SÁNCHEZ DE LA ROSA, ANTONIO. Diccionario español-bisaya para las provincias de Samar y Leyte. 3d. ed. Manila, Santos y Bernal, 1914. 2v. in 1. C

Iloko

PP18. CARRO, ANDRÉS. Vocabulario iloco-español. 2d. ed. Manila, Pérez, 1888. 294p. C, Y

PP19. VANOVERBERGH, MORICE. English-Iloko thesaurus. Baguio, Philippines, 195? 365p. C, Y

PP20. CARRO, ANDRÉS. Iloko-English dictionary. Baguio, Philippines, Catholic School Press, 1956. 370p. C, Y

Tagalog

PP21. IGNACIO, ROSENDO P. Diksiyonaryo ng wikang Pilipino; inihanda para sa nagsisipágaral sa mabá bà at matáas na páaralan. Quezon City, Samar, 1958. 230p. C, Y

Tagalog-English and English-Tagalog

PP22. NIGG, CHARLES. A Tagalog English and English Tagalog dictionary. Manila, Fajardo, 1904. 360p. Y

PP23. DÁLUZ, EUSEBIO T. Filipino-English vocabulary, with practical examples of Filipino and English grammars. Manila, 1915. 1v. Y

PP24. PHILIPPINES (REP.) INSTITUTE OF NATIONAL LANGUAGE. A national language-English vocabulary. Manila, GPO, 1940. 180p. C

PP25. PHILIPPINES (REP.) INSTITUTE OF NATIONAL LANGUAGE. A Tagalog-English vocabulary. Manila, GPO, 1940. 180p. C, Y

PP26. PANGANIBAN, JOSÉ VILLA. English-Tagalog vocabulary. Manila, University Pub. Co., 1946. 170p. C, Y

PP27. MUNDO, CLODUALDO DEL. Pocket dictionary: Tagalog-English, English-Tagalog, prepared by Clodualdo del Mundo and Andrea Amor Tablan. enl. ed. Manila, Abiva, 1948. 208p. C, Y

PP28. ENRÍQUEZ, PABLO JACOBO. Pocket dictionary: an English-Tagalog vocabulary by P. Jacobo Enríquez and Maria Odulio Guzman. Manila, Philippine Book, 1949. 135p. C

PP29. ENRÍQUEZ, PABLO JACOBO. A pocket dictionary: Tagalog-English vocabulary by P. Jacobo Enríquez and Maria Odulio Guzman. Manila, Philippine Book, 1949. 129p. C

PP30. ENRÍQUEZ, PABLO JACOBO. Pocket dictionary, talatinigang pambulsa: English-Tagalog, Tagalog-English vocabulary by P. Jacobo Enríquez and Maria Odulio Guzman. Manila, Philippine Book, 1949. 170p. Y

PP31. PHILIPPINES (REP.) INSTITUTE OF NATIONAL LANGUAGE. A national language-English vocabulary. Manila, GPO, 1950. 176p. C, Y

PP32. PHILIPPINES (REP.) INSTITUTE OF NATIONAL LANGUAGE. An English-Tagalog dictionary. Manila, GPO, 1960. 412p. C, Y

PP33. ALDAVE-YAP, FE Z. Pilipino-English, English-Pilipino dictionary. Quezon City, Phoenix, 1961. 272p. C, Y

PP34. TABLAN, ANDREA AMOR. Pilipino-English, English-Pilipino dictionary for students, teachers, laymen, professionals, and foreigners. Compiled and edited by Andrea A. Tablan and Carmen B. Mallari. New York, Washington Square, 1961. 213p. C, Y

PP35. ALEJANDRO, RUFINO. A word-building Tagalog-English dictionary by Rufino Alejandro and Amparo R. Buhain. Manila, Abiva, 1962. 110p. Y

PP36. CALDERÓN, SOFRONIO G. Combined dictionary English-Tagalog, Tagalog-English. Manila, Aklatong Lunas, 1963. 155, 109p. Y

PP37. MANALILI, FELIX MACAPINLAC. Pocket dictionary English-Tagalog vocabulary by Felix Macapinlac Manalili and Reynaldo de Dios. Quezon City, Pressman, 1963. 217p. Y

PP38. MANALILI, FELIX MACAPINLAC. English-Pilipino, Pilipino-English vocabulary pocket dictionary by Felix Macapinlac Manalili and Reynaldo de Dios. Quezon City, Pressman, 1964. 123, 83p. C

PP39. MANALILI, FELIX MACAPINLAC. English-Tagalog vocabulary and Tagalog-English vocabulary pocket dictionary by Felix Macapinlac Manalili and Reynaldo de Dios. Quezon City, Pressman, 1964. 430p. C

PP40. PHILIPPINES (REP.) INSTITUTE OF NATIONAL LANGUAGE. Selected vocabulary lists (arithmetical, biological, parliamentary, etc.) Mga piling talasalitaan (pang-aritmétika, pambiyolohiyá, pangkapulungán, atb.). Special ed. Manila, GPO, 1964. 171p. C, Y

PP40a.   PANGANIBAN, JOSE VILLA. Tesaurong Ingles-Pilipino. San Juan, Rizal, Limbagang Pilipino, 1965– C

PP41.   GUZMAN, MARIA ODULIO DE. An English-Tagalog and Tagalog-English dictionary. Rev. ed. Manila, G.O.T., 1966. 668p. C, Y

PP42.   PANGANIBAN, JOSE VILLA. Talahulugang Pilipino-Engles. Maynila, Kawanihan ng Palimbagan, 1966. 362p. C, Y

Tagalog-Spanish and Spanish-Tagalog

PP43.   SANTOS, DOMINGO DE LOS. Vocabulario de la lengua tagala. Manila, Oliva, 1835. 739, 118p. Y

PP44.   NOCEDA, JUAN JOSÉ DE. Vocabulario de la lengua tagala, compuesta par varios religiosos doctos y graves, y coordinado por el p. Juan de Noceda y el p. Pedro de Sanlucar. Manila, Ramirez y Giraudier, 1860. 642p. C, Y

PP45.   SERRANO, ROSALIO. Nuevo diccionario manual español-tagalo. Manila, Ciudad condal, 1872. 398p. Y

PP46.   SERRANO LAKTAW, PEDRO. Diccionario hispano-tagalog. Manila, La Opinión, 1889–1914. 2v. C, Y

PP47.   ARTIGAS Y CUERVA, MANUEL. La primera imprenta en Filipinas; reseña histórica bio-bibliográfica, con tres apéndices. Uno bibliográfico de las obras citadas en el texto: otro con la biografía del P. Blancas, y el último, con una reseña de los actos ilevados á cabo para celebrar por primera vez el contenario de la imprenta en Filipinas. Manila, Germania, 1910. 259p.
        (Biblioteca nacional filipina. Vol. VI de la colección) Y

PP48.   SERRANO, ROSALIO. Diccionario de términos comunes tagalo-castellano. 4. ed. Manila, Santos y Bernal, 1910. 373p. C

PP49.   SERRANO, ROSALIO. Diccionario manual de términos comunes español-tagalo. 2. ed. Manila, Martinez, 1913. 404p. C, Y

PP50.   IGNACIO, ROSENDO P. Vocabulario bilingüe Español-Tagalo, Tagalo-Español. Manila, Martinez, 1917. 212p. C, Y

PP51.   SERRANO LAKTAW, PEDRO. Diccionario Hispano-Tagalog. Madrid, Ediciones Cultura Hispanica, 1965. 2v. in 3. Y

See also   PH23

Other Philippine Languages, Arranged Alphabetically by Language

PP52.   GISBERT, MATEO. Diccionario bagobo-español. Manila, Tip. Ramírez, 1892. 2v. in 1. C, Y

PP53.   LISBOA, MARCOS DE. Vocabulario de la lengua bicol. Manila, Colegio de Santo Tomás, 1865. 417, 103p. Y

PP54.   NELSON, ANDREW M. Basic Cebuano-English and English-Cebuano vocabulary. Manila, 196? 53ℓ C, Y

PP55.   RUIJTER, JUAN. Cebuano-English dictionary. Cebu, Sacred Heart Seminary, 196? 338p. C, Y

PP56.   CONKLIN, HAROLD C. Hanunóo-English vocabulary. Berkeley, Univ. of California Pr., 1953. 290p. C, Y

PP57.   BUGARÍN, JOSE. Diccionario ybang-español. Manila, Amigos del País, 1854. 12, 280, 72p. Y

PP58.   Diccionário español-ibanag, o sea, Tesauro hispano-cagayán. Manila, Ramírez y Giraudier, 1867. 511p. Y

PP59. Diccionario español-ibatán, por varios PP Dominicos misioneros de las Islas Batanes. Manila, Sto Tomás, 1914. 574p. C

PP60. YAMADA, YUKIHIRO. A preliminary Itbayaten vocabulary. Manila, Inst. of Asian Studies, Univ. of the Philippines, 1966. 122ℓ C, Y

PP61. CLAPP, WALTER CLAYTON. A vocabulary of the Igorot language as spoken by the Bontok Igorots. Manila, GPO, 1908. 143-236p. (Philippine Islands. Ethnological survey. Publications. vol. V. pt. III) C, Y

PP62. VANOVERBERGH, MORICE. A dictionary of Lepanto Igorot or Kankanay as it is spoken at Bauco. St. Gabriel, Austria, Anthropos, 1933. 508p. (Anthropos; linguistische bibliothek t.XII) Y

PP63. WILLIAMS, HERMON P. Revised dictionary English-Ilocano, Ilocano-English. Manila, Christian Mission, 1929-30. 2v. C

PP64. McKAUGHAN, HOWARD. A Maranao dictionary compiled by Howard P. McKaughan and Batua A. Macaraya. Honolulu, Univ. of Hawaii Pr., 1967. 483, 394p. C, Y

PP65. PORTER, RALPH STRIBLING. A primer and vocabulary of the Moro dialect (Magindanau). Washington, GPO, 1903. 77p. C, Y

PP66. BERGAÑO, DIEGO. Vocabulario de la lengua pampanga en romance. 2d. ed. Manila, Ramírez y Giraudier, 1860. 343p. C, Y

PP67. FERNANDEZ COSGAYA, LORENZO. Diccionario pangasinan-español. Manila, Colegio de Santo Tomás, 1865. 330, 121p. Y

PP68. RAYNER, ERNEST A. Grammar and dictionary of the Pangasinan language. Manila, Methodist Pub. House, 1923. 96p. Y

PP69. BENNÁSAR, GUILLERMO. Diccionario tiruray-español. Manila, Chofré, 1892-93. 1v. C, Y

PT—THAI DICTIONARIES

Polyglot

PT1. PALLEGOIX, JEAN BAPTISTE. Dictionarium linguae thai sive siamensis interpretatione latina, gallica et anglica illustratum. Paris, Imperatoris im pressum, 1854. 897p. Y

PT2. PALLEGOIX, JEAN BAPTISTE. Dictionnaire siamois français anglais. Bangkok, Mission Catholique, 1896. 1165p. C

French

PT3. CUAZ, MARIE JOSEPH. Essai de dictionnaire français-siamois. Bangkok, Mission Catholique, 1903. 1012p. C, Y

PT4. LUNET DE LAJONQUÌERE, ETIENNE EDMOND. Dictionnaire français-siamois, précédé de quelques notes sur la langue et la grammaire siamoises. Paris, Leroux, 1904. 227p. C, Y

PT5. MANICH JUMSAI. Dictionnaire français-siamois. Bangkok, 1949. 192p. C [Cornell entry: Manit Chumsai]

English

PT6. English and Siamese vocabulary. Bangkok, Presbyterian Mission Pr., 1865. 343p. Y

PT7. BRADLEY, DAN BEACH. Dictionary of the Siamese language. Bangkok, 1873. 804p. Y

PT8. MICHELL, EDWARD BLAIR. A Siamese-English dictionary for the use of students in both languages. Bangkok, 1892. 323p. Y

PT9. SMITH, SAMUEL J. A comprehensive Anglo-Siamese dictionary. Bangkok, Bangkolem, 1899-1908. 5v. C

PT10. CARTWRIGHT, BASIL OSBORN. A Siamese-English dictionary. Bangkok, American Presbyterian Mission Pr., 1907. 731p. Y

PT11. BANGKOK. AMNUAY SILPA SCHOOL. Scholars' Siamese-English dictionary: a useful manual for students of both languages, containing more than 13,500 entries. 3d. ed. Bangkok, 1936. 788p. Y

PT12. SO SETHAPUTRA. The new model English-Thai dictionary. Bangkok, Khun Wathathararak, 1940. 4v. Y

PT13. McFARLAND, GEORGE BRADLEY. Thai-English dictionary. Stanford, Calif., Stanford UP, 1944. 1019, 39p. C, Y

PT14. HAAS, MARY ROSAMOND. Phonetic dictionary of the Thai language. Berkeley, Univ. of California Pr., 1947. 2v. C, Y

PT15. MANICH JUMSAI. English-Siamese dictionary. Bangkok, 1949. 610p. Y

PT16. MANICH JUMSAI. Siamese-English dictionary. 3d. ed. Bangkok, 1949. 692p. C, Y
[Cornell entry: Manit Chumsai]

PT17. SO SETHAPUTRA. New model English-Thai dictionary. 2d. ed. Bangkok, 1952. 2v. Y

PT18. HAAS, MARY ROSAMOND. Thai vocabulary. Washington, American Council of Learned Societies, 1955. 217-589p. (American Council of Learned Societies. Program in Oriental Languages. Publications. Series A: Texts, no. 2) C, Y

PT19. MANICH JUMSAI. English-Thai dictionary. 5th unabridged ed. London, Macmillan, 1955. 1568p. C, Y
[Cornell entry: Manit Chumsai]

PT20. PLANG PHLOIPHROM. Pru's standard Thai-English dictionary, with the cooperation of Brother Urbain-Gabriel by Plang Phloyphrom and Robert Dorne Golden. Bangkok, Pricha, 1955. 1774p. C

PT21. WIT SIWASARIYANON. The standard Thai-English dictionary. Bangkok, Royal Thai Institute, 1957. 762p. C

PT22. MANICH JUMSAI. Thai-English dictionary. 48th ed. Bangkok, 1958. 780p. C, Y
[Cornell entry: Manit Chumsai]

PT23. KAMON PHAOPHICHIT. Modern English-Thai, Thai-English dictionary. Bangkok, 1959. 819, 765p. C

PT24. PLANG PHLOIPHROM. Modern standard Thai-English dictionary. Bangkok, Prae Bhitthaya, 1959. 1563p. C

PT25. MANICH JUMSAI. English-Thai dictionary. 20th ed. London, Macmillan, 1960. 609, 692p. C
[Cornell entry: Manit Chumsai]

PT26. KAMON PHAOPHICHIT. Modern English-Thai, Thai-English dictionary. Bangkok, Thai Wattana Phanit, 1961. 820, 805p. C

PT27. SO SETHAPUTRA. New model English-Thai dictionary. 3d. library ed. Samud Prakan, Thailand, 1961. 2v. Y

PT28. MANICH JUMSAI. Advanced English-Thai dictionary. 7th unabridged ed. Bangkok, Chalermnit Pr., 1963. 1504p. Y

PT29. PURNELL, HERBERT C. A short northern Thai-English dictionary Tai Yuan. Chiengmai, Overseas Missionary Fellowship, 1963. 125p. C

PT30. HAAS, MARY ROSAMOND. Thai-English student's dictionary. Stanford, Calif., Stanford Univ. Pr., 1964. 638p. C, Y

PT31. SO SETHAPUTRA. New model Thai-English dictionary. Samud Prakan, Thailand, 1965. 2v. Y

PT32. SO SETHAPUTRA. New model Thai-English dictionary. Library ed. Samud Prakan, Thailand, 1965- C, Y

PT33. BORISAT PHRAE PHITTHAYA, BANGKOK. Modern standard English-Thai dictionary, compiled and edited by Technical and Educational Department of Prae Pittaya. Bangkok, 1966. 1942p. C, Y
[Cornell entry: title]

PT34. SO SETHAPUTRA. New model Thai-English dictionary. Desk ed. 2d. ed. Bangkok, 1967. 727p. C

PV—VIETNAMESE DICTIONARIES

Polyglot

PV1. SAVINA, FRANÇOIS MARIE. Dictionnaire tay-annamite, français. Hanoi, Ideo, 1910. 488p. C, Y

PV2. LE-BA-KONG. Thanh-ngu Viet-Anh-Phap; Vietnamese-English-Jrench [sic] idioms. Saigon, Zien-Hong, 1952. 303p. C

PV3. BOCHET, GILBERT. Lexique polyglotte; viêtnamien-koho-roglai-français, par Gilbert Bochet et Jacques Dournes. Saigon, Editions France-Asie, 1953. 135p. C

PV4. GOUIN, EUGÈNE. Dictionnaire vietnamien, chinois, français. Saigon, Impr. d'Extrême-Orient, 1957. 1606, 40p. C, Y

PV5. Viet-Nam bach-khoa tu-dien, co bo-chu chu Han, Phap va Anh, do Dao-dang-Vy. Dictionnaire encyclopédique vietnamien avec annotations en chinois, français et anglais. Vietnamese encyclopedic dictionary with annotations in Chinese, French and English. Saigon, 1960– C, Y

Vietnamese

PV5a. VIETNAM. DO CONG-CHANH VA GIAO-THONG. Danh-tu Ky-thuat cong-chanh va giao-thong. Saigon, Bo Quoc-gia Giao-duc, 1959– C

Chinese

PV6. DAO-DUY-ANH. Gian-yeu Han-Viet tu-dien. 3d. ed. Paris, Minh-Tan. 2v. in 1. C

PV7. DAO-DUY-ANH. Gian yeu han Viet tu dien. Dictionnaire sino-annamite. Hué, Tien Dan, 1932. 2v. C

PV8. DAO-DUY-ANH. Gian-yeu han-viet tu-dien (thuong). Paris, Minh-Tan, 1949. 605p. Y

English

PV9. EMENEAU, MURRAY BARNSON. Annamese-English dictionary prepared by M. B. Emeneau and Diether van den Steinen with an English-Annamese index on work by John Sherry. Berkeley, Army specialized training program, Univ. of California, 1945. 279ℓ C, Y

PV10. LE-BA-KONG. Tu-dien tieu-chuan Anh-Viet. Standard pronouncing English-Vietnamese dictionary. In lan thu bo, co sua lai va them 5000 chu. rev. ed. Hanoi, Dien-Hong, 1951. 512p. C

PV11. LE-BA-KHANH. Tu-dien tieu-chuan Viet-Anh. Standard pronouncing Vietnamese-English dictionary, cua Le-ba-Khanh va Le-ba-Kong. Hanoi, Dien-Hong, 1951. 382p. (Hoi Nghien-cuu Pho-Thong Giao-Duc) C

PV12. LE-BA-KHANH. Standard pronouncing Vietnamese-English and English Vietnamese dictionary by Le-ba-Khanh and Le-ba-Kong. New York, Ungar, 1955. 2v. in 1. C, Y

PV13. LE-BA-KONG. Tu-dien Anh-Viet bo tui. English-Vietnamese pocket dictionary. Saigon, Dien-Hong, 1955. 541p. C

PV14. LE-VAN-HUNG. Vietnamese-English dictionary with the international phonetic system and more than 30,000 words and idiomatic expressions.

Paris, Editions Europe-Asie, 1955. 820p. C, Y

PV15. NGUYEN-VAN-KHON. English-Vietnamese dictionary. Anh-Viet tu-dien. Saigon, Viet-Dang, 1955. 1741p. C, Y

PV16. LE-BA-KONG. Tu-dien Viet-Anh bo tai. Vietnamese-English pocket dictionary. Saigon, Zien-Hong, 1956. 496p. C

PV17. NGO-VU. Anh-Viet-phap tu-dien cua Ngo Vu va Thanh Nghi. Saigon, Thoi-The, 1956. 650p. C

PV18. NGUYEN-VAN-KHON. Tu-dien Anh-Viet pho-thong. General English Vietnamese dictionary. Saigon, 1956. 655p. C

PV19. NGUYEN-DINH-HOA. Hoa's Vietnamese-English dictionary. Saigon, Bing-Minh, 1959. 568p. C, Y

PV20. LE-BA-KHANH. Tu-dien tieu-chuan Viet-Anh. Standard pronouncing Vietnamese English dictionary cua Le-Ba-Khanh va Le-Ba-Kong. Loai moi, co sua lai va them nhieu chu. Saigon, Zien-Hong, 1964. 439p. C

PV21. LE-BA-KONG. Tu dien tieu-chuan Anh-Viet. Standard pronouncing English-Vietnamese dictionary with a guide to Vietnamese pronunciation and an outline of Vietnamese grammar. Rev. ed. Saigon, Zien-Hong, 1964. 562p. C

PV22. LE-BA-KONG. English-Vietnamese conversation dictionary. Saigon, Zien-Hong, 1966. 354p. C

PV23. LE-BA-KONG. Tu-dien dam thoai Viet-Anh. Vietnamese-English conversation dictionary. Saigon, Zien-Hong, 1966. 411p. C

PV24. NGUYEN-VAN-KHON. Viet-Anh tu-dien; Vietnamese English dictionary. Saigon, Khai-Tri, 1966. 1233p. C

PV24a. NGUYEN-DINH-HOA. Vietnamese-English student's dictionary. Rev. and enl. ed. Saigon, Vietnamese American Association, 1967. 676p. C

PV25. NGUYEN-VAN-KHON. Tu-dien Anh-Viet pho thong. General English Vietnamese dictionary. Saigon, Khai-Tri, 1967. 605p. C

French

PV26. AUBARET, LOUIS GABRIEL GALDÉRIC. Vocabulaire français-annamite et annamite-français précédé d'un traité des particules annamites, rédigé par les soins de M. Aubaret. Bangkok, Mission Catholique, 1861. 2v. in 1. C, Y

PV27. AUBARET, LOUIS GABRIEL GALDÉRIC. Grammaire annamite suivie d'un vocabulaire français-annamite et annamite-français. Paris, Imprimerie impériale, 1867. 598p. C, Y

PV28. LE GRANDE DE LA LIRAŸE. Dictionnaire élémentaire annamite-français. Saigon, Imprimerie Impériale, 1868. 184p. Y

PV29. CUA, HUYNH-TINH-PAULUS. Dictionnaire annamite. Dai nam quac am tu vi. Saigon, Rey, Curiol, 1895–96. 2v. Y

PV30. GÉNIBREL, J. F. M. Dictionnaire annamite-français, comprenant: 1º tous les caractères de la langue annamite vulgaire, avec l'indication de leurs divers sens propres ou figurés, et justifiés par de nombreux exemples; 2º les caractères chinois nécessaires à l'étude des Tú Thu, ou Quatre livres classiques chinois; 3º la flore et la faune de l'Indo-Chine. 2d.ed. Saigon, Tan Dinh, 1898. 986p. Y

PV31. BONET, JEAN. Dictionnaire annamite-français (Langue officielle et langue vulgaire). Paris, Leroux, 1899–1900. 2v. (Publications de l'École des langues orientales vivantes 5e serie, vol. 1–2) C, Y

PV32. GÉNIBREL, J. F. M. Petit dictionnaire annamite-français. 2d. ed. Saigon, Tan Dinh, 1906. 812p. Y

PV33. MASSERON, J. Nouveau dictionnaire français-annamite. Saigon, Mission, 1922. 1083p. C, Y

PV34. BARBIER, VICTOR. Dictionnaire français-annamite. 3d. ed. Hanoi, Extrême-Orient, 1924. 856p. C, Y
PV35. GÉNIBREL, J. F. M. Petit dictionnaire annamite-français. 3d. ed. Saigon, 1927. 971p. C
PV36. BARBIER, VICTOR. Dictionnaire annamite-français. Hanoi, Ideo, 1929. 951p. C
PV37. CORDIER, GEORGES. Dictionnaire annamite-français. Hanoi, Tonkinoise, 1930-32. 1433p.
Supplement. Hanoi, Tonkinoise, 1932. 403p. Y
PV38. CORDIER, GEORGES. Dictionnaire français-annamite. Hanoi, Tonkinoise, 1934-36. 3v. C, Y
PV39. DAO-VAN-TAP. Tu-dien phap-viet pho-thong. Dictionnaire général français-vietnamien. Saigon, Vinh-Bao, 1949. 1242p. Y
PV40. DAO-DANG-VY. Phap-Viet tu-dien. Dictionnaire français-vietnamien. Hué, Tao-Dan, 1950-51. 2v. C, Y
PV41. DAO-DUY-ANH. Phap-viet tu-dien (Chu them chu Han). Dictionnaire français-vietnamien avec transcription en caractères chinois des termes sino-vietnamiens. 2d. ed. Paris, Minh-Tan, 1950. 1958p. C, Y
PV42. DAO-VAN-TIEN. Danh-tu khoa-hoc. Vocabulaire scientifique. Van-vat-hoc sinh, sinh-ly, dong-vat, thuc-vat, dia-chat. Paris, Minh-Tan, 1950. 104p. C, Y
PV43. THANH-NGHI. Viet-Nam tan tu-dien. Saigon, Thoi-The, 1951. 1669p. C, Y
PV44. DAO-DONG-VY. Viet-Phap tan tu-dien. Nouveau dictionnaire vietnamien-français. Xuat-ban lan thu nhat. Saigon, 1956. 1458p. Y
PV45. THANH-NGHI. Viet-Phap-Anh tu-dien. In lan 2. Saigon, Thoi-The, 1960. 890p. C
PV46. THANH-NGHI. Viet-Nam tan tu-dien minh-hoa. Saigon, Khai-Tri, 1965. 1538p. C
PV47. DAO-DANG-VY. Viet-Phap tieu tu-dien. Petit dictionnaire vietnamien français. Saigon, 1966. 936p. C
PV48. KHAI-ANH. Phap-Viet tieu tu-dien cua Khui-Anh va Thanh Nghi. In lan 4. Saigon, Nha-Y, 1968. 789p. C

German

PV49. FERKINGHOFF, KLAUS. Deutsch-Vietnamesisches Wörterbuch. Tu-dien Duch-Viet. Wiesbaden, Harrossawitz, 1962. 110p. C, Y

Latin

PV50. PIGNEAU DE BEHAINE, PIERRE JOSEPH. Dictionarium anamitico-latinum. Serampore, Fredericnagori, 1838. 722, 128p. Y
PV51. TABERD, JEAN LOUIS. Dictionarium latino-anamiticum. Serampore, Fredericnagori, 1838. 708p. Y
PV52. TABERD, JEAN LOUIS. Dictionarium anamitico-latinum. Ninh Phu, Tunquini occidentalis, 1877. 566, 71p. Y
PV53. RAVIER, H. Dictionarium latino-annamiticum completum et novo ordine dispositum, cui accedit appendix praecipuas voces proprias cum brevi explicatione condinens. Ninh Phu, Missionis Tunquini occidentalis, 1880. 1270, 72p. C, Y

PZ—OTHER LANGUAGES OF MAINLAND SOUTHEAST ASIA, ARRANGED ALPHABETICALLY BY LANGUAGE

PZ1. AYMONIER, ÉTIENNE FRANÇOIS. Dictionnaire cam-français par Étienne

Aymonier et Antoine Cabaton. Paris, Leroux, 1906. 587p. (L'École française d'Extrême-Orient. Publications, v.7) C, Y

PZ2. HANSON, OLA. A dictionary of the Kachin language. Rangoon, Baptist Board of Publications, 1954. 739p. C, Y

PZ3. BLACKWELL, GEORGE E. The Anglo-Karen dictionary, based on the dictionary compiled by J. Wade and Mrs. J. P. Binney. Rev. and abridged by G. E. Blackwell. Rangoon, Baptist Board of Publications, 1954. 543p. Y

PZ4. SAVINA, FRANÇOIS MARIE. Dictionnaire français-mán, précédé d'une note sur les mán kim-di-mun et leur langue. Hanoi, Impr. d'Extrême-Orient, 1927. 255p. (Extrait du Bulletin de l'École française d'Extrême-Orient, t. XXVI, 1926) Y

PZ5. HALLIDAY, ROBERT. Mon-English dictionary. Bangkok, 1922. 512p. C, Y

PZ6. SHORTO, HARRY LEONARD. A dictionary of modern spoken Mon. London, Oxford Univ. Pr., 1962. 280p. C, Y

PZ7. SAVINA, FRANÇOIS MARIE. Dictionnaire étymologique français-nung-chinois. Hongkong, Société des missions étrangèrs, 1924. 528p. C, Y

PZ8. MILNE, MARY LEWIS. A dictionary of English-Palaung and Palaung-English. Rangoon, GPO, 1931. x, 383, v, 290p. Y

PZ9. HASWELL, JAMES MADISON. Grammatical notes and vocabulary of the Peguan language to which are added a few pages of phrases. 2d. ed. by Rev. E. O. Stevens. Rangoon, American Baptist Mission Pr., 1901. 357p. Y

PZ10. STEVENS, EDWARD OLIVER. A vocabulary, English and Peguan to which are added a few pages of geographical names. Rangoon, American Baptist Missionary Pr., 1896. 139p. Y

PZ11. DOURNES, JACQUES. Dictionnaire srê (köho)-français; recueile de 8,000 mots et expressions du dialecte pémsien srê, populations montagnardes du sud-indochinois, tribu des Srê. Saigon, Impr. d'Extrême-Orient, 1950. 269, 13p. C, Y

PZ12. MORÈRE. Essai de vocabulaire français-stieng, avec traduction en annamite sur le plan du vocabulaire français-laotien de Pierre Marty. Saigon, Viet, 1930. 101p. Y

PZ13. LOMBARD, SYLVIA J. Yao-English dictionary. Ithaca, 1968. 363p. (Cornell Univ. Southeast Asia Program. Data paper, no. 69) C, Y

Q—ARCHEOLOGY

QA—GENERAL

QA1. LEYDEN. INSTITUUT KERN. Annual bibliography of Indian archaeology. Leyden, Brill, 1926– C, Y
[Cornell entry: Instituut Kern. Leyden.]

QA2. COWA bibliography; current publication in Old World archaeology. Cambridge, Council for Old World Archaeology, 1957–59. 22v. in 1. C, Y
[Area 19 Southeast Asia; Area 20 Indonesia.]
[Superseded by COWA surveys and bibliographies.]

QA3. HIERCHE, HENRI. Manuel d'archéologie d'Extrême-Orient. Paris, Picard, 1966– C

QA4. LOOFS, HELMUT HERMANN ERNST. Elements of the megalithic complex in Southeast Asia, an annotated bibliography. Canberra, Centre of Oriental Studies in association with Australian National Univ. Pr., 1967. 114p. (Oriental monograph series, no. 3) C, Y

QB—BURMA

QB1. BURMA. List of ancient monuments in Burma. Rangoon, GPO, 1916. 199p. Y

QB2. DUROISELLE, C. A list of inscriptions found in Burma. Rangoon, GPO, 1921. C, Y
[Cornell entry: Burma. Archaeological Survey.]

QC—CAMBODIA

QC1. LUNET DE LAJONQUIÈRE, ETIENNE EDMOND. Atlas archeologique de l'Indo-Chine. Monuments du Champa et du Cambodge. Paris, Impr. Nationale, 1901. 24p. (Publications de l'École française d'Extrême-Orient) C, Y

QC2. LUNET DE LAJONQUIÈRE, ETIENNE EDMOND. Inventaire descriptif des monuments du Cambodge. Paris, Leroux, 1902–11. 3v. C, Y

QC3. COEDÈS, GEORGE. Listes générales des inscriptions et des monuments du Champa et du Cambodge. Inscriptions par George Coedès, monuments par Henri Parmentier. Hanoi, Extrême-Orient, 1923. 300p. C

QI—INDONESIA

QI 1. LEMBAGA KEBUDAJAAN INDONESIA. MUSEUM. Catalogus der archeologische verzameling van het Bataviaasch Genootschap van Kunsten en Wetenschappen, door W. P. Groeneveldt. Batavia, Albrecht, 1887. 391p. C, Y

See also FI 44

QM—MALAYSIA

QM1. MALAYA (FED.) MUSEUMS DEPT. Guide to ancient monuments and historic sites. Kuala Lumpur, Caxton, 1959. 1v. C, Y

QM2. MATTHEWS, JOHN. A checklist of "Hoabinhian" sites excavated in Malaya, 1860–1939. Singapore, Eastern Universities Pr., 1961. x, 59p. (Papers on Southeast Asian subjects, no. 3) C, Y

QT—THAILAND

See FT4

QV — VIETNAM

QV1. PARMENTIER, HENRI. Inventaire descriptif des monuments cams de l'Annam. Paris, Leroux, 1909–18. 2v. (L'École française d'Extrême-Orient. Publications vol. XI, XII) C, Y

QV2. FAZAKAS, DONELDA. Vietnamese art and archaeology; a selected bibliography. New York, American Friends of Vietnam, 1962. 9ℓ C, Y

R—RELIGION

RA—GENERAL

RA1. BLUMENTRITT, FERDINAND. Diccionario mitologico de Filipinas. 2d. ed. cor. y aumentada. Madrid, Minuesa de los Ríos, 1895. 120p. (In Retana, W. E. Archivo del bibliofilo filipino t. 2 p. 335-454, 511) Y

RA2. Mythology of all races. Boston, Archaeological Institute of America, 1916-32. 13v. C, Y
[V. 12 Egyptian by W. Max Müller, Indo-Chinese by J. G. Scott.]

RA3. GARD, RICHARD ABBOTT. A guide to non-Buddhist materials in western languages for Buddhist libraries in Asia. Berkeley, Cal., 1957- Y

See also PH40

RB—BUDDHISM

RB1. BHATTACHARYYA, BENOYTOSH. The Indian Buddhist iconography mainly based on the Sadhanamala and other cognate Tantric texts of rituals. London, Oxford Univ. Pr., 1924. 220p. Y

RB2. Bibliographie bouddhique, 1928/29-1954/58. Paris, Librarie d'Amérique et d'Orient, 1930-61. Fasc. 1-31. C, Y

RB3. MARCH, ARTHUR CHARLES. A Buddhist bibliography. London, The Buddhist Lodge, 1935. 257p. Y
[Annual supplements also issued.]

RB4. AKIYAMA, AISABURO. Buddhist hand-symbol. Yokohama, Yoshikawa Bookstore, 1939. 2, iii, 86p. C

RB5. NANA-TILOKA, BHIKKU [PSEUD.] Buddhist dictionary, manual of Buddhist terms and doctrines. Colombo, Ceylon, Frewin, 1950. 189p. (Island hermitage publication, no. 1) Y

RB6. NANA-TILOKA, BHIKKU [PSEUD.] Buddhist dictionary, manual of Buddhist terms and doctrines. 2d. rev. ed. Colombo, Frewin, 1956. 197p. Y

RB7. GARD, RICHARD ABBOTT. A select bibliography for the study of Buddhism in Burma in western languages. Tokyo, 1957. iii, 40p. C, Y

RB8. BHATTACHARYYA, BENOYTOSH. The Indian Buddhist iconography, mainly based on the Sadhanamala and cognate Tantric texts of rituals. 2d. ed. rev. and enl. Calcutta, Mukhopadhyay, 1958. 478p. C, Y

RB9. GARD, RICHARD ABBOTT. A select bibliography for the study of Buddhism in Thailand in western languages, compiled at the request of the Mahamakuta Library, Mahamakuta University. Bangkok, 1958. 17p. C, Y

RB10. Encyclopaedia of Buddhism, edited by G. P. Malalasekera. Colombo, GPO, 1961- C, Y

RB11. HANAYAMA, SHINSHO. Bibliography on Buddhism; ed. by the Commemoration Committee for Prof. Shinsho Hanayama's sixty-first birthday. Tokyo, Hokuseido, 1961. 869p. C, Y
[Covers the period previous to 1928.]

RB12. HUMPHREYS, CHRISTMAS. A popular dictionary of Buddhism. London, Arco, 1962. 223p. C, Y

RB13. NGUYEN-KHAC-KHAM. So-thao muc-luc thu-tich ve Phat-giao Viet-Nam. A bibliography of Vietnamese Buddhism. Saigon, Directorate of National Archives and Libraries, 1963. 32p. C, Y

RC — CHRISTIANITY

RC1. Almanak kristen. Djakarta. v.1– C

RC2. Catholic directory of the Philippines. Manila, Catholic Trade School. v.1– C, Y

RC3. Philippine directory of Christian churches, mission boards and related organizations. Manila, v.1– C, Y

RC4. NEDERLANDSE STUDENTEN ZENDINGS-BOND. Hedendaagsche zending in onze Oost; handbook voor zendingsstudie. n.p. 1909. 267p. Y

RC5. DOMINICANS. PROVINCIA DEL SANTISSIMO ROSARIO DE FILIPINAS. Catalogue conventuum, domorum et fratrum. Manilae, Universitatis S. Thamae, 1953. 129p. Y

RC6. CHURCH OF CHRIST IN THAILAND. OFFICE OF CHRISTIAN EDUCATION AND LITERATURE. Catalogue. Bangkok, 1957. 32p. C

RC7. GOWING, PETER G. Christianity in the Philippines and related subjects; a selected bibliography of books, pamphlets and articles most of which are available at Silliman University as of 1964. Dumaguete City, 1964. 9ℓ Y

RC8. ANDERSON, GERALD HARRY. Christianity in Southeast Asia, a bibliographical guide, an annotated bibliography of selected references in western languages. New York, Missionary Research Library, 1966. x, 69p. C, Y

RI — ISLAM

RI 1. Encyclopaedia of Islam; a dictionary of the geography, ethnology and biography of the Muhammadan peoples. Leyden, Brill, 1913–36. 4v. C, Y

RI 2. LEMBAGA KEBUDAJAAN INDONESIA. PERPUSTAKAAN. Daftar buku2 jang bertalian dengan agama Iselam. Djakarta, Perpustakaan Negara, 1947. 107p. C

RI 3. Encyclopaedia of Islam. New edition edited by H. A. R. Gibb, J. H. Kramers, E. Lévi-Provençal, J. Schacht under the patronage of the International Union of Academies. Leiden, Brill, 1954– C, Y

RI 4. MUNAF, HUSAIN. Ensiklopedi Islam "Ichtisari." Djakarta, Gunung Agung, 1958– C

RI 5. DJAKARTA. SEKOLAH TINGGI THEOLOGIA. Almanak. Djakarta, 1961– C

RI 6. GOWING, PETER G. Islam and Muslims in the Philippines; a bibliography of materials in English. Dumaguete City, 1963. 7ℓ Y

S—OTHER MATERIALS DEALING WITH THE HUMANITIES

SA—NUMISMATICS

SA1. LEMBAGA KEBUDAJAAN INDONESIA. MUSEUM. Catalogus der numismatische afdeeling van het Museum van het Bataviaasch Genootschap van Kunsten en Wetenschappen. Batavia, Lange, 1869. xii, 47p. C, Y

SA2. LEMBAGA KEBUDAJAAN INDONESIA. MUSEUM. Catalogus der numismatische afdeeling van het Museum van het Bataviaasch Genootschap van Kunsten en Wetenschappen. 2. druk. Batavia, Bruining, 1877. 148p. Y

SA3. LEMBAGA KEBUDAJAAN INDONESIA. MUSEUM. Catalogus der numismatische verzameling van het Bataviaasch Genootschap van Kunsten en Wetenschappen, door J. A. van der Chijs. 3. druk. Batavia, Albrecht, 1886. 229p. C, Y

SA4. LEMBAGA KEBUDAJAAN INDONESIA. MUSEUM. Catalogus der munten en amuletten van China, Japan, Corea, en Annam, behoorende tot de numismatische verzameling van het Bataviaasch Genootschap van Kunsten en Wetenschappen door H. N. Stuart. Batavia, GPO, 1904. 227p. Y

SA5. BOWKER, HOWARD FRANKLIN. A numismatic bibliography of the Far East; a checklist of titles in European languages. New York, American Numismatic Society, 1943. 144p. (Numismatic notes and monographs, no. 101) Y

SB—OTHER MATERIALS

SB1. HADDON, ALFRED CORT. Iban or sea Dayak fabrics and their patterns; a descriptive catalogue of the Iban fabrics in the Museum of archaeology and ethnology, Cambridge, by Alfred C. Haddon and Laura E. Start. Cambridge, Eng., Univ. Pr., 1936. 157p. Y

SB2. RENOU, LOUIS. L'Inde classique; manuel des études indiennes par Louis Renou et Jean Filliozat. Paris, Payot, 1947– C, Y

SB3. BANERJEA, JITENDRA NATH. The development of Hindu iconography. 2d. ed. rev. and enl. Calcutta, Univ. of Calcutta, 1956. 653p. C

SB4. BOWERS, FAUBION. Theatre in the East; a survey of Asian dance and drama. New York, Nelson, 1956. 374p. C, Y

SB5. LOS ANGELES. FERDINAND PERRET RESEARCH LIBRARY. Indice del ensayo de la Perret-enciclopedia del arte hispano-americano de la época colonial en las Américas y en las Islas Filipinas. Las secciones de pintores, escultores y grabadores de los siglos XVI, XVII y XIX. Mexico, 1958. 122p. Y

T — LIBRARIES AND THE BOOK TRADE

TA — GENERAL

TA1. HOBBS, CECIL CARLTON. An account of an acquisition trip in the countries of Southeast Asia. Ithaca, 1952. 51ℓ (Cornell Univ. Southeast Asia Program. Data paper, no. 3) C, Y

TA2. HOBBS, CECIL CARLTON. Account of a trip to the countries of Southeast Asia for the Library of Congress, 1952-53. Ithaca, 1953. 89p. (Cornell Univ. Southeast Asia Program. Data Paper, no. 11) C, Y

TA3. HOBBS, CECIL CARLTON. Southeast Asia publication sources; an account of a field trip 1958-59. Ithaca, 1960. 145p. (Cornell Univ. Southeast Asia Program. Data paper, no. 40) C, Y

TA4. USUI, JISHO. Report of survey trip concerning Southeast Asian studies in the United States, European and Southeast Asian countries by Jisho Usui, Joji Tanase, Takeshi Motooka. Kyoto, Kyoto Univ., 1961. 114p. Y

TA5. International library directory. London, Wales, 1963. 1083p. C, Y

TA6. BHATKAL, SADANAND G. Directory of Asian book trade. Bombay, Popular Prakashan, 1964. 471p. C, Y

TA7. NUNN, GODFREY RAYMOND. Resources for research on Asia at the University of Hawaii and in Honolulu. Honolulu, East-West Center, 1965. iii, 16ℓ (Hawaii. Univ. Honolulu. East-West Center. Library. Occasional papers, no. 1) Y

TA8. HOBBS, CECIL CARLTON. Account of a trip to the countries of Southeast Asia for the Library of Congress, August-December 1965. Ithaca, 1967. 92p. (Cornell Univ. Southeast Asia Program. Data Paper, no. 67) C, Y

TB — BURMA

TB1. CALDER, ROSE E. A guide to the library resources in Rangoon. Rangoon, 1960. 47p. C, Y

TI — INDONESIA

TI 1. Pekan buku Indonesia, 1954. Djakarta, Gunung Agung, 1954. 331p. Tambahan dan pembetulan. Djakarta, Gunung Agung, 1954. 99p. C, Y

TI 2. INDONESIA. DEPARTEMEN PERINDUSTRIAN RAKJAT. Daftar nama2 pertjetakan jang mendapat surat2 keputusan & lisensi. Djakarta, Kantor Penjuluhan Perindustrian, Departemen Perindustrian Rakjat, 1960. 83p. C, Y

TI 3. TAIRAS, J. N. B. Daftar subjek untuk digunakan pada penjusunan katalogus dalam perpustakaan umum. Djakarta, Jajasan Perpustakaan Indonesia, 1964. 176p. C, Y

TM — MALAYSIA

TM1. KEETH, KENT H. A directory of libraries in Malaysia. Kuala Lumpur, Univ. of Malaya Library, 1965. 163p. Y

TP — PHILIPPINES

TP1. PHILIPPINES (REP.) NATIONAL INSTITUTE OF SCIENCE AND TECHNOLOGY. DIVISION OF DOCUMENTATION. University libraries of the Philippines; a brief description of the main and unit libraries of 25 Philippine universities, illustrated by photographs and sketches of the library quarters. Manila, 1962. 200p. (Philippine libraries v.2) C

TP2. GONZAGA, FELIPE L. Directory of Philippine printers and publishers. Manila, Bureau of Public Libraries, 1964. 133ℓ C, Y

TP3. YUNESUKO HIGASHI AJIA BUNKA KENKYU SENTA, TOKYO. Research institutes and researchers of Asian studies in the Philippines. Tokyo, Center for East Asian Cultural Studies, 1966. 133p. (Its Directories, no. 5) C, Y

TT — THAILAND

TT1. SATOW, ERNEST MASON. Essay towards a bibliography of Siam. Singapore, GPO, 1886. 1v. Y

TT2. BANGKOK, THAILAND. KROM SINLAPAKON. Guide-book to the Vajiranan Library and the National Museum. Bangkok, Prachandra Pr., 1948. ii, 32p. C

TT3. YUNESUKO HIGASHI AJIA BUNKA KENKYU SENTA, TOKYO. Research institutes and researchers of Asian studies in Thailand. Tokyo, Center for East Asian Cultural Studies, 1964. 56p. (Its Directories, no. 4) C, Y

U—AGRICULTURE

UA—GENERAL

UA1. RUTGERS, ABRAHAM ARNOLD LODEWIJK. Rubber bibliographie, rubber bibliography, 1901-1916. Medan, 1917. 84p. (Mededeelingen van het Algemeen Proefstation der A. V. R. O. S. Rubberserie no. 5) Y

UA2. U.S. OFFICE OF FOREIGN AGRICULTURAL RELATIONS. Published information on foreign agriculture. Washington, 1937- C, Y

UA3. LOS BAÑOS, PHILIPPINES. INTERNATIONAL RICE RESEARCH INSTITUTE. International bibliography of rice research. New York, Scarecrow, 1951/61- C, Y

UA4. MUELLER, WOLF. Bibliographie des Kakao, seiner Geschichte, Kultur, Verwendung, Verarbeitung, wirtschaftlichen Bedeutung. Hamburg, Gordian, 1951. 120p. C

UA5. MUELLER, WOLF. Bibliographie des Kaffee, des Kakao, der Schokolade, des Tee und deren Surrogate, bis zum Jahre 1900. Bad Bocklet, Walter Krieg Verlag, 1960. 225p. (Bibliotheca bibliographica Bd. 20) C

UB—BURMA

UB1. BURMA. FOREST DEPT. A handbook of the forest products of Burma; based on the original handbook of 1921. Bombay, Times of India Pr., 1943. 162p. C

UB2. DAVIS, JOHN HENRY. Selected bibliography, Burma and adjacent regions, agriculture. Gainesville, Univ. of Florida, 1961. 80 C

UB3. NUTTONSON, MICHAEL Y. Climate, soils and rice culture of Burma: supplementary information and a bibliography to the report of the physical environment and agriculture of Burma; a study based on field survey and pertinent records, material and reports. Washington, American Institute of Crop Ecology, 1963. 21p. C, Y
[Cornell entry: American Institute of Crop Ecology.]

UH—INDOCHINA

UH1. CREVOST, CHARLES. Catalogue des products de l'Indochine par Ch. Crevost et Ch. Lemarié. Hanoi, Extrême-Orient, 1917. 337p. Y

UI—INDONESIA

UI 1. Almanak pertanian. Djakarta, Badan usaha penerbit almanak pertanian. v.1- C

UI 2. Handboek voor cultuur- en handels-ondernemingen in Nederlandsch-Indië. Amsterdam, de Bussy, 1888- Y

UI 3. KONINKLIJK INSTITUUT VOOR DE TROPEN. AFDELING TROPISCHE PRODUCTEN. Beschrijvende catalogus tevens handleiding tot de kennis der voortbrengselen van Nederlandsche overzeesche gewesten. Haarlem, Loosjes, 1894-1903. 18v. Y

UI 4. GONGGRIJP, H. Rubber-bibliographie, 1910-1928. The Hague, 1929. 440p. C, Y
[Revised edition of Dr. Rutger's rubber bibliographie.]

UI 5. DUTCH EAST INDIES. DEPARTEMENT VAN ECONOMISCHE ZAKEN. DIENST VAN DEN LANDBOUW. Lijst van mededeelingen van het algemeen proefstation voor den landbouw, 1912-1939. List of publica-

	tions of the general agricultural experiment station, 1912-1939. Buitenzorg, 1939. 11p. C
UI 6.	DUTCH EAST INDIES. DIENST VAN DEN LANDBOUW. AFDEELING ONDERNEMINGSLANDBOUW. Bergcultuurondernemingen op Java; ondernemingsgegevens. Batavia, 1947. 1v. C
UI 7.	SASTROAMIDJOGO, ACHMAD SENO. Atlas gambar2 termasak bilangan buku fungsi makanan. Jakarta, Wolters, 1953. 92p. C

UP — PHILIPPINES

UP1.	PHILIPPINES (COMMONWEALTH) COMMISSION OF THE CENSUS. Bulletin. Census of the Philippines, 1939: Agriculture. Manila, GPO, 1939- Y
UP2.	QUEZON, PHILIPPINES. UNIV. OF THE PHILIPPINES. COLLEGE OF AGRICULTURE. LIBRARY. Bibliographical contribution. Los Banos, College of Agriculture Library, 1952- C, Y [v.3-Basio, E. Bibliography of published contributions of the College of Agriculture and Central Experiment Station, 1909-1958. v.4-Gendrano, V. P. Abstract bibliography of undergraduate and graduate theses presented for graduation in the College of Agriculture 1945-62.]
UP3.	PHILIPPINES (REP.) DIVISION OF AGRICULTURAL ECONOMICS. Handbook of agriculture. Manila, 1955- C
UP4.	PHILIPPINES (REP.) DIVISION OF AGRICULTURAL ECONOMICS. Philippine agricultural atlas, 1957. Quezon City, 1960. 108p. C
UP5.	QUEZON, PHILIPPINES. UNIV. OF THE PHILIPPINES. LIBRARY. Bibliography on gardening found in the University of the Philippines. Quezon City, 1962. 46ℓ C
UP6.	VIRATA, ENRIQUE T. Agrarian reform; a bibliography. Quezon City, Community Development Research Council, Univ. of the Philippines, 1965. 239p. (A community development research council publication. Special studies series, no. 5) C, Y

V—NATURAL SCIENCES

VA—GENERAL

VA1. INDO-PACIFIC FISHERIES COUNCIL. List of scientific and other periodicals published in the Indo-Pacific area. Bangkok, Udom. v.1- C, Y

VA2. Bibliography of scientific publications of South and Southeast Asia. New Delhi, INSDOC, 1955- monthly. C, Y
[Supersedes UNESCO South Asia Science Corp. Office. Bibliography of scientific publications of South Asia.]

VA3. INDO-PACIFIC FISHERIES COUNCIL. Directory of fisheries institutions, Asia and the Far East. Bangkok, 1957- C, Y

VA4. GLENISTER, ARCHIBALD GERALD. The birds of the Malay Peninsula, Singapore and Penang; an account of all the Malayan species, with a note of their occurrence in Sumatra, Borneo and Java and a list of the birds of those islands. London, Oxford Univ. Pr., 1959. 282p. C, Y

VA5. MEDWAY, LORD. Mammals of Borneo: field keys and an annotated checklist. Singapore, Malaysian Branch of the Royal Asiatic Society, 1965. 193p. C, Y

VB—BURMA

VB1. BLANFORD, HENRY FRANCIS. A practical guide to the climates and weather of India, Ceylon and Burma and the storms of Indian seas, based chiefly on the publications of the Indian Meteorological department. London, Macmillan, 1889. 369p. C, Y

VB2. Bibliography of scientific publications of South Asia (India, Burma, Ceylon). Delhi, 1949- semiannual. Y
[Continued by VA2.]

VB3. DAVIS, JOHN HENRY. Selected bibliography: Burma and adjacent regions, biology, natural history. Gainesville, Univ. of Florida, 1961. 1v. C

VC—CAMBODIA

VC1. U.S. AGENCY FOR INTERNATIONAL DEVELOPMENT. A preliminary list of Cambodian plant diseases. Phnom-Penh, US AID, 1962. 29p. C

VH—INDOCHINA

VH1. NOYER, BORIS. Bibliographie analytique des travaux scientifiques en Indochine, 1939-41. Hanoi, Extrême-Orient, 1943. 1v. Y

VH2. NUTTONSON, MICHAEL Y. Climatological data of Vietnam, Laos, and Cambodia: a supplement to the report on the physical environment and agriculture of Vietnam, Laos, and Cambodia; a study based on field survey data and on pertinent records, material, and reports. Washington, American Institute of Crop Ecology, 1963. iii, 75p. C, Y
[Cornell entry: American Institute of Crop Ecology.]

VI—INDONESIA

VI 1. CLERCQ, FREDERIK SIGISMUND ALEXANDER DE. Nieuw plantkundig woordenboek voor Nederlandsch Indië met korte aanwijzingen van het nuttig gebruik der planten en hare beteekenis in het volksleven, en met registers der inlandsche en wetenschappelijke benamingen. Na het overlijden van den schrijver voor den druk bewerkt en uitgegeven door Dr. M. Greshoff. Amsterdam, Bussy, 1909. 395p. C

VI 2. VERBEEK, ROGIER DIEDERIK MARIUS. Opgave van geschriften over geologie en mijnbow van Nederlandsch Oost-Indië. The Hague, Geologisch Mijnbouwkundig Genootschap voor Nederland en Kolonien, 1912-36. 4v. C

VI 3. CLERCQ, FREDERIK SIGISMUND ALEXANDER DE. Nieuw plantkundig woordenboek voor Nederlandsch Indië, met korte aanwijzingen van het nuttig gebruik der planten en hare beteekenis in het volksleven en met registers der inlandsche en wetenschappelijke benamingen, na het overlijden van den schrijver voor den druk bewerkt door A. Pulle. 2. herz. en verm. druk. Amsterdam, Bussy, 1927. 443p. C, Y

VI 4. DUTCH EAST INDIES. DIENST VAN DEN MIJNBOUW. Uitgaven Dienst van den mijnbouw Nederlandsch-Indië 1910-1930. Publications of the mining and geological survey department of the Dutch East Indies during 1910-1930. Bandoeng, Drukkerij Muks, 1931. 21, 5, 2p. C, Y

VI 5. DUTCH EAST INDIES. DIENST VAN DEN MIJNBOUW. Uitgaven van den Dienst van den mijnbouw in Nederlandsch-Indië, 1900-1939. Publications of the mining and geological survey department in the Netherlands Indies during 1900-1939. Batavia, GPO, 1939. 39p. C, Y

VI 6. HONIG, PIETER. Science and scientists in the Netherlands Indies, edited by Pieter Honig and Frans Verdoorn. New York, Board for the Netherlands Indies, Surinam and Curaçao, 1945. 491p. C, Y

VI 7. SCHRIEKE, BERTRAM JOHANNES OTTO. Report of the scientific work done in the Netherlands on behalf of the Dutch overseas territories during the period between approximately 1918 and 1943. Amsterdam, North Holland Publishing, 1948. 356p. C, Y

VI 8. ORGANISATIE VOOR NATUURWETENSCHAPPELIJK ONDERZOEK IN INDONESIË. Guide of scientists in Indonesia. Djakarta, 1949- C, Y

VI 9. HOOGERWERF, A. An ornithological bibliography having particular reference to the study of the birds of Java. Djakarta, 1953. 4 nos. in 1v. (Organisatie voor Natuurwetenschappelijk Onderzoek in Indonesië. Bulletin no. 13-16) C

VI 10. POSTMUS, SIMON. Nutrition bibliography of Indonesia. Honolulu, Univ. of Hawaii Pr., 1955. 135p. (Pacific area bibliographies) C, Y

VI 11. MADJELIS ILMU PENGETAHUAN INDONESIA. Scientific publications published in Indonesia. Djakarta, 1958. 12ℓ C

VI 12. Directory of scientific institutions in Indonesia. Djakarta, 1959. 80p. (Madjelis Ilmu Pengetahuan Indonesia. Bulletin 1) C

VI 13. MADJELIS ILMU PENGETAHUAN INDONESIA. Daftar penerbitan ilmiah Indonesia jang terdaftar di Bag. Dokumentasi MIPI sampai 15 April 1960. Djakarta, 1960. 10ℓ C

VI 14. MADJELIS ILMU PENGETAHUAN INDONESIA. Indeks karangan2 ilmiah jang dimuat dalam madjalah2 Indonesia, meliputi djangka waktu 1 Djanuari-30 Djuni 1960. Djakarta, 1960. 22p. C

VI 15. MADJELIS ILMU PENGETAHUAN INDONESIA. Indeks madjalah ilmiah, 1960. Indonesian scientific periodical index. Djakarta, 1961. 89p. (Madjelis Ilmu Pengetahuan Indonesia. Bulletin, no. 3) C

VI 16. SUTTER, JOHN O. Scientific facilities and information services of the Republic of Indonesia. Honolulu, Pacific Scientific Information Center, 1961. 136p. (Pacific scientific information, no. 1) C, Y

VI 17. BOGOR, INDONESIA. KEBUN RAJA. An alphabetical list of plant species cultivated in the Hortus Botanicus Tjibodasensis by Rusdy E. Nasution. Bogor, Pertjetakan Archipel, 1963. 65p. Y

VI 18.   BOGOR, INDONESIA. KEBUN RAJA. An alphabetical list of plant species cultivated in the Hortus Botanicus Bogoriensis. Bogor, Pertjetakan Archipel, 1963. 268p. C, Y
          [Cornell entry: Bogor, Java, Kebun Raya Indonesia.]

VI 19.   PURBO HADIWIDJOJO, MULJONO. Kata2 istilah geologi dan ilmu2 jang berhubungan; Inggris-Indonesia dan Indonesia-Inggris. English-Indonesian and Indonesian-English terms of geology and related sciences. Bandung, Departemen Pertambangan, 1965. ix, 83p. (Publikasi teknik, seri geologi chusus, no. 2A) C

VI 20.   SUPARDI, RADEN. Medicines from forest products. A translation of the book Obat-obatan dari hasil hutan, translated by Setijati Notoatmodjo. Honolulu, East-West Center, 1967. 116ℓ (Hawaii. Univ. Center for Cultural and Technical Interchange between East and West. Institute of Advanced Projects. Research Translations. Occasional papers. Translation series, no. 24) C, Y

VM — MALAYSIA

VM1.   GIMLETTE, JOHN DESMOND. A dictionary of Malayan medicine. London, Oxford Univ. Pr., 1939. 259p. C, Y

VM2.   GIBSON-HILL, CARL ALEXANDER. Check-list of the birds of the Malay Peninsula. Singapore, 1949. 1v. (Bulletin of the Raffles Museum, no. 20) C, Y

VM3.   KESTEVEN, GEOFFREY LEIGHTON. Malayan fisheries; a handbook prepared for the inaugural meeting of the Indo-Pacific Council, Singapore, March 1949. Singapore, Malaya Publishing House, 1949. viii, 88p. C, Y
         [Cornell entry: Indo-Pacific Fisheries Council.]

VM4.   LEONG, PENG CHONG. Nutrition bibliography of Malaya. Honolulu, Univ. of Hawaii Pr., 1952. 23p. (Pacific area bibliographies) C, Y

VM5.   SUTTER, JOHN O. Scientific facilities and information services of the Federation of Malaya and State of Singapore. Honolulu, Pacific Scientific Information Center, 1961. 43p. (Pacific scientific information, no. 2) C, Y

VP — PHILIPPINES

VP1.   Philippine index medicus. Manila, National Science Development Board. v.1- Y
         [V. 1 covers the period 1900-16.]

VP2.   PHILIPPINE ISLANDS. BUREAU OF FORESTRY. Dictionary of names applied to trees of the first, second and third groups. Manila, GPO, 1923. 40p. (Its Bulletin no. 23) C, Y

VP3.   PHILIPPINE ISLANDS. BUREAU OF SCIENCE. SCIENTIFIC LIBRARY. Bibliography on mines and mining in the Philippines compiled by Cirilo B. Perez and L. Estrella-Villaneuva. Manila, GPO, 1937. 100p. (Its Bibliographic contributions no. 1) C

VP4.   PHILIPPINE ISLANDS. BUREAU OF SCIENCE. Publications of the Bureau of Science. Manila, 1938. 26ℓ C

VP5.   An annotated bibliography of nutrition and related topics with special emphasis on experimental researches. Quezon City, Institute of Nutrition and the Dept. of Physiology and Biochemistry of the College of Medicine, Univ. of the Philippines, 1953. 155p. C

VP6.   TEVES, JUAN S. Bibliography of Philippine geology, mining and mineral resources. Presented at the eighth Pacific Science Congress, Manila, November 16-28, 1953. Manila, GPO, 1953. 155p. (Philippines (Rep.) Bureau of Mines. Bibliography series, no. 1) C, Y

VP7. Philippine abstracts. Manila, National Institute of Science and Technology, Division of Documentation, 1960– C, Y

VP8. PHILIPPINES (REP.) NATIONAL INSTITUTE OF SCIENCE AND TECHNOLOGY. DIVISION OF DOCUMENTATION. Union catalog of Philippine publications on science and technology, compiled by Concordia Sanchez. Manila, 1962. 1v. C, Y

VT — THAILAND

VT1. SUVATTI, CHOTE. Index to fishes of Siam. Bangkok, Bureau of Fisheries, 1936. 226p. C, Y
[Cornell entry: Chot Suwatthi]

VT2. SUVATTI, CHOTE. A checklist of aquatic fauna in Siam, excluding fishes. Bangkok, Bureau of Fisheries, 1937. 116p. C, Y
[Cornell entry: Chot Suwatthi]

VT3. THAILAND. FOREST DEPT. Siamese plant names. Bangkok, 1948. 1v. Y

VT4. SUVATTI, CHOTE. Fauna of Thailand. Bangkok, Dept. of Fisheries, 1950. 1100p. C, Y
[Cornell entry: Chot Suwatthi]

VT5. THAILAND. SUN BORIKAN QEKKASAN KANWICHAI. List of scientific reports relating to Thailand. Bangkok, 1964– C

VT6. THAILAND. KROM KASIKAM. A host list of the insects of Thailand. Bangkok, Dept. of Agriculture, 1965. 149p. C

VV — VIETNAM

VV1. SUTTER, JOHN O. Scientific facilities and information services of the Republic of Viet-Nam. Honolulu, Pacific Scientific Information Center, 1961. 36p. (Pacific scientific information, no. 3)
Supplement. Honolulu, 1964. 11p. C, Y

W—GENERAL STATISTICS, ARRANGED ALPHABETICALLY

WA—GENERAL

WA1. AJIA KEIZAI KENKYUJO, TOKYO. Bibliography of the statistical materials on Southeast Asia. Tokyo, 1960. 66p. C, Y

WA2. BALL, JOYCE. Foreign statistical documents. Stanford, Stanford Univ. Hoover Institution on War, Revolution and Peace, 1967. 173p. (Its Bibliographical Series, no. 28) Y

WB—BURMA

WB1. BURMA. District gazetteer, volume B, statistics. Rangoon, GPO, 1906-07. 36v. Y

WB1a. BURMA. CHIEF COMMISSIONER. Notes and statistics in four parts. 3d. ed. for the combined provinces corrected up to 1st April 1893. Rangoon, 1893. 4pts. Y

WB2. BURMA. LOCAL GOVERNMENT DEPT. Statistics of district councils and deputy commissioners local funds in Burma. Rangoon, 1930- Y

WB3. BURMA. LOCAL GOVERNMENT DEPT. Statistics of municipalities (except Rangoon) and notified areas in Burma. Rangoon, 1930- Y

WB4. BURMA (UNION) CENTRAL STATISTICAL AND ECONOMICS DEPT. Report on the 1958 survey of household expenditure in Rangoon. Rangoon, 1959. 60p. C

WB5. BURMA (UNION) CENTRAL STATISTICAL OFFICE. The national income of Burma. Rangoon, 1951- annual. Y

WB6. BURMA (UNION) CENTRAL STATISTICAL OFFICE. Quarterly bulletin of statistics. Rangoon. v.1- C

WB7. BURMA (UNION) CENTRAL STATISTICAL OFFICE. Report on the survey of rural household expenditures. Rangoon. v.1- Y

WB8. BURMA (UNION) CENTRAL STATISTICAL OFFICE. Selected economic indicators. Rangoon. v.1- monthly. C, Y

WB9. BURMA (UNION) CENTRAL STATISTICAL OFFICE. Statistical yearbook. Rangoon, 1961- Y

WB10. BURMA (UNION) CENTRAL STATISTICAL OFFICE. The union budget in brief. Rangoon. v.1- annual. C, Y
[Cornell entry: Burma (Union) Central Statistical and Economics Dept.]

WB11. BURMA (UNION) MINISTRY OF NATIONAL PLANNING AND RELIGIOUS AFFAIRS. The national income of Burma. Rangoon, 1951- annual. C, Y

WB12. HAUSER, PHILIP MORRIS. Development of statistics in Burma, 1951-52, prepared for the Government of Burma. New York, 1954. 35p. (U.N. Document ST/TAA/K/Burma/4) C
[A reissue of ST/TAA/J/Burma/R5 issued on 24 Sept. 1953 for restricted distribution.]

WB13. NIHON BIRUMA KYÔKAI. Biruma tôkei sho, edited by Kamachi Kiyoshi. Tokyo, Kokusai Nihon Kyôkai, 1942. 234p. (Dai Tôa tôkei sôsho, Dai I bu, 6) Y

WC—CAMBODIA

WC1. CAMBODIA. DIRECTION DE LA STATISTIQUE. Bulletin mensuel de statistique. Phnom-Penh. v.1- C

WC2.   CAMBODIA. MINISTÈRE DU PLAN. Annuaire statistique retrospectif du Cambodge. Direction de la Statistique et des Études Économiques. v.1- annual. Y

WH—INDOCHINA

WH1.   Annuaire statistique de l'Indochine. v.1-12. Saigon, 1913/22-1947/48. C, Y
[Superseded by: Vietnam. Institut de la statistique et des études économiques. Viet-Nam nien-giam thong-ke; by Annuaire statistique de Laos; and by Annuaire statistique du Cambodge.]

WH2.   BRENIER, HENRI. Essai d'atlas statistique de l'Indochine française, Indochine physique, population, administration, finances, agriculture, commerce, industrie. Hanoi, Ideo, 1914. 256p. C, Y

WH3.   INDOCHINA, FRENCH. DIRECTION DES SERVICES ÉCONOMIQUES. Résumé statistique relatif aux années 1913 à 1940. Hanoi, Extrême-Orient, 1941. 48p. Y

WH4.   INDOCHINA, FRENCH. INSPECTION GÉNÉRALE DES MINES ET DE L'INDUSTRIE. Statistique générale de l'Indochine, résumé rétrospectif, 1913-29. Hanoi, Extrême-Orient, 1931. xxvp. C

WH5.   INDOCHINA, FRENCH. SERVICE DE LA STATISTIQUE GÉNÉRALE. Annuaire statistique de l'Indochine. Hanoi, 1927- C, Y
[Vol. 1 "Recueil de statistiques" and supplement cover the years 1913 to 1926.]

WH6.   INDOCHINA (FEDERATION) SERVICE DE LA STATISTIQUE GÉNÉRALE. Bulletin économique de l'Indochine. Supplement nos. 13 and 17. Saigon, 1948-49. C, Y
[Title for volumes 13 and 17: Bulletin statistique de l'Indochine 1947 and 1948.]

WI—INDONESIA

WI 1.   DUTCH EAST INDIES. CENTRAL KANTOOR VOOR DE STATISTIEK. Crimineele statistiek van Nederlandsch-Indië . . . Criminal statistics of Netherlands-India. Weltevreden, 1932- C, Y

WI 2.   DUTCH EAST INDIES. CENTRAAL KANTOOR VOOR DE STATISTIEK. Grafieken betreffende de economische en maatschappelijke ontwikkeling van Nederlandsch-Indië. Batavia, 1936. 4, 79p. C

WI 3.   DUTCH EAST INDIES. CENTRAAL KANTOOR VOOR DE STATISTIEK. Jaarbericht. Batavia, 1939- C, Y
[Cornell title: Jaaroverzicht van den in- en uitvoer van Nederlandsch-Indië.]

WI 4.   DUTCH EAST INDIES. CENTRAL KANTOOR VOOR DE STATISTIEK. Kosten van levensonderhoud der inlandsche bevolking op Java en Madoera, 1920-1924. Cost of living of the native population on Java and Madura 1920-24. Weltevreden, 1925. 2, 12p. Y

WI 5.   DUTCH EAST INDIES. CENTRAAL KANTOOR VOOR DE STATISTIEK. Mededeelingen van het Centraal Kantoor voor de Statistiek. Weltrevreden, 1920- C, Y
[Title varies: no. 1-17, Mededeelingen van het Statistisch Kantoor; no. 18-180, Mededeelingen van het Centraal Kantoor voor de Statistiek; no. 109, 113, 181- Publicatie.]
[At head of title: no. 1-117, Departement van landbouw, nijverheid en handel; no. 118- Departement van economische zaken.]

WI 6.   DUTCH EAST INDIES. CENTRAAL KANTOOR VOOR DE STATISTIEK. Onderwijs-statistiek. Statistics of education. Weltevreden, 1928- C, Y

WI 7.   DUTCH EAST INDIES. CENTRAAL KANTOOR VOOR DE STATISTIEK.
        Onderzoek naar gezinsuitgaven in Nederlandsch-Indië gederunde Augustus 1925, en het jaar 1926. Inquiry into family budgets in the Dutch East Indies, during August 1925, and the year 1926. Weltevreden, 1927. 225p. C, Y

WI 8.   DUTCH EAST INDIES. CENTRAAL KANTOOR VOOR DE STATISTIEK.
        Prijslijst der publicaties van het Centraal Kantoor voor de Statistiek. Batavia, 1938. 8p. C

WI 9.   DUTCH EAST INDIES. CENTRAAL KANTOOR VOOR DE STATISTIEK.
        Statistical pocketbook of Indonesia. Batavia, Kolff, 1941– annual. C, Y
        [Supersedes the Statistical abstract of the Netherlands Indies, pocket edition.]

WI 10. DUTCH EAST INDIES. CENTRAAL KANTOOR VOOR DE STATISTIEK.
        Statistiek van de inschrijvingen in de registers van den Burgerlijken Stand voor Europeanen, 1929. Statistics of registrations of Europeans in the civil registrar's office, 1929. Batavia, GPO, 1931. 3, 42p. C, Y

WI 11. DUTCH EAST INDIES. CENTRAAL KANTOOR VOOR DE STATISTIEK.
        Statistik pengadjaran rendah di Indonesia. Statistiek van het lager onderwijs in Indonesië (1/6 1947) Batavia, 1948. xiv, 97p. C

WI 12. DUTCH EAST INDIES. CENTRAAL KANTOOR VOOR DE STATISTIEK.
        Statistisch jaaroverzicht voor Nederlandsch-Indië. Statistical abstract for the Netherlands East Indies; new series of the statistical annual of the Netherlands (Colonies). Batavia, 1924–40. 17v. C, Y

WI 13. DUTCH EAST INDIES. CENTRAAL KANTOOR VOOR DE STATISTIEK.
        Statistisch zakboekje voor Nederlandsch Indië. Batavia, Kolff. v.1– C, Y

WI 14. DUTCH EAST INDIES. CENTRAAL KANTOOR VOOR DE STATISTIEK.
        Uitkomsten van het onderzoek naar het verschil in duurte tusschen de verschillende standplaatsen van gouvernementsambtenaren in Nederlandsch-Indië. Weltevreden, 1925– Y

WI 15. DUTCH EAST INDIES. DEPARTEMENT VAN ONDERWIJS EN EEREDIENST. Eenige statistische gegevens betreffende het hooger onderwijs in Nederlandsch-Indië. Batavia, GPO, 1933. 2, 27p.
        [Supersedes the publication "Het hooger onderwijs in Nederlandsch-Indië" issued as no. 4 of the series "Korte mededeelingen van het Centraal Kantoor voor de Statistiek" 1932, which contained several errors.]

WI 16. GERMANY (FEDERAL REPUBLIC, 1949–) STATISTISCHES BUNDESAMT. Länderberichte: Indonesien. Stuttgart, 1958– (Its Allgemeine Statistiek des Auslandes) C

WI 17. GRAAFF, E.A. VAN DER. De statistiek in Indonesië. The Hague, van Hoeve, 1955. 198p. C, Y

WI 18. INDONESIA. BIRO PUSAT STATISTIK. Berita ringkas perdagangan antarpulau beras, ikan asin, barang2 tenunan jang didjual meteran, semen, gula dan kopra. Djakarta. v.1– monthly. C, Y
        [PL 480 Indo-S-116.]

WI 19. INDONESIA. BIRO PUSAT STATISTIK. Budget materials, 1958–64. Djakarta, 1962–63. 1v. Y

WI 20. INDONESIA. BIRO PUSAT STATISTIK. Grafik2 perkembangan ekonomi di Indonesia. Graphs on the economic development of Indonesia. Djakarta. v.1– C, Y
        [Supersedes Its Grafik2 tentang keadaan ekonomi di Indonesia.]

WI 21. INDONESIA. BIRO PUSAT STATISTIK. Outline of information available at the Central Office of Statistics, Djakarta. Djakarta, 1952. 4, 4p. C

WI 21a. INDONESIA. BIRO PUSAT STATISTIK. Pengadjaran perguruan tinggi. Djakarta. v.1- C

WI 22. INDONESIA. BIRO PUSAT STATISTIK. Statistical abstracts, 1950-1955. Djakarta, Central Bureau of Statistics, 1956. 138p. C

WI 23. INDONESIA. BIRO PUSAT STATISTIK. Statistical abstracts. Djakarta, 1955- C
[English edition of Statistik Konjunktur.]

WI 24. INDONESIA. BIRO PUSAT STATISTIK. Statistical pocketbook of Indonesia. Djakarta, 1956- annual. C, Y

WI 25. INDONESIA. BIRO PUSAT STATISTIK. Statistik konjunktur (monthly survey). Djakarta. v.1- monthly. C, Y

WI 26. INDONESIA. BIRO PUSAT STATISTIK. Statistik pengadjaran mengenai permulaan tahun peladjaran (sekolah2 rendah). Djakarta. v.1- C

WI 27. INDONESIA. BIRO PUSAT STATISTIK. Statistik perindustrian: Pabrik "dan perusahaan" "Besar" dari beberapa djenis-perindustruan di Indonesia. Djakarta, 1953- C

WI 28. INDONESIA. BIRO PUSAT STATISTIK. Warta B. P. S. Djakarta, 1966- monthly. Y

WI 29. INDONESIA. DEPARTEMEN AGAMA. Statistik. Djakarta. v.1- annual. C, Y
[PL 480 Indo-S-205]

WI 30. INDONESIA. DEPARTEMEN PENDIDIKAN DASAR DAN KEBUDAJAAN. Educational statistics, 1939/40-1960/61. Djakarta, 1959-62. 16 sheets of tables. C

WI 31. INDONESIA. KANTOR PUSAT STATISTIK. Harga2 pasar di Djakarta dalam rupiah. Djakarta. v.1- C

WI 32. INDONESIA. KEMENTERIAN PENDIDIKAN, PENGADJARAN DAN KEBUDAJAAN. Daftar adanja sekolah landjutan negeri, subsidi dan bantuan dimasing-masing kabupaten dan kota (achir 1955). Djakarta, 1956. 36ℓ C

WI 33. INDONESIA. KEMENTERIAN PEREKONOMIAN. Ichtisar naik turunnja harga beberapa hasil dipasar2 jang terpenting. Djakarta. v.1- C

WI 34. INDONESIA. MONETARY SUB-BOARD. Beberapa statistik terpenting. Selected statistics. Djakarta. v.1- Y

WI 35. NETHERLANDS (KINGDOM, 1815-) CENTRAL BUREAU VOOR DE STATISTIEK. Maandcijfers en andere periodieke opgaven betreffende Nederland en de Koloniën. Nieuwe volgreeks. The Hague, 1898- C, Y

WI 36. NETHERLANDS (KINGDOM, 1815-) DEPARTEMENT VAN ZAKEN OVERZEE. Indisch verslag. The Hague, 1931- annual. C, Y
[Supersedes in part the Department's Verslag van bestuur en staat van Nederlandsch-Indië, Suriname en Curaçao.]
[Cornell entry: Dutch East Indies. Centraal Kantoor voor de Statistiek.]

WI 37. PUSPONEGORO, SUDJONO DJUNED. Masalah kesehatan anak2 di Indonesia; pidato diutjapkan pada penerimaan djabatan sebagai gurubesar biasa dalam ilmu penjakit anak2 pada Fakultet Kedokteran daripada Universitet Indonesia di Djakarta pada tanggal 7 Februari 1963. Djakarta, Pembangunan, 1963. 19p. C

WL— LAOS

WL1. Annuaire statistique du Laos. Vientiane, 1949/50- C

WL2. CALIFORNIA. UNIVERSITY. UNIV. AT LOS ANGELES. DEPT. OF ANTHROPOLOGY AND SOCIOLOGY. Government statistics by Joel M. Halpern. Los Angeles, 1961. 9ℓ (Its Laos project paper no. 8) C, Y
[Cornell entry: Halpern, Joel Martin.]

WL3. CALIFORNIA. UNIVERSITY. UNIV. AT LOS ANGELES. DEPT. OF ANTHROPOLOGY AND SOCIOLOGY. Laotian educational statistics by Joel M. Halpern. Los Angeles, 1961. 15ℓ (Its Laos project paper no. 7) C, Y
[Cornell entry: Halpern, Joel Martin.]

WL4. CALIFORNIA. UNIVERSITY. UNIV. AT LOS ANGELES. DEPT. OF ANTHROPOLOGY AND SOCIOLOGY. Laotian health statistics, by Joel M. Halpern. Los Angeles, 1961. 7ℓ (Its Laos Project paper no. 10) C, Y
[Cornell entry: Halpern, Joel Martin.]

WL5. LAOS (KINGDOM) OFFICE OF ELEMENTARY AND ADULT EDUCATION. Elementary school statistics: 1966-1967 school year, as of April 1, 1967. Unofficial translation by Education Division US AID/Laos. Vientiane, 1967. 3p. 15 tables. C

WL6. LAOS (KINGDOM) SERVICE DE LA STATISTIQUE. Bulletin de statistiques du Laos. Vientiane, 1951- C

WL7. U.S. AGENCY FOR INTERNATIONAL DEVELOPMENT. MISSION TO LAOS. Laos; annual statistical report. Vientiane. v.1- C

WL8. U.S. AGENCY FOR INTERNATIONAL DEVELOPMENT. OFFICE OF ECONOMIC AFFAIRS. Laos; statistical report. Vientiane, 1959- Y

WM— MALAYSIA-SINGAPORE

WM1. KOKUSAI NIHON KYÔKAI. Marê tôkei sho, edited by Ide Kiwata. Tokyo, 1942. 134p. (Dai Tôa tôkei sôsho, Dai I bu 4) Y

WM2. MALAYA (FED.) DEPT. OF STATISTICS. Household budget survey of the Federation of Malaya, 1957-58. Report on the sample survey of consumption and expenditure, income and housing conditions of 2,760 Malay, Chinese and Indian households in urban and rural areas, undertaken by the Department of Statistics in order to secure the necessary information regarding patterns of consumption and expenditure for the preparation of new indices of retail prices. Kuala Lumpur, 1959. 66p. C, Y

WM3. MALAYA (FED.) DEPT. OF STATISTICS. Monthly statistical bulletin. Kuala Lumpur. v.1- monthly. C

WM4. MALAYA (FED.) DEPT. OF STATISTICS. National accounts of the Federation of Malaya. Kuala Lumpur. v.1- C, Y

WM5. MALAYA (FED.) DEPT. OF STATISTICS. Statistical bulletin of the Federation of Malaya. Kuala Lumpur. v.1- monthly. Y

WM6. MALAYA (FED.) ELECTION COMMISSION. Local Council elections 1962: results and statistics of voting. Kuala Lumpur, 1963. 183p. C

WM7. Malaya . . . Malayan statistics. London, Malayan information agency. v.1- C, Y

WM8. MALAYSIA. DEPT. OF STATISTICS. Annual bulletin of statistics. Kuala Lumpur, 1964- annual. C, Y

WM9. MALAYSIA. DEPT. OF STATISTICS. Bulletin of statistics: Sabah. Kuala Lumpur, 1964- annual. C, Y

WM10. MALAYSIA. DEPT. OF STATISTICS. Monthly statistical bulletin of West Malaysia. Kuala Lumpur. v.1- monthly. C

WM11. MALAYSIA. DEPT. OF STATISTICS. Quarterly development progress statistics: States of Malaysia. Kuala Lumpur. v.1- quarterly. C

WM12. SARAWAK. DEPT. OF STATISTICS. Bulletin of statistics. Kuching, 1964- C, Y

WM13. SARAWAK. EDUCATION DEPT. Statistics of schools and enrollment, 1955-1958. Kuching, 1958. 53p. C

WM14. SINGAPORE. DEPT. OF STATISTICS. Digest of statistics. Singapore, 1962– monthly. Y
[Supersedes Malayan statistics; digest of economic and social statistics (Colony of Singapore and Federation of Malaya).]

WM15. SINGAPORE. DEPT. OF STATISTICS. Monthly digest of statistics. Singapore, 1962– monthly. C, Y
[Supersedes Digest of economics and social statistics section of the department's Malayan statistics.]

WM16. Statistical handbook of Sarawak. Kuching, Sarawak dept. of Statistics, 1966– C

WM17. STRAITS SETTLEMENTS. STATISTICAL OFFICE. Statistical summary. Singapore, 1927– C

WO— BRUNEI

WO1. BRUNEI. DEPT. OF CUSTOMS AND EXCISE. Statistics for the year. Kuching. v.1– C

WP— PHILIPPINES

WP1. CAVADA Y MENDEZ DE VIGO, AGUSTIN DE LA. Historia geográfica, geológica y estadístico de Filipinas. Manila, 1876. 2v. in 1. C, Y

WP2. CENTRAL BANK OF THE PHILIPPINES. DEPT. OF ECONOMIC RESEARCH. Statistical bulletin. Manila. v.1– quarterly. C, Y

WP3. HÔKI, SUBURÔ. Hirippin tôkei sho. Tokyo, Kokusai Nihon Kyôkai, 1942. 211p. (Dai Tôa tôkei sôsho, Dai I bu 3) Y

WP4. Journal of Philippine statistics. Manila, 1941– quarterly. C, Y

WP5. PHILIPPINE ISLANDS. BUREAU OF JUSTICE. Criminal statistics accompanying the report of the Bureau of Justice corresponding to the fiscal year. Manila. v.1– Y

WP6. PHILIPPINE ISLANDS. BUREAU OF JUSTICE. Criminality in the Philippine Islands, 1903–1908 by Ignacio Villamor. Manila, 1908. 102p. C, Y

WP7. PHILIPPINE ISLANDS. BUREAU OF JUSTICE. Judicial statistics accompanying the report of the Bureau of Justice corresponding to the fiscal year 1912, by Ignacio Villamor, attorney-general. Manila, 1912. 103p. Y

WP8. PHILIPPINE ISLANDS. DEPT. OF AGRICULTURE AND COMMERCE. DIV. OF STATISTICS. The Philippine statistical review. Manila, 1934– quarterly. C

WP9. PHILIPPINE ISLANDS. DEPT. OF AGRICULTURE AND COMMERCE. DIV. OF STATISTICS. Statistical handbook of the Philippine islands. Manila, 1933– Y
[Superseded by the Philippine statistical review.]

WP10. The Philippine statistician. Manila, 1952– C, Y

WP11. Philippine statistics. Manila, Grace Trading Co., 1960/61– annual. C, Y
[Cornell entry: Yap, Thomas.]

WP12. PHILIPPINES (COMMONWEALTH) BUREAU OF THE CENSUS AND STATISTICS. Bulletin of Philippine statistics. Manila. v.1– C

WP12a. PHILIPPINES (COMMONWEALTH) DEPT. OF AGRICULTURE AND COMMERCE. Atlas of Philippine statistics. Manila, GPO, 1939. 43p. C

WP13. PHILIPPINES (REP.) BUREAU OF LANDS. Basic statistical information. Manila. v.1– C

WP14. PHILIPPINES (REP.) BUREAU OF THE CENSUS AND STATISTICS. Economic census of the Philippines, 1961. Manila, 1964–65. 8v. in 10. C, Y

WP15.   PHILIPPINES (REP.) BUREAU OF THE CENSUS AND STATISTICS. Food prices index for the Philippines. Manila. v.1- monthly. Y
WP16.   PHILIPPINES (REP.) BUREAU OF THE CENSUS AND STATISTICS. Number of cities, municipalities and municipal districts by province. Manila, 1963. 95ℓ C, Y
WP17.   PHILIPPINES (REP.) BUREAU OF THE CENSUS AND STATISTICS. The Philippine statistical survey of households. Manila. v.1-
WP18.   PHILIPPINES (REP.) BUREAU OF THE CENSUS AND STATISTICS. Philippine statistics, 1903-1959; handbook. Manila, 1960. 144p. C
WP19.   PHILIPPINES (REP.) BUREAU OF THE CENSUS AND STATISTICS. Statistical handbook of the Philippines. Manila, 1952- C
[Title varies: 1952, Digest of Philippine statistics.]
WP20.   PHILIPPINES (REP.) BUREAU OF THE CENSUS AND STATISTICS. Statistical service sheet. Manila. v.1- weekly. C, Y
WP21.   PHILIPPINES (REP.) BUREAU OF THE CENSUS AND STATISTICS. Yearbook of Philippine statistics. Manila, 1940- C, Y
WP22.   PHILIPPINES (REP.) DEPT. OF FINANCE. Statistical bulletin. Manila. v.1- C
WP23.   PHILIPPINES (REP.) DEPT. OF HEALTH. DISEASE INTELLIGENCE CENTER. Philippines health statistics. Manila. v.1- annual. Y
WP24.   PHILIPPINES (REP.) NATIONAL ECONOMIC COUNCIL OFFICE OF STATISTICAL COORDINATION AND STANDARDS. Statistical progress report. Manila. v.1- Y
WP25.   PHILIPPINES (REP.) OFFICE OF STATISTICAL COORDINATION AND STANDARDS. An annotated bibliography of official statistical publications of the Philippine Government. Manila, 1963. 25ℓ C, Y
WP26.   PHILIPPINES (REP.) OFFICE OF STATISTICAL COORDINATION AND STANDARDS. Philippine housing programs and statistics. Manila, 1963. 48ℓ C, Y
WP27.   PHILIPPINES (REP.) OFFICE OF STATISTICAL COORDINATION AND STANDARDS. Planning for statistical development in the Philippines. Manila, 1963. C, Y
WP28.   PHILIPPINES (REP.) OFFICE OF STATISTICAL COORDINATION AND STANDARDS. Statistical progress report. Manila. v.1- C
WP29.   PHILIPPINES (REP.) OFFICE OF STATISTICAL COORDINATION AND STANDARDS. Statistical services of the Philippine Government, July 1957. Rev. ed. Manila, 1957. 61p. C
WP30.   PHILIPPINES (REP.) OFFICE OF STATISTICAL COORDINATION AND STANDARDS. Statistical services of the Philippine Government, July 1964. 3d. ed. Manila, 1964. 115p. C, Y
WP31.   PHILIPPINES (REP.) PHILIPPINE FISHERIES COMMISSION. FISHERIES INFORMATION DIVISION. Fisheries statistics of the Philippines. Manila. v.1- annual. C, Y
[Cornell entry: title]
WP32.   QUEZON, PHILIPPINES. UNIV. OF THE PHILIPPINES. STATISTICAL CENTER. Statistical services of the Philippine government. Description of statistics collected, processed and published. Manila, 1955. iii, 45ℓ C
WP33.   The statistical reporter. Manila, Office of Statistical Coordination and Standards, National Economic Council, 1957- quarterly. C, Y

WT—THAILAND

WT1.   BANGKOK. CHULALONGKORN UNIVERSITY. FACULTY OF COMMERCE

	AND ACCOUNTANCY. Bulletin of statistics. Bangkok. v.1- monthly. Y
WT2.	BANK OF THAILAND. Current statistics. Bangkok, 1952- monthly. C, Y [Cornell entry: Thanakhan haeng Prathet Thai.]
WT3.	GERMANY (FEDERAL REPUBLIC, 1949-) STATISTICHES BUNDESAMT. Länderberichte: Thailand. Stuttgart, Kohlhammer. v.1- (Its Allgemeine Statistik des Auslandes) Y
WT4.	THAILAND. Statistical tables. Bangkok, 1967. 56ℓ Y
WT5.	THAILAND. CENTRAL STATISTICAL OFFICE. Bulletin of statistics. Bangkok, 1952- quarterly. C, Y [Cornell entry: Thailand. Samnakngan Sathiti haeng chat.]
WT6.	THAILAND. CENTRAL STATISTICAL OFFICE. Food consumption in Thailand. Bangkok, 1963. 6p. (Special family expenditure survey report no. 1) Y
WT7.	THAILAND. CENTRAL STATISTICAL OFFICE. Household expenditure survey, 1963. Bangkok, 1965. 6v. Y
WT8.	THAILAND. CENTRAL STATISTICAL OFFICE. Report of tourist expenditure survey. Bangkok. 1v. Y
WT9.	THAILAND. CENTRAL STATISTICAL OFFICE. Reports on family expenditure survey, round 1-2, survey period August-September 1957-58. Bangkok, 1963. 2v. Y
WT10.	THAILAND. CENTRAL STATISTICAL OFFICE. Statistical bibliography; an annotated bibliography of Thai Government statistical publications. Bangkok, 1961. 34p. C, Y [Cornell entry: Thailand. Samnakngan Sathiti haeng chat.]
WT11.	THAILAND. CENTRAL STATISTICAL OFFICE. Statistical bibliography, an annotated bibliography of Thai Government statistical publications. Bangkok, 1964. 175p. C, Y [Cornell entry: Thailand. Samnakngan Sathiti haeng chat.]
WT12.	THAILAND. CENTRAL STATISTICAL OFFICE. Statistical yearbook. Bangkok, 1916- annual. C, Y [Cornell entry: Thailand. Samnakngan Sathiti haeng chat.]
WT13.	THAILAND. CENTRAL STATISTICAL OFFICE. Working women in the Bangkok-Thonburi municipal area, from result of the household expenditure survey B.E. 2505 and labor force survey Round 1, B.E. 2506. Bangkok, 1964. 10p. (Special family expenditure survey report) Y
WT14.	THAILAND. KROM KANPOKKHRONG. Changwat-Amphoe statistical directory, dept. of local administration, USOM. Bangkok, 1965. A-I, 71p. C
WT15.	THAILAND. SAMNAKNGAN SATHITI HAENG CHAT. Advance report: school and teacher census 1965. Bangkok, 1967. 40p. Y
WT16.	THAILAND. SAMNAKNGAN SATHITI HAENG CHAT. Advance report school census 2507. Bangkok, Ministry of Education, 1965. 17p. C
WT17.	WIRA BUNYANURAK. Survey on statistical data in Thailand. Bangkok, Thailand Management Development and Productivity Center, 1964. 20ℓ C

WV—VIETNAM

WV1.	U.S. AGENCY FOR INTERNATIONAL DEVELOPMENT. VIETNAM. Annual statistical bulletin. Saigon, 1957- C, Y
WV2.	U.S. OPERATIONS MISSION TO VIETNAM. Annual statistical bulletin. Saigon, 1957- annual. Y

WV3. VIETNAM. VIEN QUOC-GIA THONG-KE. Recensement des éstablishments au Viet-Nam, 1960. Saigon, Institut National de la Statistique, 1962–
C

WV4. VIETNAM. VIEN QUOC-GIA THONG-KE. Thong-ke nguyet-san. Monthly bulletin of statistics. Saigon. v.1– monthly. C, Y

WV5. VIETNAM. VIEN QUOC-GIA THONG-KE. Vietnam nien-giam thong-ke. Annuaire statistique du Viet-Nam. Statistical yearbook of Vietnam. Saigon, 1949/50– annual. C, Y
[Title varies: 1949/50, Thong-ke nien giam Viet-Nam.]

X—AGRICULTURAL STATISTICS, ARRANGED ALPHABETICALLY

XB—BURMA

XB1.   BURMA. FOREST DEPT. Certain statistics relating to the Forest Department in Burma. Rangoon, 1947. 224p. C

XI—INDONESIA

XI 1.   DUTCH EAST INDIES. CENTRAAL KANTOOR VOOR DE STATISTIEK. Landbouwatlas van Java en Madoera. Agricultural atlas of Java and Madura. Weltevreden, 1926. 2v. C, Y

XI 2.   DUTCH EAST INDIES. CENTRAAL KANTOOR VOOR DE STATISTIEK. De landbouwexport gewassen van Nederlandsch Indië. The export crops of the Netherlands East Indies. Weltevreden, 1925- C, Y
[Succeeds Its Beplante uitgestrektheden en producties in het grootlandbouwbedrijf in Nederlandsch Indië.]

XI 3.   DUTCH EAST INDIES. CENTRAAL KANTOOR VOOR DE STATISTIEK. Maandgemiddelden en bouwgrondoccupaties per district van de negen belangrijkste inlandsche landbouwgewassen op Java en Madoera in de jaren 1920 tot en met 1925. Monthly averages and occupation of the arable lands per district of the nine most important native crops on Java and Madura during the years 1920–1925 inclusive, door C. W. Bagchus. Weltevreden, 1929. 269p. Y

XI 4.   DUTCH EAST INDIES. CENTRAAL KANTOOR VOOR DE STATISTIEK. Raming der voor het verbruik op Java en Madoera beschikbare hoeveelheden der voornaamste plantaaridge voedingsmiddelen. Estimates of the quantities of the principal vegetable foodstuffs available for consumption in Java and Madura, 1916/19- Batavia, 1921- Y

XI 5.   DUTCH EAST INDIES. CENTRAAL KANTOOR VOOR DE STATISTIEK. Rubber in Nederlandsch-Indië (Aanplant, producties en uitvoeren). Weltevreden, 1925. 2, 45p. Y

XI 6.   DUTCH EAST INDIES. CENTRAAL KANTOOR VOOR DE STATISTIEK. Statistische gegevens nopens de geoogste en beplante uitgestrektheden der voor naamste inlandsche landbouwproducten, 1916/20- Statistics of the harvested and planted areas of the principal native crops. Weltevreden, 1921- Y

XI 7.   INDONESIA. BIRO PUSAT STATISTIK. Berita ringkas panen dan penanaman beberapa tanam2an jang berumur pendek di Djawa dan Madura. Djakarta. v.1- C

XI 8.   INDONESIA. BIRO PUSAT STATISTIK. Berita ringkas pemakaian dan produksi perusahaan remilling karet. Summary report: materials used and production of rubber remilling mills. Djakarta. v.1- quarterly. C, Y
[PL 480 Indo-S-113]

XI 9.   INDONESIA. BIRO PUSAT STATISTIK. Berita ringkas produksi dan persediaan tanaman perkebunan jang terpenting dalam. Concise bulletin of production and stock of principal estate crops. Djakarta. v.1- monthly. C, Y

XI 10.   INDONESIA. BIRO PUSAT STATISTIK. Harga beras dan djagung didaerah perkebunan di Djawa. Price of rice and corn in the plantation region of Java. Djakarta. v.1- C, Y

XI 11.   INDONESIA. BIRO PUSAT STATISTIK. Harga etjeran rata2 dari beberapa

	matjam barang, terutama barang dalam negeri, dipasar bebas (dalam rupiah) di Djakarta. Djakarta. v.1- C, Y
XI 12.	INDONESIA. BIRO PUSAT STATISTIK. Luas panen dan penanaman tanam2an rakjat berumur pendek Djawa dan Madura. Penerbitan bulanan. Djakarta. v.1- monthly. C, Y
XI 13.	INDONESIA. BIRO PUSAT STATISTIK. Luas panen dan produksi tanam2an rakjat berumur pendek Djawa dan Madura; angka2 sementara. Djakarta. v.1- C, Y
XI 14.	INDONESIA. BIRO PUSAT STATISTIK. Luas panen dan produksi tanam2an rakjat berumur pendek Djawa dan Madura; angka2 tetap. Djakarta. v.1- annual. C, Y
XI 15.	INDONESIA. BIRO PUSAT STATISTIK. Luas-tanaman, produksi dan persediaan tanam2an perkebunan jang terpenting. Planted area, production and stocks of principal estate crops. Djakarta. v.1- C, Y
XI 16.	INDONESIA. BIRO PUSAT STATISTIK. Panen dan penanaman beberapa tanam2an jang berumur pendek, di Djawa dan Madura. Berita ringkas. Djakarta. v.1- monthly. Y
XI 17.	INDONESIA. BIRO PUSAT STATISTIK. Panen dan penanaman tanaman bahan makanan rakjat jang terutama di Djawa dan Madura. Djakarta. v.1- C
XI 18.	INDONESIA. BIRO PUSAT STATISTIK. Panen dan penanaman tanam2an jang berumur pendek didaerah Bali. Djakarta. v.1- C
XI 19.	INDONESIA. BIRO PUSAT STATISTIK. Panen dan penanaman tanam2an jang berumur pendek didaerah Sumbawa. Djakarta, 1958- C
XI 20.	INDONESIA. BIRO PUSAT STATISTIK. Produksi bahan makanan utama di Indonesia. Production of principal foodstuffs in Indonesia. Djakarta. v.1- C
XI 21.	INDONESIA. BIRO PUSAT STATISTIK. Rubber: area, production, trade and consumption. Djakarta, 1958- C
XI 22.	INDONESIA. BIRO PUSAT STATISTIK. Sensus pertanian 1963. Agricultural census 1963. Djakarta, 1964- C
XI 23.	INDONESIA. BIRO PUSAT STATISTIK. Taksiran pertama produksi padisawah (termasuk gogorantjah), padigogo dan djagung di Djawa dan Madura. Djakarta. v.1- annual. C
XI 24.	INDONESIA. BIRO PUSAT STATISTIK. Tanam2an perdagangan perkebunan. Commercial crops of estates. Djakarta. v.1- annual. C, Y
XI 25.	INDONESIA. KANTOR PUSAT STATISTIK. Hasil, persediaan dan luas-tanaman perkebunan karet. Dihitung menurut tjara pertjobaan (sampling) dalam tiap2 bulan tahun. Djakarta, 1952- C
XI 26.	ODENKIRCHER, TH. J. Nederlandsch-Indië. Batavia, Kolff, 193? 27p. C
XI 27.	SUMATRA PLANTERS ASSOCIATION. Cultuur-statistiek. v.1-5, 1917-1923. Medan. 5v. annual. Y [Superseded by Handelsvereniging, Medan. Statistiek van aanplant, produceeren aanplant en productie van de groote cultures van Sumatra's Oostkust, Atjeh en Tapanoeli.]

XL— LAOS

XL1.	CALIFORNIA. UNIVERSITY. UNIV. AT LOS ANGELES. DEPT. OF ANTHROPOLOGY AND SOCIOLOGY. Laotian agricultural statistics by Joel M. Halpern. Los Angeles, 1961. 16ℓ (Its Laos project paper no. 9) C, Y

XM — MALAYSIA-SINGAPORE

XM1. MALAYA (FED.) DEPT. OF AGRICULTURE. Census of agriculture, 1960. Banchi pertanian, 1960. Administrative report. Kuala Lumpur, 1962. 1v. C, Y
[Cornell entry: Malaya (Fed.) Kementerian Pertanian dan Sharikat Kerjasama.]

XM2. MALAYA (FED.) DEPT. OF AGRICULTURE. Census of agriculture, 1960. Banchi pertanian, 1960. Preliminary report. Penyata permulaan. Kuala Lumpur, 1960-65. 16v. C, Y
[Cornell entry: Malaya (Fed.) Kementerian Pertanian dan Sharikat Kerjasama.]

XM3. MALAYA (FED.) DEPT. OF STATISTICS. Rubber statistics handbook. Kuala Lumpur. v.1- annual. Y

XM4. MALAYA (FED.) DEPT. OF STATISTICS. Statistical bulletin of the Federation of Malaya, rice supplement. Kuala Lumpur, 1951- annual. Y

XM5. MALAYA (FED.) KEMENTERIAN PERTANIAN DAN SHARIKAT KERJASAMA. Census of Agriculture, 1960. Census monograph. Kuala Lumpur, 1961- C

XM6. MALAYSIA. DEPT. OF STATISTICS. Oil palm, coconut and tea statistics. Kuala Lumpur. v.1- C, Y

XM7. MALAYSIA. DEPT. OF STATISTICS. Rubber statistics, preliminary bulletin. Kuala Lumpur, 1964- Y
[Superseded by Its Rubber statistics handbook.]

XM8. MALAYSIA. DEPT. OF STATISTICS. Rubber statistics handbook. Kuala Lumpur. v.1- C

XM9. SABAH. DEPT. OF AGRICULTURE. Census of agriculture, 1961. Jesselton, 1962. 27, 75ℓ C

XM10. SARAWAK. DEPT. OF AGRICULTURE. A digest of agricultural statistics. Kuching, 1965- C

XO — BRUNEI

XO1. BRUNEI, BORNEO (STATE). Report on the 1964 census of agriculture. Brunei, GPO, 1966. 330p. C, Y

XP — PHILIPPINES

XP1. PHILIPPINES (REP.) AGRICULTURAL CREDIT AND COOPERATIVE FINANCING ADMINISTRATION. Statistical digest on progress of ACCFA operations and accomplishments. Manila. v.1- C

XP2. PHILIPPINES (REP.) BUREAU OF THE CENSUS AND STATISTICS. Census of the Philippines, 1960: agriculture. Manila, 1965- C, Y

XP3. PHILIPPINES (REP.) BUREAU OF THE CENSUS AND STATISTICS. Summary report on the 1948 census of agriculture, under ECA counterpart project no. 5. Manila, GPO, 1952. 1174p. C, Y

XP4. PHILIPPINES (REP.) DIVISION OF AGRICULTURAL ECONOMICS. Crop and livestock statistics. Manila, 1954/55- Y

XP5. PHILIPPINES (REP.) DIVISION OF AGRICULTURAL ECONOMICS. Philippine agricultural statistics. Manila, GPO, 195?-1956. 2v. C

XT — THAILAND

XT1. THAILAND. CENTRAL STATISTICAL OFFICE. Census of agriculture. Bangkok, 1963- C, Y

XT2. THAILAND. CENTRAL STATISTICAL OFFICE. ECONOMIC SURVEY DIVISION. Report of crop cutting survey 1966. Bangkok, 1968. ii, 40p. (E-Su R. no. 1, 1968) Y

XT3. THAILAND. DIVISION OF AGRICULTURAL ECONOMICS. Agricultural statistics of Thailand. Bangkok, 1954– annual. Y
[Title varies: 1954, Statistical review of Thai agriculture.]

XT4. THAILAND. KHANA KAMMAKAN SANGSOEM KANLANGTHUN PHUA KITCHAKAN QUTSAHAKAM. Agricultural statistics of Thailand. Bangkok. v.1– C

XT5. THAILAND. KONG SETTHAKIT KANKASET. A statistical review of Thai agriculture, 1954. Bangkok, 1956. 146p. C

XV — VIETNAM

XV1. VIETNAM. SO THONG-KE VA KINH-TE NONG-NGHIEP. Nien-giam thong-ke nong-nghiep. Agricultural statistics yearbook. Saigon, 1961– C

XV2. VIETNAM. SO THONG-KE VA KINH-TE NONG-NGHIEP. Phuc-trinh ve cuoc kiem-tra canh-nong tai Viet-Nam. Report on the agricultural census of Viet-Nam 1960–61. Saigon, 1962. 188p. C

XV3. VIETNAM. SO THONG-KE VA KINH-TE NONG-NGHIEP. Vietnam thong-ke canh-nong. Saigon. v.1– C

Y—COMMERCIAL STATISTICS, ARRANGED ALPHABETICALLY

YA—GENERAL

YA1. Afro-Asian trade directory, 1957. Djakarta, National UPMI, 1957. 220p. C

YA2. AJIA KEIZAI KENKYUJO, TOKYO. Asian trade statistics. Statistics on foreign trade between the Asian countries and industrial nations classified by commodities, 1956-58. Tokyo, Institute of Asian Economic Affairs, 1961. 503p. Y

YA3. Banking, finance and investments annual and directory. 1959- C
[Annual supplement to The Insurance and finance journal.]

YA4. U.S. BUREAU OF FOREIGN AND DOMESTIC COMMERCE. Quarterly trade review of Southeastern Asia. Singapore. v.1- Y
[Monthly until 1931; 1932-40 quarterly.]
[Title varies: Nov. 1931-2d quarter 1932, Quarterly review of economic conditions in middle Asia; 1933-34, Quarterly review of economic conditions in Southeastern Asia; 1935-38, Quarterly trade report, Southeastern Asia; 1939-40, Quarterly trade review of Southeastern Asia.]
[Ceased publication 1940.]

YB—BURMA

YB1. BURMA. Report on the trade and navigation of Burma for the year 1885/86- Rangoon, 1886- Y

YB2. BURMA. CUSTOMS DEPT. Annual statement of the sea-borne trade and navigation of Burma with foreign countries and Indian ports. Rangoon, 18??- Y

YB3. BURMA. CUSTOMS DEPT. Report on the inland trade of Burma for the year 1885/86-1888/89. Rangoon, 1886-89. 4v. Y
[Continued the Report on the inland trade of British Burma. Continued by Memorandum on the internal trade of Burma.]

YB4. BURMA. CUSTOMS DEPT. Report on the trade and customs administration of Burma for the official year. Rangoon. v.1- C, Y
[Cornell entry: Report on the maritime trade and customs administration of Burma.]

YB5. BURMA. DEPT. OF LAND RECORDS AND AGRICULTURE. Memorandum on the trade between Burma and the adjoining foreign countries. Rangoon. v.1- Y
[Continues the report on the inland trade of Burma.]

YB6. BURMA. DEPT. OF LAND RECORDS AND AGRICULTURE. Memorandum on the internal trade of Burma. Rangoon, 1889/90-1896/97. 8v. Y
[Continued the report on the inland trade of Burma.]

YB7. BURMA (UNION) CENTRAL STATISTICAL AND ECONOMICS DEPT. Retail prices and consumer price index at Rangoon. Rangoon. v.1- C

YB8. BURMA (UNION) CENTRAL STATISTICAL AND ECONOMICS DEPT. CENSUS DIV. Survey of manufactures. Rangoon, 1955/56- annual. C

YB9. BURMA (UNION) CENTRAL STATISTICAL OFFICE. Bulletin of export trade. Rangoon. v.1- monthly. C, Y

YB10. BURMA (UNION) CENTRAL STATISTICAL OFFICE. Bulletin of import trade. Rangoon. v.1- monthly. C, Y

YB11. BURMA (UNION) CENTRAL STATISTICAL OFFICE. Survey of manufactures. Rangoon. v.1- annual. Y

YB12.   BURMA (UNION) OFFICE OF THE COLLECTOR OF CUSTOMS. Statement of the trade and navigation of Burma. Rangoon, 1946/47- annual. C
[Supersedes Burma. Customs Dept. Report on the trade and navigation of Burma.]

YB13.   BURMA, LOWER. Report on the inland trade of British Burma. Rangoon, 1877/78- Y

YB14.   BURMA, LOWER. Report on the trade and navigation of British Burma. Rangoon, -1884/85. Y
[Continues Report on the trade and customs of British (Lower) Burma.]
[Continued by Report on the trade and navigation of Burma.]

YB15.   Burma business directory and national trade register. Rangoon, Burma Publicity Services, 1956- annual. C, Y

YB16.   Burma trade directory. Rangoon, Burma Commerce, 1952- C

YB17.   GREAT BRITAIN. BOARD OF TRADE. Burma; review of commercial conditions. London, GPO, 1953- Y

YB18.   Khosla's industrial and commercial directory of India, Burma, Ceylon and Afganistan including Japan and foreign section. Delhi, Khosla. v.1- annual. C, Y
[Title varies.]

YB19.   KOOP, JOHN CLEMENT. Sample survey of labour force in Rangoon: a study in methods. Rangoon, GPO, 1955. 101p. Y

YB20.   Tabular statements of the commerce and shipping of the ports of Rangoon, Bassein, Moulmein, Tavoy, Mergui, Kyouk Phyoo and Akyab. Calcutta. v.1- C

YC—CAMBODIA

YC1.   CAMBODIA. DIRECTION DES DOUANCES ET RÉGIES. Bulletin de statistiques des échanges commerciaux. Phnom-Penh. v.1- C

YC2.   CAMBODIA. MINISTÈRE DE L'ÉCONOMIE NATIONALE. Annuaire statistique du Cambodge. Phnom-Penh, Imprimerie Nouvelle, 1949- C

YC3.   INDIA (REP.) DIRECTORATE OF COMMERCIAL PUBLICITY. Importers of Indian products: Cambodia. Delhi, GPO, 1963. 15p. C, Y

YH—INDOCHINA

YH1.   Annuaire général, commercial, administratif et industriel de l'Indo-Chine. Hanoi. v.1- C, Y

YH2.   INDOCHINA, FRENCH. SERVICE DE LA STATISTIQUE GÉNÉRALE. Indices économiques indochinois. Hanoi, 1932- C

YH3.   INSTITUT D'EMISSION DES ÉTATS DU CAMBODGE DU LAOS ET DU VIETNAM. SERVICE DES ÉTUDES ÉCONOMIQUES ET FINANCIÈRES. Statistiques économiques et financières. Saigon, 195?- C

YI—INDONESIA (TRADE STATISTICS)

YI 1.   BERG, NORBERT PIETER VAN DEN. De handel van Java, gedurende de laaste acht jaren. Batavia, Kolff, 1883. 98p. C, Y

YI 2.   DUTCH EAST INDIES. CENTRAAL KANTOOR VOOR DE STATISTIEK. De betalingsbalans van Nederlandsch-Indië. The balance of international payments of the Netherlands East Indies. Weltevreden, 1926/27- Y

YI 3.   DUTCH EAST INDIES. CENTRAAL KANTOOR VOOR DE STATISTIEK. Beplante uitgestrektheden en producties in het grootland bouwbedrijf in Nederlandsch-Indië, 1920/21-1924. Weltevreden, 1922-25. 4v. C, Y
[Succeeded in 1925 by Its De landbouwexportgewassen van Nederlandsch-

Indië . . . The export crops of the Netherlands East Indies.]
YI 4. DUTCH EAST INDIES. CENTRAAL KANTOOR VOOR DE STATISTIEK. Exportcultures van Nederlandsch-Indië, 1830–1937. Batavia, 1939. xii, 86p. Y

YI 5. DUTCH EAST INDIES. CENTRAAL KANTOOR VOOR DE STATISTIEK. Jaaroverzicht van den in- en uitvoer van Nederlandsch-Indië gedurende het jaar. Weltevreden, 1925– Y
[Succeeds Dutch East Indies. Hoofdbureau der in- en uitvoerrechten en accijnzen. Statistiek van handel en de in- en uitvoerrechten in Nederlandsch-Indië.]

YI 6. DUTCH EAST INDIES. CENTRAAL KANTOOR VOOR DE STATISTIEK. Meerjarige overzichten van den in- en uitvoer van Nederlandsch-Indië. Abstract tables of imports and exports into and from the Netherlands East Indies. Weltevreden, 1924– annual. Y

YI 7. DUTCH EAST INDIES. CENTRAAL KANTOOR VOOR DE STATISTIEK. Statistiek van de handelsbeweging der buitenbezittingen gedurende de jaren 1917, 1918, en 1919. Buitenzorg, 1921. 209p. C, Y

YI 8. DUTCH EAST INDIES. CENTRAAL KANTOOR VOOR DE STATISTIEK. Statistiek van de intergewestelijke handelsbeweging der buitengewesten, 1917/1919– Weltevreden, 1921– C, Y
[Title varies: 1917/19–1920, Statistiek van de handelsbeweging der buitenbezittingen; 1921, Statistiek van de intergewestelijke handelsbeweging der buitenbezittingen; 1923– Statistiek van de intergewestelijke handelsbeweging der buitengewesten.]

YI 9. DUTCH EAST INDIES. DEPARTEMENT DER BURGERLIJKE OPENBARE WERKEN. Statistiek van het vervoer op de spoorwegen en tramwegen met machinale beweegkracht in Nederlandsch-Indië. Batavia, 1891–1914. 14v. Y

YI 10. DUTCH EAST INDIES. DEPARTEMENT VAN FINANCIËN. Statistiek van den handel, de scheepvaart en de in- en uitvoerregten op de bezittingen buiten Java en Madura. Batavia, 1846–73. 13v. Y
[Title varies: 1846/48–68/69, Overzigt van den handel en de scheepvaart in de Nederlandsche bezittingen in Oost-Indië, buiten Java en Madura.]
[Superseded by: Dutch East Indies. Dienst der In- en Uitvoerrechten en Accijnzen. Statistiek van den handel de scheepvaart en de in- en uitvoerrechten in Nederlandsch-Indië.]

YI 11. DUTCH EAST INDIES. DEPARTEMENT VAN FINANCIËN. Statistiek van den handel, de scheepvaart en de in- en uitvoerregten op Java en Madura. Batavia, 1825–73. 49v. annual. C, Y
[Title varies: 1829–69, Verslag van de handel, de inkomende en uitgaande regten op Java en Madura.]
[Superseded by: Dutch East Indies. Dienst der In- en Uitvoerrechten en Accijnzen. Statistiek van den handel, de Scheepvaart en de in- en uitvoerrechten in Nederlandsch-Indië.]

YI 12. DUTCH EAST INDIES. DEPARTEMENT VAN LANDBOUW, NIJVERHEID EN HANDEL. Exporter's directory of the Netherlands East Indies. Batavia, Division of Industry and Commerce of the Dept. of Agriculture, Industry and Commerce, 1916– C, Y
[Cornell entry: Dutch East Indies. Departement van economische zaken.]

YI 13. DUTCH EAST INDIES. DIENST DER IN- EN UITVOERRECHTEN EN ACCIJNZEN. Meerjarige overzichten van den in- en uitvoer van Nederlandsch-Indië. Abstract tables of imports and exports into and from Nederlands-India. Weltevreden. v.1– Y

[Succeeded in 1924 by Dutch East Indies. Central Kantoor voor de Statistiek. Meerjarige overzichten . . .]

YI 14.   DUTCH EAST INDIES. DIENST DER IN- EN UITVOERRECHTEN EN ACCIJNZEN. Statistiek van den handel, de scheepvaart en de in- en uitvoerrechten in Nederlandsch-Indië. Weltevreden, 1867-1923. 118v. annual. C, Y

[Volumes for 1874-1906 issued by the Departement van Financiën; 1907-23 by the Dienst under its earlier names; 1907-18, Hoofdbureau der In- en Uitvoerrechten en Accijnzen; 1919-23, Hoofdkantoor der In- en Uitvoerrechten en Accijnzen.]

[Superceded by Dutch East Indies. Centraal Kantoor voor de Statistiek. Jaaroverzicht van den in- en uitvoer van Nederlandsch-Indië.]

YI 15.   DUTCH EAST INDIES. HOOFDKANTOOR VAN SCHEEPVAART. Statistiek van de scheepvaart in Nederlandsch-Indië. Batavia, 1909- C, Y

YI 16.   Importer's directory of the Netherlands East Indies. Weltevreden, GPO, 1916- C, Y

[Cornell entry: Dutch East Indies.]

YI 17.   INDONESIA. BIRO PUSAT STATISTIK. Berita ringkas ekspor Indonesia menurut djenis2 barang2 golongan ekonomi. Djakarta. v.1- C, Y

YI 18.   INDONESIA. BIRO PUSAT STATISTIK. Berita ringkas impor Indonesia menurut djenis2 barang golongan ekonomi. Djakarta. v.1- C

YI 19.   INDONESIA. BIRO PUSAT STATISTIK. Ekspor karet diperintji menurut mutu perdagangan. Rubber export by trade qualities. Djakarta. v.1- C, Y

YI 20.   INDONESIA. BIRO PUSAT STATISTIK. Ekspor menurut djenis barang diperintji menurut negeri tudjuan dan pelabuhan ekspor jang utama. Export by commodity specified by the most important countries of destination and ports of export. Djakarta, 1957- monthly. C, Y

YI 21.   INDONESIA. BIRO PUSAT STATISTIK. Ekspor menurut negeri diperintji menurut djenis2 barang golongan edonomi. Export specified by items of the economic groups. Djakarta. v.1- quarterly. C, Y

YI 22.   INDONESIA. BIRO PUSAT STATISTIK. Impor dan ekspor menurut djenis barang. Indonesian trade statistics, 1951-1961; imports and exports by commodities. Djakarta. 404p. C

YI 23.   INDONESIA. BIRO PUSAT STATISTIK. Impor dan ekspor menurut djenis barang. Trade by commodity. Djakarta. v.1- C

YI 24.   INDONESIA. BIRO PUSAT STATISTIK. Impor dan ekspor menurut negeri. Trade by country. Djakarta. v.1- C

YI 25.   INDONESIA. BIRO PUSAT STATISTIK. Impor Indonesia menurut djenis2 barang golongan ekonomi. Berita ringkas. Djakarta. v.1- monthly. Y

YI 26.   INDONESIA. BIRO PUSAT STATISTIK. Impor menurut djenis barang diperintji menurut negeri asal dan pelabuhan impor jang utama. Import by commodity specified by the most important countries of origin and ports of import. Djakarta. v.1- quarterly. C, Y

YI 27.   INDONESIA. BIRO PUSAT STATISTIK. Impor menurut negeri diperintiji menurut djenis2 barang golongan ekonomi. Import by country specified by items of the economic groups. Djakarta. v.1- quarterly. C, Y

YI 28.   INDONESIA. BIRO PUSAT STATISTIK. Penerbitan bulanan. Statistik perdagangan: ekspor. Djakarta, -1956. C

[Title varies: -July 1954, Warta bulanan, ekspor Indonesia.]

YI 29.   INDONESIA. BIRO PUSAT STATISTIK. Penerbitan bulanan. Statistik perdagangan: ekspor ke beberapa negeri. Djakarta, 1956- C

YI 30.   INDONESIA. BIRO PUSAT STATISTIK. Penerbitan bulanan. Statistik

perdagangan: impor. Djakarta, 1951-56. C
[Title varies: 1951-July 1954, Warta bulanan; impor Indonesia.]

YI 31. INDONESIA. BIRO PUSAT STATISTIK. Penerbitan bulanan. Statistik perdagangan: impor dari beberapa negeri. Djakarta, 1956- C

YI 32. INDONESIA. BIRO PUSAT STATISTIK. Perdagangan antar pulau. Beras, ikan asin, barang2 tenunan jang didjual meteran, semen gula dan kopra. Berita ringkas. Djakarta. v.1- monthly. Y

YI 33. INDONESIA. BIRO PUSAT STATISTIK. Perdagangan antar pulau menurut djenis barang. Interinsular trade by commodity. Djakarta. v.1- quarterly, C, Y

YI 33a. INDONESIA. BIRO PUSAT STATISTIK. Seri statistik pengangkutan air. Water transport statistics series. Djakarta, 1963- C

YI 34. INDONESIA. BIRO PUSAT STATISTIK. Seri statistik pengangkutan djalan. Djakarta, 1963- C

YI 35. INDONESIA. BIRO PUSAT STATISTIK. Seri statistik pengangkutan kerata api. Djakarta, 1963- C

YI 36. INDONESIA. BIRO PUSAT STATISTIK. Seri statistik pengangkutan udara. Air transport statistics. Djakarta, 1963- C, Y

YI 37. INDONESIA. BIRO PUSAT STATISTIK. Warta bulanan; ekspor beberapa pelabuhan Indonesia. Djakarta. v.1- C

YI 38. INDONESIA. BIRO PUSAT STATISTIK. Warta bulanan; impor beberapa pelabuhan Indonesia. Djakarta. v.1- C

YI 39. INDONESIA. BIRO PUSAT STATISTIK. Warta bulanan; impor dan ekspor dari Indonesia. Djakarta. v.1- C

YI 40. INDONESIA. BIRO PUSAT STATISTIK. SEKSI STATISTIK PENGANGKUTAN. Statistik tahunan dari inpentaris pesawat terbang niaga; pembelian pesawat terbang baru; lalu lintas P. N. Garuda; dan lalu lintas dipelabuhan Udara Internasional Kemajoran (Djakarta). Annual statistics on inventory of commercial aircraft; purchases of new aircraft and traffic of Garuda Indonesian airways; traffic at Kemjoran (Djakarta) International Airport. Djakarta, 1963- annual. Y

YI 41. INDONESIA. BIRO PUSAT STATISTIK. SEKSI STATISTIK PENGANGKUTAN. Statistik tahunan dari kapal laut dari 100 B. R. T. keatas jang digunakan dalam pengangkutan niaga Indonesia dan lalu lintas pelajaran niaga di pelabuhan2 Indonesia. Annual statistics on seagoing vessels 100 gross registered tons or more engaged in Indonesian commercial transportation, and seaborne commercial traffic at Indonesian ports. Djakarta, 1963- annual. Y

YI 42. INDONESIA. BIRO PUSAT STATISTIK. SEKSI STATISTIK PENGANGKUTAN. Statistik tahunan dari pandjang djalan dibawah wewenang pemerintah pusat, daerah tingkat I dan daerah tingkat II (atau daerah jang setingkat) dan impor kendaraan bermotor dan pemasangan kendaraan bemotor. Annual statistics on length of roads under the jurisdiction of the national, provincial and regency governments (or government of a similar level) and motor vehicles imported and motor vehicles assembled. Djakarta, 1963- annual. Y

YI 43. INDONESIA. BIRO PUSAT STATISTIK. SEKSI STATISTIK PENGANGKUTAN. Statistik tahunan dari pandjang djalan kereta api dan inpentaris bakal pelanting, pembelian baru bakal pelanting, belandja modal dan lalu lintas barang da penumpang. Annual statistics on length of railway track, rolling stock inventory, purchases of new rolling stock, capital expenditures and freight and passenger traffic. Djakarta, 1963- annual. Y

YI 44. INDONESIA. DJAWATAN BEA DAN TJUKAI. Instruksi mengenai penjusunan statistik perdagangan dan statistik bea-masuk dan bea-keluar. Djakarta, 1955- C

YI 45. INDONESIA. DJAWATAN KERETA API. Statistical report, year, 1954–1958. Bandung, 1959. 47p. C

YI 46. INDONESIA. KANTOR PUSAT STATISTIK. Angka2 tahunan sementara impor dan ekspor selama tahun 1950. Djakarta, 1951. 2v. in 1. C

YI 47. INDONESIA. KANTOR PUSAT STATISTIK. Daftar nama barang dan negeri untuk statistik impor dan ekspor Indonesia. Djakarta. v.1– C

YI 48. INDONESIA. KANTOR PUSAT STATISTIK. Ichtisar impor dan ekspor Indonesia mengenai beberapa tahun. Meerjarige overzichten van de in- en uitvoer van Indonesië, 1936/41–1946/49. Djakarta, 1950. 50p. C

YI 49. INDONESIA. KANTOR PUSAT STATISTIK. Statistik perdagangan impor dan ekspor. Djakarta. v.1– C

YI 50. KOPS, GEORGE FRANÇOIS DE BRUIJN. Statistiek von den handel en de scheepvaart op Java en Madura van 1855–1866, uit de officiele handelsverslagen bijeenverzameld. Batavia, GPO, 1869. 2v. in 1. C, Y

YI 51. LOMBOGIA, D. Buku prosedur impor, ekspor dan statistik barang2 impor, ekspor disusun menurut abdjad. Djakarta, 1964. 373p. Y

YI 52. LOMBOGIA, D. Buku statistik barang2 impor; dususun menurut nomor urut 10 s/d nomor 11660 dan dibahagi dalam 15 Kelompok; lihat pengumuman L. A. A. P. L. N. /B. D. P. tgl.25–1–1962 no. C-58/593. Djakarta, 1962. iii, 38ℓ C, Y

YI 53. LOMBOGIA, D. Buku statistik barang2 impor dan ekspor dalam bahasa Indonesia, Belanda, Inggeris. Djakarta, 1964. 114p. C, Y

YI 54. National importers-exporters and manufacturers in Indonesia, compiled by Godfried A. Simandjuntak. Djakarta, Indonesian Trade Directory, 196? 98p. C

YJ—INDONESIA (OTHER COMMERCIAL STATISTICS)

YJ1. BERITA EKONOMI. Petundjuk tjara mengisi pormulir permohonan idzin devisen; daftar barang2 golongan I, II, III, & IV. Djakarta, 1955. 120p. C

YJ1a. BERITA EKONOMI. REDAKSI. Petundjuk impor. Djakarta, 1956. 253p. C

YJ2. Buku alamat dagang. Surabaja, 1961– C

YJ3. Business directory of Indonesia. Djakarta. v.1– C

YJ4. DUTCH EAST INDIES. CENTRAAL KANTOOR VOOR DE STATISTIEK. De betalingsbalans van Nederlandsch-Indië in de jaren 1925 tot en met 1929. The balance of international payments of the Netherlands East Indies over the years 1925 to 1929 inclusive. Weltevreden, 1930. 32p. C, Y

YJ5. DUTCH EAST INDIES. CENTRAAL KANTOOR VOOR DE STATISTIEK. Groot- en kleinhandelsprijzen en index-cijfers in Nederlandsch-Indië voor de jaren 1913–1923. Wholesale and retail prices and index-numbers in the Netherlands Indies for the years 1913–1923. Batavia, 1923. 59p. C, Y

YJ6. DUTCH EAST INDIES. CENTRAAL KANTOOR VOOR DE STATISTIEK. Prijzen, indexcijfers en wisselkoersen op Java. Prices, price indexes and exchange rates in Java, 1913–24– Weltevreden, 1925– C, Y

YJ7. DUTCH EAST INDIES. DEPARTEMENT VAN ECONOMISCHE ZAKEN. Trade directory of Indonesia, 1949. Batavia, 1949. 964p. C

YJ8. DUTCH EAST INDIES. GENERALE THESAURIE. Statistische en grafische gegevens betreffende de ontvangsten en uitgaven van de landskassen in de Buitengewesten over de jaren 1917 t/m 1926. Weltevreden, 1927. 29p. C

YJ9. DUTCH EAST INDIES. WELVAARTSCOMMISSIE. Alfabetisch register op de Welvaartsedita 1904-1914. Batavia, Gedrukt bij Ruygrok, 1919. 454p. Y

YJ10. HANDELSVEREENIGING TE MEDAN. Maand-statistiek van den uitvoer van Sumatra's Oostkust en Langsa naar het buitenland. Medan, Typ. Varekamp. 1v. Y

YJ11. INDONESIA. BIRO PUSAT STATISTIK. Angka2 index ditimbang dari harga 18 matjam bahan makanan (tidak pakai beras) dipasar bebas. Djakarta. v.1- quarterly. C, Y

YJ12. INDONESIA. BIRO PUSAT STATISTIK. Angka2 index ditimbang dari harga 19 matjam bahan makanan (pakai beras) dipasar bebas. Djakarta. v.1- quarterly. C, Y

YJ13. INDONESIA. BIRO PUSAT STATISTIK. Berita ringkas pemakaian dan produksi triko dan tenun. Summary report: materials used and production knitting weaving mills. Djakarta. v.1- quarterly. C, Y
[PL 480 Indo-S-114)

YJ14. INDONESIA. BIRO PUSAT STATISTIK. Harga etjeran rata2 dipasar bebas di Djakarta. Djakarta. v.1- monthly. C, Y

YJ15. INDONESIA. BIRO PUSAT STATISTIK. Harga2 beras dipasar bebas di Indonesia. Djakarta. v.1- monthly. C, Y

YJ16. INDONESIA. BIRO PUSAT STATISTIK. Perusahaan2 industri. Manufacturing industries. Djakarta, 1953- C

YJ17. INDONESIA. BIRO PUSAT STATISTIK. Perusahaan2 industri besar dan perusahaan2 listrik umum dan gas. Large manufacturing industries and public electric light and power plants and town gas works. Djakarta. v.1- quarterly. C, Y

YJ18. INDONESIA. BIRO PUSAT STATISTIK. Perusahaan2 industri dan perusahaan2 listrik umum dan gas. Manufacturing industries and public electric light and power plants and gas works. Djakarta, 1954- annual. Y

YJ19. INDONESIA. DEPARTEMEN PERBURUHAN. Laporan penjelidikan angkatan kerdja berdasarkan sample di Djawa dan Madura. Djakarta, 1961. 1v. C

YJ20. Industrial directory of Indonesia. Almanak industri Indonesia. Djakarta, Indonesian Chamber of Industries, 1957/58- C

YJ20a. MEDAN, INDONESIA. STADSGEMEENTE. Begrooting van het woningbedrijf, pasarbedrijf, slachthuisbedrijf, ziekenhuis. Medan. v.1- annual. Y

YJ21. National business register of Indonesia. Djakarta, Indonesian Trade Directory, 1954/55- biennial. C, Y
[Title varies: 1954-55, Trade directory of Indonesia; 1956/57-60/61, Indonesian trade directory.]

YJ22. New commercial directory of the Dutch East Indies of 1932. Batavia, Nam Tiong Boek Handel, 1932. 2, 700, 10, 10p. C

YJ23. U.S. DEPT. OF COMMERCE. Netherlands East Indies and British Malaya, a commercial and industrial handbook by John A. Fowler. Washington, 1923. 411p. C, Y

YM—MALAYSIA-SINGAPORE

YM1. CH'EN CHAN-I. Singapore and Johore Bahru Oversea-Chinese commercial directory. Singapore, 1957. 26, 365, 19p. C

YM2. Directory of registered business names and companies of Singapore. Singapore, 1949- C

YM3. Hsin chia p'o hua ch'iao shang yeh chih nan. Singapore Oversea-Chinese commercial directory. Singapore, Wen I Yin Wu Kung Ssu, 1952- Y

YM4. INDIA (REP.) DIRECTORATE OF COMMERCIAL PUBLICITY. Importers of Indian products: Malaya. New Delhi, 1964. 61p. C, Y
[PL 480-I-E-3374]

YM5. MALAYA (FED.) DEPT. OF INLAND REVENUE. Statistical abstracts showing particulars of all assessments made and tax collected with details of assessments. Kuala Lumpur. v.1– C

YM6. MALAYA (FED.) DEPT. OF MINES. Bulletin of statistics relating to the mining industry. Kuala Lumpur, 1950/55– C

YM7. MALAYA (FED.) DEPT. OF STATISTICS. Annual statistics of external trade. Kuala Lumpur, 1961– annual. C, Y
[Supersedes in part Its quarterly Statistics of external trade, published through 1961.]
[Supplements Its Monthly statistics of external trade.]

YM8. MALAYA (FED.) DEPT. OF STATISTICS. Census of manufacturing industries in the Federation of Malaya. Kuala Lumpur, 1958. Y

YM9. MALAYA (FED.) DEPT. OF STATISTICS. Imports and exports including trade with Singapore. Kuala Lumpur, 1955– C

YM10. MALAYA (FED.) DEPT. OF STATISTICS. Monthly statistics of external trade. Kuala Lumpur. v.1– monthly. Y
[Supersedes in part Its quarterly Statistics of external trade, published through 1961.]
[Supplemented by Its Annual statistics of external trade.]

YM11. MALAYA (FED.) DEPT. OF STATISTICS. Statistics of external trade. Kuala Lumpur. v.1– quarterly. C, Y

YM12. MALAYA (FED.) DEPT. OF STATISTICS. Survey of manufacturing industries, 1960– Kuala Lumpur, 1962– annual. C, Y

YM13. MALAYA (FED.) INCOME TAX DEPT. Statistical abstracts showing details of assessments made for . . . with particulars of assessments made and tax collected. Kuala Lumpur. v.1– C, Y

YM14. Malayan statistics; digest of economic and social statistics (Colony of Singapore and Federation of Malaya) Singapore, GPO. v.1– monthly. C, Y
[Cornell entry: Malaya (Fed.) Dept. of Statistics.]

YM15. Malayan statistics; external trade of Malaya (Colony of Singapore and Federation of Malaya). Singapore, GPO. v.1– monthly. Y

YM16. Malayan trade annual (the Straits Settlements, the Federated Malay States, and the Unfederated Malay States). London, Low, Marston, 1925– Y

YM17. MALAYSIA. DEPT. OF STATISTICS. Census of manufacturing industries in the states of Malaya, 1963. Kuala Lumpur, 1965. 1v. C

YM18. MALAYSIA. DEPT. OF STATISTICS. Census of mining industries in the states of Malaya (incorporating supplementary data), 1964– Kuala Lumpur, 1965– C, Y
[Continuation of Its Mining census 1963.]

YM19. MALAYSIA. DEPT. OF STATISTICS. Malaysia statistics of external trade excluding trade between Singapore, Sabah, Sarawak and States of Malaya. Kuala Lumpur, 1964– quarterly. C

YM20. MALAYSIA. DEPT. OF STATISTICS. Mining census, 1963. Kuala Lumpur, 1965. v. Y
[Superseded by Its Census of mining industries in the States of Malaya.]

YM21. MALAYSIA. DEPT. OF STATISTICS. Survey of construction industries. Kuala Lumpur. v.1– C

YM22. MALAYSIA. DEPT. OF STATISTICS. Survey of manufacturing industries in West Malaysia. Kuala Lumpur. v.1– C
[Issued annually except during census years.]

YM23. Produce of Singapore. Singapore, Jay Birch, 1957- C
YM24. SABAH. DEPT. OF STATISTICS. Statistics of external trade. Jesselton. v.1- C
YM25. SARAWAK. Statistics of external trade. Kuching. v.1- C, Y
[Cornell entry: Sarawak. Dept. of Statistics.]
YM26. SARAWAK. DEPT. OF TRADE AND CUSTOMS. Annual statistics for the year. Kuching. v.1- Y
YM27. SINGAPORE. DEPT. OF STATISTICS. Singapore external trade statistics including trade with West Malaysia. Singapore, 1956- annual. C, Y
[Continues Its Singapore external trade.]
YM28. SINGAPORE (CITY). The tabular statement of the commerce and shipping of Singapore, during the years 1840-44, compiled from official documents by C. P. Holloway. Singapore, 1845. 113p. Y
YM29. STRAITS SETTLEMENTS. Return of imports and exports. Singapore. v.1- Y
[Issued as an appendix to the Straits Settlements Blue Book until 1887.]
YM30. STRAITS SETTLEMENTS. Tabular statements of the commerce and shipping of Prince of Wales' Island, Singapore and Malacca, for the official year 1843-1854. Calcutta, 1845-55. 4v. Y
YM31. STRAITS SETTLEMENTS. STATISTICAL OFFICE. The foreign trade of Malaya. Singapore. v.1- annual. C

YP— PHILIPPINES

YP1. A. B. Commercial directory of the Philippines. Manila, Briones, 1946- C, Y
YP2. ABRERA, JOSEFA B. An annotated bibliography of the history of the sugar industry in Panay and Negros. Manila, Ateneo de Manila, 1963. 143ℓ (Quezon, Philippines. Ateneo de Manila. Dept. of History and Government. Occasional papers. Bibliographical series, no. 1) C, Y
YP3. AMERICAN CHAMBER OF COMMERCE OF THE PHILIPPINES, MANILA. List of new and necessary industries granted tax exemption under Republic act nos. 35 & 901 as of July 1955. Manila, 1955. 9, 34ℓ C
YP4. AMERICAN CHAMBER OF COMMERCE OF THE PHILIPPINES, MANILA. New and necessary industries granted tax exemption under R. A.'s 35 & 901; from inception June 20, 1949 to June 30, 1958. Manila, 1958. 104ℓ C
YP5. American-Philippine yearbook. Manila, American Chamber of Commerce of the Philippines, 1962/63- C, Y
[A directory and guide to American business, government, civic and educational activities in the Republic of the Philippines.]
YP6. CEBU, PHILIPPINES. CHAMBER OF COMMERCE. Directory of Cebu. Cebu. v.1- annual. Y
YP7. Cebu trade directory; 25th anniversary Cebu City 1937-1962. Cebu, Altonaga, 1962. 1v. C, Y
YP8. CENTRAL BANK OF THE PHILIPPINES. Statistical classification of commodities. Manila, 1960. 71ℓ C
YP9. CENTRAL BANK OF THE PHILIPPINES. Statistical classification of commodities; revised July 1, 1964. Manila, 1964. 111ℓ C
YP10. CHAMBER OF COMMERCE OF THE PHILIPPINES. Directory as of December 1964. Manila, 1964. 135p. C
YP11. Directory catalog of Philippine manufacturers and producers. Manila, Philippine Industry and Business Journals, 1964- annual. C, Y
YP12. Manual of Philippine securities. Manila. v.1- C, Y
[Title varies: 1937-39?, The investor's guide.]

YP13.   PHILIPPINE ISLANDS. BUREAU OF COMMERCE AND INDUSTRY. Commercial handbook of the Philippine Islands. Manila, 1924. 204p. C, Y

YP14.   PHILIPPINE ISLANDS. BUREAU OF COMMERCE AND INDUSTRY. Statistical bulletin. Manila, 1918– C, Y

YP15.   Philippine-China yearbook and business directory. Manila, Philippine-China Society, 1938– C, Y
["Annual review of Philippine-Chinese relations, documentary statement of China's case in the current Oriental crisis, directory of Chinese business firms and other Chinese organizations in the Philippines, and general reference book on Philippine economic conditions and contemporary progress."]

YP16.   Philippine Chinese practical directory of commerce. n.p. 1951. 607p. C

YP17.   Philippine directory; manufacturers, producers, commercial banks, insurance companies. Makati, Economic Development Foundation, 1965/66– Y

YP18.   Philippine foreign trade directory and guidebook. Manila, Bureau of Commerce, 1961– C, Y

YP19.   Philippine industry and trade. Manila, 1955– annual. C, Y
[Cornell entry: Philippines (Rep.) Dept. of Commerce and Industry.]

YP20.   Philippine yearbook of commerce and industry. Manila, Dept. of Commerce and Industry, 1952– C, Y

YP21.   PHILIPPINES (COMMONWEALTH) BUREAU OF CUSTOMS. The port of Manila, a yearbook devoted to foreign commerce and shipping of Manila and the Philippines. Manila, 1924– annual. C, Y
[Cornell entry: title]

YP22.   PHILIPPINES (REP.) BUREAU OF COMMERCE. Directory of industrial establishments in the Philippines. Manila, 1940/41– C, Y

YP23.   PHILIPPINES (REP.) BUREAU OF COMMERCE. Directory of Philippine exporters. Manila. v.1– C

YP24.   PHILIPPINES (REP.) BUREAU OF COMMERCE. Trade directory of the Philippines. Manila. v.1– Y

YP25.   PHILIPPINES (REP.) BUREAU OF THE CENSUS AND STATISTICS. Foreign trade statistics of the Philippines. Manila. v.1– C, Y
[Title varies: Resume of Philippine foreign trade statistics.]

YP26.   PHILIPPINES (REP.) BUREAU OF THE CENSUS AND STATISTICS. Philippine trade with countries represented in the ECAFE, 1946–1952. Manila, GPO, 1953. iv, 80ℓ C

YP27.   PHILIPPINES (REP.) BUREAU OF THE CENSUS AND STATISTICS. Survey of manufactures. Manila, 1956– annual. C, Y

YP28.   PHILIPPINES (REP.) COOPERATIVES ADMINISTRATION OFFICE. Handbook on non-agricultural cooperatives. 3d. ed. Manila, Central Cooperative Educational Board, 1960. 172p. C, Y

YP29.   PHILIPPINES (REP.) DEPT. OF COMMERCE AND INDUSTRY. The Philippines; a handbook of trade and economic facts and figures. Manila, 1948– C, Y

YP30.   PHILIPPINES (REP.) LABOR STATISTICS DIV. Quarterly labor statistics. Manila, 1956– quarterly. C

YP31.   PHILIPPINES (REP.) NATIONAL EMPLOYMENT SERVICE. Directory of key establishments in the Philippines in selected non-agricultural industries employing five or more workers during 1955, with brief description and selected statistics on type of industries, and business, and employment. Manila, Dept. of Labor, 1956. 554p. C, Y
[Cornell entry: title]

YP32. Philippines business directory. Manila, Mahar-Escolta. v.1- Y
YP33. Philippines business guidebook, 1949; facts and figures on the postwar economic problems, potentials and resources. Manila, Chamber of Commerce of the Philippines, 1949. 380p. C, Y
YP34. VILLASIN, OLIMPIO S. Tops in Philippine business. Manila, Superprom, 1962. 1v. C, Y

YT — THAILAND

YT1. AMERICAN CHAMBER OF COMMERCE IN THAILAND. Classified list of members, trades and professions and list of American firms represented in Thailand by members. Bangkok, 1966. 70p. C

YT2. BANGKOK BANK, LTD. RESEARCH AND STATISTICS DIV. Facts and figures: an investors' guide to Thailand. Bangkok, 1966. 63p. C, Y
[Cornell entry: Thanakhon Krungthep Chamkat, Bangkok.]

YT3. BANGKOK BANK, LTD. RESEARCH AND STATISTICS DIV. A statistical portrait of Thailand's economy. Bangkok, 1962. 85p. C, Y
[Cornell entry: Thanakhon Krungthep Chamkat, Bangkok.]

YT4. Commercial directory of Thailand. Bangkok, Dept. of Commercial Intelligence. v.1- annual. C, Y
[Title varies: -1947 Commercial directory of Siam.]

YT5. GOULD, JOSEPH S. Preliminary estimates of the gross geographical product and domestic national income of Thailand, 1938/39, 1946-1950, as presented to the National Economic Council. Bangkok, National Economic Council, 1952. 68p. C, Y

YT6. THAI CHAMBER OF COMMERCE. Directory. Bangkok. v.1- biennial. C, Y
[Earlier volumes issued under its earlier name, Bangkok Chamber of Commerce.]
[Cornell entry: Ho Kankha Thai.]

YT7. THAILAND. CENTRAL STATISTICAL OFFICE. Census of business trade or services, 1966. Bangkok, 1968. 17p. Y

YT8. THAILAND. CENTRAL STATISTICAL OFFICE. Report of labor force survey, round, 1. Bangkok, 1963- Y

YT9. THAILAND. CUSTOMS DEPT. Annual statement of the foreign trade and navigation of the Kingdom of Siam. Bangkok, 1926- annual. Y
[Title varies: Annual statement of foreign trade of Thailand.]

YT10. THAILAND. DEPT. OF LABOUR. Yearbook of labour statistics. Bangkok, 1965- annual. Y

YT11. THAILAND. KROM KANSONTHET. Exportable products of Thailand, with a list of exporters, classified by products. Rev. ed. Bangkok, Dept. of Commercial Intelligence, 1956. 31p. C

YT12. THAILAND. KROM SETTHASAMPHAN. List of exporters of Thailand. Bangkok, Min. of Economic Affairs, 1964. 55p. C

YT13. THAILAND. SAMNAKNGAN SAPAHA PHATTHANAKAN SETTHAKIT CHAENG CHAT. National income statistics of Thailand. Bangkok, 1964- Y

YT14. Trades guide for Thailand. Bangkok, Business Information Dept., Howard and Watson. v.1- C

YV — VIETNAM

YV1. A.I.C. Viet-Nam. Saigon, Tring-Hu'ng. v.1- C, Y
[Vols. for 1962/63 have subtitle: Annuaire industriel et commercial. Industrial and commercial directory. Cong thuong nien giam.]

YV2. SAIGON. CHAMBRE DE COMMERCE. Situation commerciale. Statistiques, importations et exportations. Mouvement général maritime et commercial de la Cochinchine pendant l'année 1912. Saigon, 1913. 159p. Y

YV3. VIETNAM. NHA THONG GIAN DOC QUAN-THUE. Viet-Nam thong-ke ngoai-thuong. Statistiques du commerce extérieur du Viêt-Nam. Saigon. v.1- C

YV4. VIETNAM. TONG NHA THUE VU. Tax statistics 1960-1963. Saigon, Tax Directorate General, 1964. 297p. C

Z—DEMOGRAPHIC STATISTICS, ARRANGED CHRONOLOGICALLY

ZA—GENERAL

ZA1.   TEXAS. UNIV. POPULATION RESEARCH CENTER. International population census bibliography: Asia. Austin, 1966. 1v. Y

ZB—BURMA

ZB1.   BURMA, LOWER. Report on the census of British Burma, taken in August 1872. Rangoon, GPO, 1875. 1, 2, iii, 34, 19, 5, 6 lxxvp. Y

ZB2.   BURMA, LOWER. Report on the census of British Burma taken on the 17th February 1881. Rangoon, GPO, 1881. 96, 2, ccxii, 86p. (India. Census Commissioner. Imperial census of 1881. Burma) Y

ZB3.   INDIA. CENSUS COMMISSIONER. Burma. Part II. Tables by C. Morgan Webb. Rangoon, GPO, 1912. 286p. C, Y

ZB4.   INDIA. CENSUS COMMISSIONER. Census of India, 1911, Burma. Rangoon, 1912-13. 7v. Y

ZB5.   BURMA. Extracts from the Burma census report and tables of 1921 relating to languages and races, for official use. Rangoon, GPO, 1923. 58p. Y

ZB6.   INDIA. CENSUS COMMISSIONER. Census of India, 1921. Volume 10 (2 parts) Burma. Special edition containing the supplementary provincial tables III and VIII inclusive, by S. G. Grantham. Rangoon, GPO, 1923. 572p. C, Y
[Cornell omits the phrase "Census of India, 1921" in its entry.]

ZB7.   INDIA. CENSUS COMMISSIONER. Census of India, 1931. Appendix A with Burma linguistic map. Rangoon, GPO, 1933. 5p. C, Y

ZB8.   INDIA. CENSUS COMMISSIONER. Census of India, 1931; volume XI Burma by J. S. Bennison. Rangoon, GPO, 1933. 2v. C, Y

ZB9.   BURMA (UNION) CENTRAL STATISTICAL AND ECONOMICS DEPT. CENSUS DIVISION. First stage census, 1953. Rangoon, GPO, 1957-58. 3v. in 2. C

ZB10.   SUNDRUM, R. M. Population statistics in Burma. Rangoon, Economics Statistics and Commerce Depts. Univ. of Rangoon, 1957. 54p. C

ZI—INDONESIA

ZI 1.   INDONESIA. BIRO PUSAT STATISTIK. Penduduk Indonesia. Djakarta. v.1- Y

ZI 2.   DUTCH EAST INDIES. KANTOOR VOOR DE VOLKSTELLING 1920. Uitkomsten der in de maand November 1920 gehouden volkstelling. Batavia, Ruygrok, 1922. 2v. C

ZI 3.   TILLEMA, HENDRIK FREERK. Zonder tropen geen Europa. Bloemendaal, 1926. 264p. C, Y

ZI 4.   STRAUB, MANUEL. Kindersterfte ter oostkust van Sumatra. Amsterdam, Paris, 1927. 194p. C, Y

ZI 5.   DUTCH EAST INDIES. KANTOOR VOOR DE VOLKSTELLING 1930. Eerste nota, nopens de grondslagen der in 1930 hier te lande te houden volkstelling. Weltevreden, GPO, 1928. iv, 55p. C

ZI 6.   DUTCH EAST INDIES. KANTOOR VOOR DE VOLKSTELLING 1930. Volkstelling 1930; voorloope uitkomsten. Preliminary results of the census of 1930 in the Netherlands East Indies. Batavia, 1931. 2v. in 1. C

ZI 7.   DRIEL, B. M. De sterfte der ondernemingsarbeiters in de buitengewestern (behalve ter Oostkust van Sumatra en in Atjeh) in 1930. Death rates and causes of death among 187,106 estate-laborers in the outer provinces (except East coast of Sumatra and Atjeh) of the Netherlands East Indies in 1930. Medan, Varekamp, 1932. 62p. (Mededeelingen van het Pathologische Laboratorium te Medan, Sumatra, no. 13) C

ZI 8.   DUTCH EAST INDIES. TIJDELIJK KANTOOR VOOR DE VOLKSTELLING. Volkstelling 1930. Census of 1930 in Netherlands India. Batavia, GPO, 1933–36. 8v. C, Y

ZI 9.   DRIEL, B. M. Van. De sterfte der ondernemingsarbeiters in de buitengewestern van Nederlandsch-Indië in 1931 en 1932. Death rates and causes of death among 404,983 estate-laborers in the outer provinces of the Netherlands East Indies in 1931 and among 313,790 laborers in 1932. Medan, Varekamp, 1934. 175p. (Mededeelingen van het Pathologische Laboratorium te Medan, Sumatra. no. 14) C

ZI 10.   DUTCH EAST INDIES. CENTRAAL KANTOOR VOOR DE STATISTIEK. Verslag van verwerking en de resultaten der in Babadan en Noord-Cheribon gehouden proeftellingen. Batavia, 1939. 1v. C

ZI 11.   INDONESIA. BIRO PUSAT STATISTIK. Recapitulasi pembagian daerah (administratief) serta penduduknja seluruh Indonesia dalam tahun 1952, menurut laporan dari pada bupati atau kepala daerahnja masing2. Djakarta, 1952. 12ℓ C

ZI 12.   LIEM TJAY TIE. Tentang angka kematian baji Indonesia di kota Semarang dalam tahun 1952 & 1953. Jogjakarta, Universitet Negeri Gadjah Mada, 1955. 22p. C

ZI 13.   INDONESIA. BIRO PEMILIHAN. Daftar angka2 hasil pemilihan D. P. R. D. tahun 1957–58. Djakarta, 1957–58. 1v. C

ZI 14.   INDONESIA. BIRO PUSAT STATISTIK. Apakah sensus itu? Disusun oleh Biro Pusat Statistik, Bagian Sensus. Djakarta, Departemen Penerangan, 1960. 42p. C, Y

ZI 15.   INDONESIA. BIRO PUSAT STATISTIK. Sensus penduduk 1961 mengenai 90 kartu perseorangan. Djakarta, 1961. 49ℓ C

ZI 16.   INDONESIA. BIRO PUSAT STATISTIK. Sensus penduduk Republik Indonesia tahun 1961. Djakarta, 1961. 5p. C

ZI 17.   INDONESIA. BIRO PUSAT STATISTIK. Sensus penduduk 1961 Republik Indonesia. Population census 1961. Djakarta, 1962. 13ℓ C

ZI 18.   INDONESIA. BIRO PUSAT STATISTIK. Sensus penduduk 1961, Republik Indonesia angka sementara penduduk Indonesia menurut kelamin per daerah tingkat I. Population census 1961 preliminary census figures by sex and province. Djakarta, 1962. 15p. C, Y

ZI 19.   INDONESIA. BIRO PUSAT STATISTIK. Sensus penduduk 1961 D. C. I. Djakarta Raya, angka2 tetap. Djakarta, 1963. 62p. C, Y

ZI 20.   INDONESIA. BIRO PUSAT STATISTIK. Sensus penduduk 1961, Republik Indonesia; angka2 sementara. Population census 1961, Republic of Indonesia; preliminary figures. Djakarta, 1963. viii, 13p. C, Y
        [PL 480 Indo-2571]

ZI 21.   INDONESIA. BIRO PUSAT STATISTIK. Sensus penduduk 1961. Republik Indonesia; angka2 sementara hasil pengolahan 1% sample diperluas. Population census 1961, Republic of Indonesia (extended 1% sample) preliminary figures. Djakarta, 1963. 64p. C, Y
        [PL 480 Indo-2573]

ZI 22.   INDONESIA. BIRO PUSAT STATISTIK. Sensus penduduk 1961 seluruh Indonesia, angka2 sementara hasil pengolahan 1% sample diperluas. Population census 1961, extended 1% sample. Djakarta, 1963. 55, 37a–37i p. C, Y

ZI 23. INDONESIA. BIRO PUSAT STATISTIK. Sensus penduduk 1961. Republik Indonesia; hasil pendaftaran rumah-tangga bln. Maret 1961, seluruh Indonesia. Population census 1961; the result of household listing in March 1961, all Indonesia. Djakarta, 1965. 22p. C, Y

ZI 24. WIDJOJO NITISASTRO. Beberapa data kwantitatif tentang penduduk wanita Indonesia. Djakarta, Lembaga Ekonomi dan Kemas Kemas ja rakatan rakatan Nasional, 1965. ii, 55ℓ C

ZL— LAOS

ZL1. LAOS (KINGDOM) SERVICE DE LA STATISTIQUE. Population officielle du Laos, 1956–1959. Vietiane, 1959–60. 10pts. in 1v. C

ZL2. CALIFORNIA. UNIVERSITY. UNIV. AT LOS ANGELES. DEPT. OF ANTHROPOLOGY AND SOCIOLOGY. Population statistics and associated data. Los Angeles, 1961. iv, 59ℓ (Its Laos Project. Paper no. 3) C, Y
[Cornell entry: Halpern, Joel Martin.]

ZL3. LAOS (KINGDOM) SERVICE DE LA STATISTIQUE. Population statistiques, 1954–1958. Ithaca, Photo Science Studios, Cornell Univ., 1965. 1 reel microfilm. C

ZL4. HAIGHT, H. E. Lao provincial leaders and population statistics. 2d. ed. Vientiane, 1966. 13ℓ C

ZM— MALAYSIA-SINGAPORE

ZM1. SARAWAK. REGISTRATION OF BIRTHS AND DEATHS OFFICE. Report on the registration of births and deaths. Kuching. v.1– C, Y
[Cornell entry: Sarawak. Registrar-General of births and deaths.]

ZM2. SINGAPORE. REGISTRAR-GENERAL OF BIRTHS AND DEATHS. Report on the registration of births and deaths, marriages and persons. Singapore. v.1– C, Y
[Title varies: –1954, Report on the registration of births and deaths.]

ZM3. STRAITS SETTLEMENTS. REGISTRAR GENERAL OF BIRTHS AND DEATHS. Annual report on the registration of births and deaths in the Straits Settlements for the year. Singapore, GPO. v.1– annual. Y

ZM4. STRAITS SETTLEMENTS. Report on the census of the Straits Settlements taken on the 1st March 1901 by J. R. Innes. Singapore, 1901. 152p. Y

ZM5. MALAY STATES, FEDERATED. Federated Malay States census of the population 1901, compiled by George Thompson Hare. Kuala Lumpur, 1902. 172p. cxxvp. Y

ZM6. STRAITS SETTLEMENTS. The census of British Malaya (the Straits Settlements, Federated Malay States and protected states of Johore, Kedah, Perlis, Kelantan, Trengganu and Brunei) 1921 by J. E. Nathan. London, Waterlow, 1922. 406p. Y

ZM7. NORTH BORNEO. Report on the census of the State of North Borneo, taken on the night of 26th April 1931 by A. N. M. Garry. Hong Kong, Noronha, 1931. 110p. C

ZM8. STRAITS SETTLEMENTS. British Malaya (The colony of the Straits Settlements and the Malay states under British protection, namely the federated states of Perak, Selangor, Negri Sembilan and Pahang and the states of Johore, Kedah, Kelantan, Trengganu, Perlis and Brunei) a report on the 1931 census and on certain problems of vital statistics by C. A. Vlieland. London, Waterlow, 1932. viii, 389p. Y

ZM9. MALAYA (FED.) CHIEF REGISTRATION OFFICE. Report of the registrar-general on population, births, deaths, marriages and adoptions. Kuala Lumpur, 1948– annual. C, Y

ZM10.   MALAYAN UNION. REGISTRAR GENERAL OF BIRTHS AND DEATHS. Report on the registration of births and deaths, 1941-46/47. Kuala Lumpur, 1948. 2v. in 1. Y

ZM11.   TUFO, MOROBOË VINCENZO DEL. Malaya, comprising the Federation of Malaya and the colony of Singapore. A report on the 1947 census of population. London, Crown Agents, 1949. 597p. C, Y
[Cornell entry: Del Tufo, M. V.]

ZM12.   NOAKES, J. L. Sarawak and Brunei (the colony of Sarawak and the British protected state of Brunei), a report on the 1947 population census. Kuching, GPO, 1950. 282p. C

ZM13.   NORTH BORNEO. A preliminary report on the census of population 1951. Jesselton, 1952. 15p. C

ZM14.   NORTH BORNEO. Report on the census of population held on 4th June, 1951 by L. W. Jones. London, Crown Agents, 1953. 237p. C

ZM15.   MALAYA (FED.). The 1957 census; a preliminary report based on "First count total" returns by T. E. Smith. Kuala Lumpur, 1957. 57p. C, Y
[Cornell entry: Malaya (Fed.) Dept. of Statistics.]

ZM16.   MALAYA (FED.) DEPT. OF STATISTICS. 1957 population census report. Kuala Lumpur, 1958-60. 14v. in 4. C, Y

ZM17.   SINGAPORE. DEPT. OF STATISTICS. Monthly demographic bulletin. Singapore, 1959- C

ZM18.   NORTH BORNEO. Census of population, 1960; preliminary release. Population by sex, community and age. Sarawak, GPO, 1960. 19 tables. C

ZM19.   NORTH BORNEO. Report on the housing census held in four towns, May-August, 1960 by L. W. Jones. Kuching, 1961. ii, 52p. C

ZM20.   SARAWAK. Report on the housing census held in eight towns, March-June 1960 by L. W. Jones. Kuching, 1961. 74p. C

ZM21.   NORTH BORNEO. Report on the census of population taken on 10th August 1960 by L. W. Jones. Kuching 1962. 305p.
Additional tables. Kuching, 1962. 35p. C, Y

ZM22.   SARAWAK. Report on the census of population taken on 15th June 1960 by L. W. Jones. Kuching, 1962. 337p.
Additional tables. Kuching, 1962. 55p. C, Y

ZM23.   SINGAPORE. DEPT. OF STATISTICS. Report on the census of population, 1957, by S. C. Chua. Singapore, 1964. 319p. C

ZO—BRUNEI

ZO1.   BRUNEI. Report on the census of population taken on 10th August, 1960 by L. W. Jones. Kuching, GPO, 1961. 180p. C

ZP—PHILIPPINES

ZP1.   PHILIPPINES (REP.) BUREAU OF THE CENSUS AND STATISTICS. Vital statistics report. Manila. v.1- annual. C, Y

ZP2.   SPAIN. INSTITUTO GEOGRÁFICO Y ESTADÍSTICO. Censo de la población de España, Segun el empadronamiento Gecho en 31 de diciembre de 1877 por la Dirección General del Instituto Geográfico y Estadístico. Madrid, 1883-84. 2v. C
["Poblacion de las islas . . . y del archipiélago Filipino" t.1 p. 677-836.]

ZP3.   U.S. BUREAU OF THE CENSUS. Census of the Philippine Islands. Bulletin 1-3. Washington, GPO, 1904. 3v. C, Y

ZP4.   U.S. BUREAU OF THE CENSUS. Census of the Philippine Islands taken under the direction of the Philippine Commission in the year 1903. Washington, GPO, 1905. 4v. C, Y

ZP5. PHILIPPINE ISLANDS. CENSUS OFFICE. Census of the Philippine islands taken under the direction of the Philippine Legislature in the year 1918. Manila, GPO, 1920-21. 4v. in 6. C, Y

ZP6. PHILIPPINES (COMMONWEALTH) COMMISSION OF THE CENSUS. Bulletin no. 1-50. Census of the Philippines 1939: population. Manila, GPO, 1939-40. 50v. Y

ZP7. PHILIPPINES (COMMONWEALTH) COMMISSION OF THE CENSUS. Census of the Philippines 1939. Manila, GPO, 1940-43. 5v. in 8. C, Y

ZP8. PHILIPPINES (COMMONWEALTH) COMMISSION OF THE CENSUS. Special bulletin. Manila, 1940- Y

ZP9. PHILIPPINES (REP.) BUREAU OF THE CENSUS AND STATISTICS. A social census of Vigan, Ilocos Sur and Lipa, Batangas; a study of postwar human resources of the Philippines based on data secured from the population of two communities, December 1947. Manila, 1948. 167p. C

ZP10. PHILIPPINES (REP.) BUREAU OF THE CENSUS AND STATISTICS. 1948 census of the Philippines. Population classified by province, by city, municipality, and municipal district,and by barrio. Manila, 1951. 258p. C, Y
[Cornell title omits 1948]

ZP11. PHILIPPINES (REP.) BUREAU OF THE CENSUS AND STATISTICS. Census of the Philippines 1948. Manila, 1954-56. C, Y

ZP12. PHILIPPINES (REP.) BUREAU OF THE CENSUS AND STATISTICS. Enumeration manual, 1960 census of population and housing. Manila, 1960. 103p. C

ZP13. PHILIPPINES (REP.) BUREAU OF THE CENSUS AND STATISTICS. Population of the Philippines by province and municipality, February 15, 1960. Manila, 1960. v, 55p. C

ZP14. PHILIPPINES (REP.) BUREAU OF THE CENSUS AND STATISTICS. Census of the Philippines, 1960: population and housing. Manila, 1963. 2v. in 5. C, Y

ZP15. PHILIPPINES (REP.) OFFICE OF STATISTICAL COORDINATION AND STANDARDS. The population and other demographic facts of the Philippines. Manila, 1963. 37ℓ C, Y

ZP16. PHILIPPINES (REP.) BUREAU OF THE CENSUS AND STATISTICS. Fertility survey of 1963 in the Philippines. Manila, 1964. 25ℓ Y

ZT—THAILAND

ZT1. THAILAND. MINISTRY OF THE INTERIOR. Kansamruat sammanokhrua prachakorn. Bangkok, 1953. 7v. in 6. Y

ZT2. THAILAND. MINISTRY OF THE INTERIOR. Kansamruat sammanokhrua kankaset. Bangkok, 1954. 2v. Y

ZT3. THAILAND. CENTRAL STATISTICAL OFFICE. Thailand population census, 1960: Changwat series. Bangkok, 1961-62. 71v. C, Y
[Cornell entry: Thailand. Samnakngan Sathiti haeng chat.]

ZT4. THAILAND. CENTRAL STATISTICAL OFFICE. Thailand population census, 1960: Northeast region. Bangkok, 1962. 48p. C, Y
["Summarizes for the fifteen changwads of the Northeast the information that has already been published in Changwad series."]
[Cornell entry: Thailand. Samnakngan Sathiti haeng chat.]

ZT5. THAILAND. CENTRAL STATISTICAL OFFICE. Thailand population census, 1960: whole Kingdom. Bangkok, 1962. 59p. C, Y
["All of the basic data appearing in this bulletin has been previously published in a separate bulletin for each of the 71 changwads of the kingdom."]
[Cornell entry: Thailand. Samnakngan Sathiti haeng chat.]

ZV — VIETNAM

ZV1. VIETNAM. VIEN QUOC-GIA THONG-KE. Enquête demographique à Saigon en 1958. Saigon, Institut National de la Statistique, 1958. 122p. C

ZV2. VIETNAM. VIEN QUOC-GIA THONG-KE. Recensement pilote de la province de Phuoc-tuy, effectué le 6 novembre 1959. Saigon, Institut national de la Statistique, 1959. x, 68ℓ C

ZV3. VIETNAM. VIEN QUOC-GIA THONG-KE. Enquête démographique à Saigon en 1962. Saigon, Institut National de la Statistique, 1963. 232p. C

ZV4. VIETNAM. VIEN QUOC-GIA THONG-KE. Dan-so Viet-Nam theo don-vi hanh-chanh. Saigon, 1964- C

INDEX

Abdul Rahman bin Yusop: PH190
Abdullah bin Nuh: PH19, PH20
About, P. E.: FH3
Abrahamson, H. M.: FP10
Abrera, J. B.: YP2
Academia de la Historia, Madrid. Biblioteca.: AA5
Académie des Sciences Coloniales: DH1
Adatrechtbundel: HI 12
Adatrechtstichting te Leiden: HI 7, HI 8
Adinda, A. M.: PH71
Adinegoro, D.: EI 38, PH37, PH110, PH228
Adriani, N.: AI 8, PI 37
Aebersold, W. E.: PI 54
Aëtius, Brother: PH214
Agarwal, R. C. S.: PB14
Agoncillo, T. A.: CP4
Ahmad bin Ismail: PH56
Ahmady, S.: PH12
Ajia Keizai Kenkyujo, Tokyo: AA32, AA34, WA1, YA2
Akademiia Nauk SSSR. Institut Narodov Azii: AA41
Akiyama, A.: RB4
Aldave-Yap, F. Z.: PP33
Alejandro, R.: PP35
Algemeen Proefstation der AVROS: UA1
Algué, J.: NP2
Alisjahbana, S. T.: PH123
Alkema, B.: KI4
Allied Forces: AA11
Aluit, A. J.: FP14
Amara Raksasataya: GT3
Ambekar, C. G.: AV3
Ambtelijke Boekerij: BE8
American Association of Collegiate Registrars and Admissions Officers. Committee on Foreign Students: LT2
American Association of the Philippines: FP11
American Baptist Foreign Mission Society: PB13
American Chamber of Commerce in Thailand: YT1
American Chamber of Commerce of the Philippines: YP3, YP4
American Council of Learned Societies: PT18
American Friends of Vietnam: AV6, AV7, LV1, QV2
American Institute of Crop Ecology: UB3, VH2
American Institute of Pacific Relations: AA17, KA6

American Numismatic Society: SA5
American Oriental Society. Library: BA3
American University. Foreign Areas Studies Division: EB11, EC5, EI 41, EL2, EM20, ET7, ET10, EV3-EV5
Amsterdam. Bali Instituut: AI 5
Amsterdam. Minangkabau Instituut: AI 7
Amsterdam. Molukken Instituut: AI 9
Amsterdam. Rijksinstituut voor Oorlogsdocumentatie: CI 7
Amyot, J.: GT1
Anak Minang (pseud.): PI 52
Ananda: FI 23a, FI 26
Ananda Kusama, I Gusti: PI 36
Andaya, A.: HP6
Anderson, B. R.: CI 8
Anderson, G. H.: RC8
Andreatta, L.: AV7, LV1
Andronov, M. S.: OM15
Anthropos Institute: PI 53, PP62
Antonio, C. M.: KP3
Antonio, J.: FT1
Antonissen, A: PI 42
Anwir, B. S.: PH12a, PH17, PH130, PH134
Arief, M. I.: PH41
Arndt, P.: PI 45, PI 53
Arnowo, D.: PH129
Artigas y Cuerva, M.: PP47
Asiatic Society of Japan: JP3
Aspillera, P. S.: PH23
Atjeh en Onderhoorigheden (Residency). Ambtelijke Boekerij, Banda Atjeh: BE8
Atmadi, E. T.: FI 27
Aubaret, L. G. G.: PV26, PV27
Australian National University. Centre of Oriental Studies: QA4
Australian National University. Dept. of Anthropology and Sociology: KI 12
Automobile Association of Malaya: FM6
Auvade, R.: AH7
Ayala y Compañía. Library: BH5
Ayer, E. E.: BA2
Ayer, Firm, Newspaper Advertising Agents: CP1
Aymonier, E. F.: PC2, PZ1

Ba, M.: PB18
Baden, A. L.: JP4
Badings, A. H. L.: PH5, PH93, PH99
Bahar, S. M.: PH50

Bailey, D. J. S.: PI 55
Bakoenoen, Publisher: FI 19
Bakry, O.: PH19
Balfour, E. G.: EA3, EA5
Bali Instituut, Amsterdam: AI 5
Ball, J.: WA2
Bambang Sutarno: FI 40
Banerjea, J. N.: SB3
Bangkok. Amuag Silpa School: PT11
Bangkok. Chamber of Commerce: YT6
Bangkok. Chulalongkorn University: LT1
Bangkok. Chulalongkorn University. Faculty of Commerce and Accountancy: WT1
Bangkok. Chulalongkorn University. Faculty of Political Science: GT1
Bangkok. Chulalongkorn University. Library: AT4
Bangkok. Dept. of Fine Arts: TT2
Bangkok. Mahamakuta University: RB9
Bangkok. National Library: BI 1, HT2, OT1
Bangkok. Thammasat University. Institute of Public Administration: HT3
Bangkok Bank. Research and Statistics Division: YT2, YT3
Bank of Thailand: WT2
Baranera, F. X.: EP4, FP3
Barbier, V.: PV34, PV36
Barnett, L. D.: BB2
Barquissau, R.: OH3
Bartholomew, J.: NB2
Baruch, J.: OH4
Basio, E.: UP2
Bataksch Instituut, Leiden: PI 43
Bataviaasch Genootschap van Kunsten en Wetenschappen: AI 3, BE4, BE5, BE10, BE11, BR3, CI 3, CI 5, DI 4- DI 6, KI 1, KI 2, OM4, PI 24, QI 1, SA1- SA4
Bautista, J. A.: PP8
Beatty, A. C.: BB8
Behavior Sciences Bibliographies: AA20, AB4, AB5, AC1, AP25, KI 7, KI 11, MA5
Behn, H. U.: CA5
Belfield, H. C.: EM7, EM8
Bemmelen, J. F. van: FI 4, FI 5, FI 8
Bennásar, G.: PP69
Bennison, J. S.: ZB8
Berg, L. W. C. van den: BR2, HI 3, HI 5
Berg, N. P. van den: YI 1
Bergaño, D.: PP66
Berita Ekonomi: YJ1, YJ1a
Bernard, J. B.: PC4
Bernardo, G. A.: OP4
Bernath, F. A.: BA15
Beus, G. de: MI 3

Bezemer, T. J.: KI 4, PI 8, PI 13
Bhatkal, S. G.: TA6
Bhatta, J. N.: GI 3
Bhattacharyya, B.: RB1, RB8
Bibliographia Belgica: OA3
Bibliographical Society of the Philippines: AA24, DP24, HP7, HP15
Bibliography Bulletin: AP28
Biblioteca Nacional Filipina: PP47
Bibliotheca Bibliographica: UA5
Bijdragen Tot eene Nederlandsche Bibliographie: KA1
Binney, Mrs. J. P.: PZ3
Blackmore, T.: JB2
Blackwell, G. E.: PZ3
Blagden, C. O.: KM1
Blair, E. H.: AP16
Blake, F. R.: OP2
Blanchard, W.: ET6
Blanford, H. F.: VB1
Bloomfield, B. C.: LA6
Bloys van Treslong Prins, P. C.: DI 10
Blumentritt, F.: AP4, AP20, RA1
Bodin de Galembert, J. de: HH2
Boer, D.: PH122
Bogor, Indonesia. Kebun Raja: VI 17, VI 18
Bonet, J.: PV31
Bons, L.: PH11, PH13, PH15
Books That Matter: JA5
Borisat Phrae Phitthaya, Bangkok: PT33
Bork-Feltkamp, A. J. van: KI 5
Bouchet, G.: PV3
Boudet, P.: AH2, AH4
Bowers, F.: SB4
Bowker, H. F.: SA5
Boze, P.: PH203
Bradley, D. B.: PT7
Bragghen, W. van der: BE14
Bravo, F.: EP1
Brebion, A.: DH1
Brenier, H.: WH2
Brissaud, L. D.: PH208
British Museum. Dept. of Oriental Printed Books and Manuscripts: BB2
British Overseas Airways Corp.: FM10, FM25
Brondgeest, B. T.: PH73
Brondgeest, H.: FI 10
Brooks, R. J.: PH21
Broughton, J. D.: GT2
Brown, C. C.: OM8
Bruijn, C. A. L. van T. de: DI 7
Brunei: XO1, ZO1
Brunei. Dept. of Customs and Excise: WO1
Brussels. Université Libre. Centre d'Étude du Sud-Est Asiatique: AA38

Buddhist Lodge: RB3
Bugarín, J.: PP57
Buhain, A. R.: PP35
Bulletin of Bibliography: AP11
Burkill, I. H.: IM2
Burma: FB7, HB1, MB4, QB1, WB1, YB1, ZB5
Burma. Accounts Dept.: HB2
Burma. Archaeological Survey: QB2
Burma. Chief Commissioner: WB1a
Burma. Commissioner of Settlements and Land Records: NB1
Burma. Customs Dept.: YB2-YB4, YB12
Burma. Dept. of Land Records and Agriculture: YB5, YB6
Burma. Education Dept.: PB4
Burma. Forest Dept.: UB1, XB1
Burma. Government Book Depot: BD1, HB3
Burma. Local Government Dept.: WB2, WB3
Burma. Public Works Dept. Secretariat Library: BD3
Burma. Secretariat Library: BD2
Burma. Superintendent, Government Printing: OB1, OB2
Burma (Union): FB8
Burma (Union) Central Statistical and Economics Dept.: WB4, WB10, YB7, YB8, ZB9
Burma (Union) Central Statistical Office: WB5-WB10, YB9-YB11
Burma (Union) Dept. of Information and Broadcasting: EB7, FB11
Burma (Union) Foreign Office: HB4
Burma (Union) Government Book Depot: BD1
Burma (Union) Historical Commission. Library: BD5
Burma (Union) Institute of Public Administration. Library: HB5
Burma (Union) Linguistic Survey: OB4
Burma (Union) Ministry of Information: CB1, EB1, EB7, EB10, FB10, FB12, FB13
Burma (Union) Ministry of National Planning and Religious Affairs: WB11
Burma (Union) Office of the Collector of Customs: YB12
Burma, Lower: EB3, YB13, YB14, ZB1, ZB2
Burma Historical Commission: BD5
Burma Pamphlets: EB6
Burnell, A. C.: EA6
Burns, P. L.: HM5
Bussy, J. H. de, Publisher: NI 12
Buzeta, M.: EP1

COWA: QA2
Cabaton, A.: BM2
Cahen, C.: JA6
Calder, R. E.: TB1
Calderón, S. G.: PP3, PP4, PP36
California. University. University at Los Angeles. Dept. of Anthropology: AL2, KA7, WL2-WL4, XL1, ZL2
Caltex (Philippines) Inc.: FP8
Cambodia: EC1
Cambodia. Direction de la Statistique: WC1
Cambodia. Direction des Douanes et Régies: YC1
Cambodia. Ministère de l'Économie Nationale: YC2
Cambodia. Ministère des Affaires Étrangères: HC1
Cambodia. Ministère du Plan: WC2
Cammack, F. M.: AA31
Campbell, F. B. F.: HA1
Canberra, Australia. National Library: AI 20
Carnegie Endowment for International Peace. Library: HP5
Carnegie Institution of Washington: PP16
Carro, A.: PP18, PP20
Cartwright, B. O.: PT10
Case, M. H.: JA5
Castro, J. L.: CP11
Catálogos de Archivos y Bibliotecas: BB6
Cavada y Mendez de Vigo, A. de la: WP1
Cebu, Philippines. Chamber of Commerce: YP6
Cense, A. A.: OM10
Central Bank of the Philippines: WP2, YP8, YP9
Centre d'Étude des Relations Internationales, Paris: JA1
Chabert, O. de: NH3
Chalid Rasjidi: LI 5
Chamber of Commerce of the Philippines: YP10
Chawit Rangthong: FI 9
Cheeseman, H. A. R.: AM5
Cheminaud, G.: PL3
Ch'en Chan-I: YM1
Cheng, E. L. S.: CM7
Chicago. University: AC1
Chicago. University. Dept. of Anthropology: KP1
Chicago. University. Division of Social Sciences: EC2
Chicago. University. Philippine Studies Program: AP25, EP21
Chieng, A.: BB7
Chijs, J. A. van der: AI 3, BE5, BE6, KI 2, SA3

Chot Suwatthi: VT1, VT2, VT4
Chua, S. C.: ZM23
Church of Christ in Thailand: RC6
Clapp, W. C.: PP61
Clercq, F. S. A. de: PH90, VI 1, VI 3
Coates, J.: AV9
Codices Manuscripti, Univ. of Leiden: BN12
Coedès, G.: BM6, QC3
Collins, D.: PL1
Colorado. University. Institute of Asiatic Affairs: DI 15, DM14, DP17, DT2
Committee for Coordination of Investigations of the Lower Mekong Basin: NA6
Conklin, H. C.: KP4, PP56
Conover, H. F.: AI 12
Cook, T., Firm Publishers: FA3, FA4, FB2-FB6
Coolhaas, W. P.: JI 6
Coolsma, S.: PI 24a, PI 25, PI 27
Coope, A. E.: PH155
Copenhagen. Kongelige Bibliotek: BM6
Cordero, F. V.: HP20
Cordier, G.: PV37, PV38
Cordier, H.: AH1
Cornell University. Libraries: BA9, CI 8, CI 11
Cornell University. Modern Indonesia Project: AI 27, CI 11, OM9
Cornell University. Southeast Asia Program: AT1, BA10, ET5
Cornell University. Southeast Asia Program. Data Papers: AA25, AT1, BA6, BA9, BA14, BA15, BA18, BA19, CI 8, LA4, LA8, PZ13, TA1-TA3, TA8
Cornell University. Thailand Project: AT1, AT5, AT7, AT9
Cornets de Groot, A. D.: PI 1
Cotter, C. P.: AM8, GM1, KM2
Council for Old World Archaeology: QA2
Country Survey Series: EC3, EM14, ET6
Cowie, A.: PP2
Crawfurd, John, EA2, PH141
Crevost, C.: UH1
Crow, Carl, Inc., Firm, Advertising Agents: CA1
Cteme a Studujeme: AA21
Cua, H. T. P.: HV1, PV29
Cuaz, M. J.: PT3
Cuesta, L.: BB6
Cuesta, M.: BB6
Culture et Civilisation: DC2

Daguio, A. O.: DP20
Dahar, R. W.: LI 6
Dai Tôa Tôkei Sôsho: WB13, WM1, WP3

Dáluz, E. T.: PP23
Daniel, H.: MA4
Daniel, P.: BG3
Dao-Dang-Vy: PV40, PV44, PV47
Dao-Duy-Anh: PV6-PV8, PV41
Dao-Van-Tap: PV39
Dao-Van-Tien: PV42
Daoed, Radja Medan: PI 50
Datje Rahajukusumah: PH217
Davis, J. H.: UB2, VB3
Del Tufo, M. V.: ZM11
Deli-Archief: BE9
Denny, R. M.: AA41
Dennys, N. B.: EM6
Derfelden van Hinderstein, G. F. von: NI 1
Deutsche Morgenländische Gesselschaft: OA1
Dilmy, N.: PH162
Dios, R. de: PP37-PP39
Dirdja Suprabha, R. M. A.: PI 6
Djajadiningrat, H.: PI 35
Djakarta. Centrale Natuurwetenschappelijke. Bibliotheek: BE14
Djakarta. Djawatan Penerangan: FI 36
Djakarta. Lembaga Administrasi Negara: HI 17
Djakarta. Lembaga Ekonomi dan Kemasjarakatan Nasional: BE16
Djakarta. Lembaga Ekonomi dan Kemasjarakatan Nasional. Perpustakaan: AI 28
Djakarta. Perpustakaan Sedjarah Politik dan Sosial: BE15
Djakarta. Sekolah Tinggi Theologia: RI 5
Djakarta. Universitet Indonesia: WI 37
Djakarta. Universitet Indonesia: Lembaga Bahasa dan Budaja: PH39, PH45-PH48, PH51, PH53, PH54, PH58, PH135
Djambatan Uitgeversbedrijf, N. V. Amsterdam: NA5
Djambek, S.: EI 18
Doble, M.: PH18
Documentation dans les Sciences Sociales: HA5
Documents on Asian Affairs: AA28
Dominicans. Provincia del Santissimo Rosario de Filipinas: RC5
Dornselffen, I.: NI 9
Dotson, L. O.: KA4
Dournes, J.: PV3, PZ11
Drewes, G. W. J.: PI 35
Driel, B. M.: ZI 7, ZI 9
Dumont, C. F. H.: MI 6
Dunn, C. W.: PB11
Duroiselle, C.: QB2
Dutch East Indies: EI 36, HI 1, HI 2, MI 10, YI 16

Dutch East Indies. Algemene Secretarie: BE7, MI 4, MI 5, MI 8
Dutch East Indies. Centraal Kantoor voor de Statistiek: WI 1–WI 15, WI 36, XI 1–XI 6, YI 2–YI 8, YI 13, YI 14, YJ4–YJ6, ZI 10
Dutch East Indies. Departement der Burgerlijke Openbare Werken: YI 9
Dutch East Indies. Departement van Economische Zaken: NI 16, UI 5, WI 5, YI 12, YJ7
Dutch East Indies. Departement van Financiën: YI 10, YI 11
Dutch East Indies. Departement van Landbouw, Nijverheid en Handel: EI 26, EI 33, WI 5, YI 12
Dutch East Indies. Departement van Onderwijs en Eeredienst: PH117, WI 15
Dutch East Indies. Dienst der In- en Uitvoerrechten en Accijnzen: YI 10, YI 11, YI 13
Dutch East Indies. Dienst van den Landbouw: UI 6
Dutch East Indies. Dienst van den Mijnbouw: NI 5, NI 6, NI 14, NI 15, VI 4, VI 5
Dutch East Indies. Generale Thesaurie: YJ8
Dutch East Indies. Hoofbureau der In- en Uitvoerrechten en Accijnzen: YI 5
Dutch East Indies. Hoofdkantoor van Scheepvaart: YI 15
Dutch East Indies. Kantoor voor de Volkslectuur: NI 13
Dutch East Indies. Kantoor voor de Volkstelling: MI 11, ZI 2, ZI 5, ZI 6, ZI 8
Dutch East Indies. Leger: PH7
Dutch East Indies. Topographische Dienst: MI 12, NZ 6, NZ 7
Dutch East Indies. Welvaartscommissie: YJ9

Eala, Q. A.: CP7
East and West Association, New York: AP23
Eberhardt, P.: FV2
Echols, J. M.: AI 27, AI 29, BA 13, CI 11, OM9, PH181, PH188
École des Langues Orientales Vivantes: PV31
École Française d'Extrême-Orient: AH1, AL4, NH1, PZ1, PZ4, QC1, QV1
Editions du Comité Littéraire: BP2
Eggan, F.: AP25
Egges Post, A.: PH119
Egner, D. W.: PI 10
Elmer, E. O.: HP4

Elout, C. P. J.: PH1, PH86
Embree, J. F.: AA14, AA22, AA23, KA3, KA4, KA6
Emeneau, M. B.: PV9
Ennen, H.: PH120
Enríquez, P. J.: PP6–PP9, PP28–PP30
Erard, E.: HH2
Erickson, G. E.: AA37
Errington de la Criox, J.: PH207, PH210
Escobar y Lozano, J.: FP2
Estrade: PL2
Estrella-Villaneuva, L.: VP3
Études Orientales: OH4

Fadlullah, M.: PH73
Far Eastern Economic Review: FA5
Favre, P. E. L.: PH205, PH206, PI 3
Fazakas, D.: QV2
Fegan, E. S.: KA2
Fegen, W. W.: FT1
Feith, P. R.: JI 3
Feliciano, M.: HP19
Felix de la Encarnación, J.: PP14
Ferkinghoff, K.: PV49
Fernandez Cosgaya, L.: PP67
Feucreisen, F.: CA6
Filliozat, J.: SB2
Fischer, H. T.: KI 11
Fisher, F. C.: FP4
Fisher, J.: AB3
Florentino, A. S.: OP9
Florida. University. Libraries: AT3
Fokker, A. A.: PH98
Forbes, D. C.: PH172, PH183
Foreign Area Fellowship Program: DA2
Fowler, J. A.: YJ23
Fox, R. B.: KP1
France. Commission Archéologique de l'Indochine: PC6
France. Direction de la Documentation: AB6
France. Ministère de l'Instruction Publique et des Beaux-Arts: NH2, PC6
France. Ministère des Affaires Étrangères: NH2
France. Ministère des Colonies: NH2
Franfurter, O.: OT1
Franzén, C. G. F.: LT2
Frei, E. J.: AA24
Friederich, R.: BR1
Fryer, G. E.: EB3
Fuller, Mrs. C. F.: FI 37
Furnivall, J. S.: AB7

Galang, Z. M.: EP11, EP15
Gallas, V.: PP5
Gallois, L. L. J.: NH3, NH4

Garcia, M.: DP24
Gard, R. A.: RA3, RB7, RB9
Garde, P. K.: AA19
Gardner, R. K.: CV1
Garry, A. N. M.: ZM7
Garuda Indonesian Airways: FI 21
Gaspardone, E.: AV1
Gazali Gelar Sutan Maharadja: PH34
Gelder, W. van: NI 4, NI 7, NI 10, NI 11, NI 17
Gendrano, V. P.: UP2
Génibrel, J. F. M.: PV30, PV32, PV35
Geographical Handbook Series: EH4, EI 35
Geography Publications at Dartmouth: MP5
Geologisch Mijnbouwkundig Genootschap voor Nederland en Kolonien: VI 2
Gericke, J. F. C.: PI 2, PI 7
Germany (Federal Republic, 1949-) Statistisches Bundesamt: WI 16, WT 3
Gerungan, W. A.: LI 7
Geschriften over Atjeh: BE8
Gibb, H. A. R.: RI 3
Gibson-Hill, C. A.: VM2
Gimlette, J. D.: VM1
Gisbert, M.: PP52
Glen San Lwin: PB15
Glenister, A. G.: VA4
Golden, R. D.: PT20
Gonggrijp, G. F. E.: EI 34, UI 4
Gonzaga, F. L.: TP2
Gougenheim, G.: PH210a
Gouin, E.: PV4
Gould, J. S.: YT5
Gowing, P. G.: RC7, RI 6
Graaff, E. A. van de: WI 17
Graham, W. A.: EM9, ET3
Grantham, S. G.: ZB6
Grashuis, G. J.: PH92
Great Britain. Admiralty: EI 31
Great Britain. Board of Trade: YB17
Great Britain. Central Office of Information: JH1
Great Britain. Colonial Office: HA4, HM1
Great Britain. Commonwealth Relations Office. India Office Library: BM4
Great Britain. India Office. Library: BM3
Great Britain. Naval Intelligence Division: EH4, EI 35
Great Britain. Public Record Office: HM1
Grenzenberg, J. M.: FI 35
Greshoff, M.: VI 1
Griffin, A. P. C.: BA1
Guesdon, J.: PC6

Guides des Colonies Françaises: FH3
Guignard, T.: PL4
Gunning, J. G. H.: PI 7
Gunung Agung, Djakarta: AI 1, AI 18, AI 25
Guzman, M. O. de: PP10, PP28-PP30, PP41

Haas, M. R.: PT14, PT18, PT30
Habeyb: PH68
Haddon, A. C.: KA2, SB1
Hague. Koloniale Bibliotheek: BC2
Hague. Koninklijke Bibliotheek: HI 10
Haight, H. E.: ZL4
Hale, A.: DM12
Halkema, H.: PH104
Hall, D. G. E.: JA3, NA5
Halliday, R.: PZ5
Halpern, J. M.: WL2-WL4, XL1, ZL2
Hamilton, A. W. H.: PH149, PH171
Hamilton, W.: EA1, MA1-MA3
Hanayama, S.: RB11
Handelsvereeniging, Medan: XI 27, YJ10
Hanson, O.: PZ2
Harahap, E. S.: PH24-PH26, PH28, PH30, PH35
Hare, G. T.: ZM5
Harris, G. L.: EM14
Harris, L. J.: CM11
Harrison, C. W.: FM2, FM3
Hart, D. V.: AA26, AA29, CP7, HA8, HP21, LA5
Hartmann, A.: CI 2
Harvard University. Graduate School of Business Administration: IA3
Harvard University. Library: AH5, BA21
Haswell, James Madison: PZ9
Hauser, P. M.: WB12
Hawaii. University. Dept. of Asian Studies: KM2
Hawaii. University. East-West Center: AA41, VI 20
Hawaii. University. East-West Center. Library: AA39, AP29, CP12, TA7
Hawaii. University. Industrial Relations Center: IA2
Hay, S. N.: JA5
Hazra, N. K.: CM7
Helfrich, O. L.: AI 6
Hellman, F. S.: AI 12, AM4
Helsloot, N.: PH8
Hendershot, V. E.: PH151
Hendriks, H.: PI 47
Hendry, R. S.: NP6
Hermosisima, T. V.: PP12
Hickey, G. C.: EL1
Hicks, G. L.: II 1, II 4

Hierche, H.: QA3
Hobbs, C. C.: AA13, AA15, AA36, AH6, TA1–TA3, TA8
Hoi Nghien-Cuu Pho-Thong Giao-Duc: PV11
Hoki, S.: WP3
Holle, K. F.: OM3
Hollyman, K. J.: OA5
Honig, P.: VI 6
Hoogerwerf, A.: VI 9
Hooyer, G. B.: FI 5, FI 8
Hooykaas, J. C.: JI 2
Horne, N. P.: AA30
Hough, G. H.: PB2
Houston, C. O.: AP27
Houten, H. van: DI 8
Howard, J. H.: BP5
Howell, W.: PI 55
Howison, J.: PH139
Hsu, Y. C.: AA27
Htun Aun Jo: PB16
Htun Nyein: PB7, PB16
Hudson, R.: FT20
Huke, R. E.: MP5
Hull. University. Dept. of Geography: LM6
Human Relations Area Files: EB8, EC2–EC4, EI 40, EL1, EM12, EM13, EP21, ET5, ET6, KA8, KI 7, KI 11
Humphreys, C.: RB12

INSDOC: VA2
Ibnu Rasjid: PH42
Ignacio, R. P.: PP21, PP50
Iken, D.: PH24
Illinois. Northern Illinois University. Library: BA20, BA22
Ilustración Filipina, Periódico Quincenal: CP9
India. Census Commissioner: ZB2–ZB4, ZB6–ZB8
India (Rep.) Directorate of Commercial Publicity: YC3, YM4
Indian Council of World Affairs: AA28
Indian Library Association: CA2
Indo-Pacific Fisheries Council: VA1, VA3, VM3
Indochina: EC1
Indochina (Fed.) Service de la Statistique Générale: WH5, WH6
Indochina, French. Direction des Archives et des Bibliothèques: AH3
Indochina, French. Direction des Services Économiques: IH1, WH3
Indochina, French. Inspection Générale des Mines et de l'Industrie: WH4

Indochina, French. Laws, Statutes, etc.: HH1, HH3
Indochina, French. Service de la Statistique: YH2
Indochina, French. Service Géographique: NH5, NZ5
Indologische Studentencorps, Delft: LI 1
Indologische Vereeniging, Delft: LI 1
Indonesia. Angkatan Darat: GI 3
Indonesia. Angkatan Laut. Djawatan Hidrografi: MI 17
Indonesia. Arsip Nasional: BE6
Indonesia. Badan Penjelenggara Partisipasi New York World's Fair, 1964–65: FI 33
Indonesia. Biro Pemilihan: ZI 13
Indonesia. Biro Perpustakaan: AI 30, CI 10
Indonesia. Biro Pusat Statistik: WI 18–WI 28, XI 7–XI 24, YI 17–YI 39, YJ11–YJ18, ZI 1, ZI 11, ZI 14–ZI 23
Indonesia. Biro Pusat Statistik. Seksi Statistik Pengangkutan: YI 40–YI 43
Indonesia. Departemen Agama: WI 29
Indonesia. Departemen Pendidikan Dasar dan Kebudajaan: WI 30
Indonesia. Departemen Penerangan: CI 1, FI 16, FI 18, FI 20, FI 32, HI 4, HI 15, HI 16, HI 19, JI 7, JI 8, ZI 14
Indonesia. Departemen Perburuhan: YJ19
Indonesia. Departemen Perguruan Tinggi dan Ilmu Pergetahuan: LI 2
Indonesia. Departemen Perindustrian Rakjat: TI 2
Indonesia. Departemen Pertambangan: VI 19
Indonesia. Dewan Tourisme: FI 22
Indonesia. Djawatan Bea dan Tjukai: YI 44
Indonesia. Djawatan Hidrografi: MI 17
Indonesia. Djawatan Kereta Api: YI 45
Indonesia. Djawatan Pendidikan Kedjuruan: LI 3
Indonesia. Kantor Bibliografi Nasional: AI 19, AI 22, GI 2
Indonesia. Kantor Pusat Statistik: WI 31, XI 25, YI 46–YI 49
Indonesia. Kementerian Pendidikan, Pengadjaran dan Kebudajaan: FI 44, HI 13, NI 21, WI 32
Indonesia. Kementerian Pendidikan, Pengadjaran dan Kebudajaan. Perpustakaan Perguruan: AI 14
Indonesia. Kementerian Penerangan: DI 18, EI 27, FI 20, FI 29–FI 31, HI 4
Indonesia. Kementerian Perekonomian: WI 33

Indonesia. Laws, Statutes, etc.: HI 19
Indonesia. Lembaga Administrasi Negara: HI 17
Indonesia. Lembaga Bahasa dan Kesusasteraan: OM16, PH61, PH72
Indonesia. Lembaga Ekonomi dan Kemas ja Rakatan Nasional: ZI 24
Indonesia. Lembaga Pers dan Pendapat Umum: OM1
Indonesia. Monetary Sub-Board: WI 34
Indonesian Chamber of Industries: YJ20
Innes, J. R.: ZM4
Institut d'Emission des États du Cambodge du Laos et du Vietnam. Service des Études Économiques et Financières: YH3
Institute for Defense Analysis: AV9
Institute of Asian Economic Affairs, Tokyo: AA32, AA34, WA2, YA2
Institute of Philippine Culture: AP30
Instituut Kern, Leyden: QA1
Instituut voor Taal-, Land- en Volkenkunde: BC2, BN10, BN11, GI 1, JI 6, JI 10, KI 8, NZ3, NZ4, OM7, OM10, OM12, OM14
Insurance and Finance Journal: YA3
International Association of Legal Science: HA5, HA7
International Association of Tamil Research: OM15
Ipoh, Malaysia. Public Library: BG1, BG7
Irikura, J. K.: AA20, BA4
Island Hermitage Publications: RB5
Italy. Ambasciata. Indonesia: PH219

Jackson, J. C.: LM6
Jacobini, H. B.: HP9
Jacquet, C. H.: AP24
Jaivid Rangthong: FT7
Jamolangue, F. J.: PP8
Janert, K. L.: LA2
Janse, O. R. T.: KH1
Jansz, P.: PI 5, PI 9, PI 11, PI 14
Japan. Dept. of Railways: FA2
Jaspan. M. A.: KI 9, KI 10
Java (Japanese Military Administration, 1942-45) Bunkyokyoku: PH223
Java (Japanese Military Administration, 1942-45) Komisi Bahasa Indonesia: PH114
Java Motor Club: FI 12
Jesus, D. D. de: FP12, NP4, NP5
Jogjakarta, Indonesia. Universitet Negeri Gadjah Mada: ZI 12
Joint Thai United States Military Research and Development Center: AT8

Jones, G. N.: AI 26
Jones, L. W.: ZM14, ZM19-ZM22, ZO1
Josephson, A. G. S.: AP11
Joustra, M.: AI 4, AI 7, PI 38, PI 43
Juanmarti, J.: PP1
Judson, A.: PB5, PB6, PB8-PB10
Jumper, R.: JV2, JV3
Jumsai, Manich: PT5, PT15, PT16, PT19, PT22, PT25, PT28
Juynboll, H. H.: BN3, NB4, BN6, PI 44

Kaelan: FI 23
Kafton, M.: AA21
Kahler, H.: OM17
Kahlo, G.: PH6, PH211, PH213, PH216, PH218
Kamon Phaophichit: PT23, PT26
Kamsta (pseud.): PH202
Kan, C. M.: MI 2, NZ2
Kanchananago, N. T.: FM4
Kaplan, I.: EM12
Karim, M. A.: PH16
Karow, O.: PH215
Kaufmann, J.: PP13
Kawabe, T.: AT2
Keasberry, B. P.: PH142, PH154
Keeth, K. H.: TM1
Kéne, T.: AL1, BP2
Kennedy, R.: KI 6, KI 7, KI 11
Kennedy, T. F.: NP9
Kern, R. A.: BN9
Kesteven, G. L.: VM3
Keyes, E. J.: BA14, BA18
Keyes, J. G.: BA14, BA18
Khai-Anh: PV48
Khin, U.: PB15
Kiliaan, H. N.: PI 46
Kim Korwong: FI 7
Kleiweg de Zwaan, J. P.: KI 5
Klinkert, H. C.: PH100, PH101, PH106, PH109, PH112
Koch, D. M. G.: DI 19
Kokuritsu Kokkai Toshokan, Tokyo. Ippan Kosabu: AA18, CA3
Kokusai Nihon Kyôkai: WM1
Koninklijk Instituut voor de Tropen: KI 5, UI 3
Koninklijk Instituut voor de Tropen. Afdeling Tropische Producten. Bibliotheek: BC3
Koninklijke Akademie van Wetenschappen: BN8
Koninklijke Paketvaart Maatschappij: FI 9
Koninklijke Vereeniging Java Motor Club, Semarang: FI 12, II 1
Koop, J. C.: YB19
Kops, G. F. de B.: YI 50

Korigodsky, R. N.: PH230
Korwong, K.: FI 7
Kramer, A. L. N.: PH115, PH116, PH121, PH125, PH137, PH164
Kramers, J. H.: RI 3
Kuala Lumpur. Pustaka Antara: OM13
Kuala Lumpur. Rubber Research Institute: CM4
Kuala Lumpur. University of Malaya: BP5, CM11
Kuala Lumpur. University of Malaya. Dept. of Indian Studies: OM15
Kuala Lumpur. University of Malaya. Library: BG8, TM1
Kuching, Sarawak. Rural District Council: DM2
Kusbini: PH38
Kusnodiprodjo: PH43
Kwee, O. G.: PH180
Kyriak, T. E.: AA33, AA35

Labberton, D. van H.: CI 3, EI 29, HI 11
Labrousse, P.: PH210a
LaDage, J. H.: PH185
Lafont, P. B.: AL4
Laist, A.: EP4
Language Series: OP2
Laos (Kingdom) Ministère des Affaires Étrangères: DL1
Laos (Kingdom) Office of Elementary and Adult Education: WL5
Laos (Kingdom) Service de la Statistique: WL6, ZL1, ZL3
Lasker, B.: AA22, KA6
Lathief, A. K.: PH156
Latif, I.: FI 7, FI 24, FI 45
Laygo, A.: AP32
Le-Ba-Khanh: PV11, PV12, PV20
Le-Ba-Kong: PV2, PV10-PV13, PV16, PV20-PV23
Le-Qui-Don: JV1
Le-Van-Hung: PV14
LeBar, F. M.: KA8
Leclerc, C.: AP2, AP3
Lee, Y. K.: PH189
Legge, J.: PH3
Le Grand de la Liraÿe: PV28
Leigh, M. B.: BA19
Lekkerkerker, C.: NI 17, NI 20
Lemarie, C.: UN1
Lembaga Bahasa Indonesia, Medan: PH27
Lembaga Kebudajaan Indonesia: BE10, CI 3, CI 5, DI 4-DI 6, JI 5, NZ1
Lembaga Kebudajaan Indonesia. Museum: BR3, KI 1, KI 2, QI 1, SA 1-SA 4
Lembaga Kebudajaan Indonesia. Perpustakaan: BE1-BE5, BE11, BE13, BR1, OM4, RI 2

Leong, P. C.: VM4
Lev, D. S.: BA9
Lévi-Provençal, E.: RI 3
Lewin, E.: HA3
Leyden. Bataksch Instituut: PI 43
Leyden. Instituut Kern: QA1
Leyden. Rijksuniversiteit: BN12
Leyden. Rijksuniversiteit. Bibliotheek: BN1, BN3-BN7, BN9
Lezer, L. A.: PI 28
Lie, J. K.: PH9, PH74, PH79-PH81
Liem Tjay Tie: ZI 12
Lietz, P. S.: BA8
Lim, B.: AM7
Linguistic Society of New Zealand: OA5
Lisboa, M. de: PP53
Lombard, S. J.: PZ13
Lombogia, D.: YI 51-YI 53
London. Commonwealth Institute: AM15
London. University. School of Oriental and African Studies: JA3, JA4
London. University. School of Oriental and African Studies. Library: BB9, CA4
London Oriental Bibliographies: OA6
Loofs, H. H. E.: QA4
Lopez, C.: GP1
Lopez Memorial Museum, Manila: BH6, BH7
Lordkipanidze, A. G.: PH231
Los Angeles. Ferdinand Perret Research Library: SB5
Los Baños, Philippines. International Rice Research Institute: UA3
Luang Prabang. Bibliothèque Royale: BF1
Luce, G. H.: JB3
Lummel, H. J. van: KI 3
Lunet de Lajonquière, E. E.: NH1, PT4, QC1, QC2

Macaraya, B. A.: PP64
McFarland, G. B.: PT13
McKaughan, H.: PP64
McKinstry, J.: AL2, AL3
McNicoll, G.: II 3, II 4
McVey, R. T.: AA25
Madjelis Ilmu Pengetahuan Indonesia: VI 11-VI 15
Madrid. Academia de la Historica. Biblioteca: AA5
Madrid. Biblioteca Nacional: BB6
Madrolle, C.: FA1, FC1, FH1, FH4, FH5, FV1
Madrolle Guides: FC1, FH1, FH4, FH5
Mager, J. F.: PI 41
Maggs Bros., London: AP21
Magsaysay, R.: HP11
Maimoon binti Abdullah: PH184, PH199
Mai's Weltführer: FT13

Makagiansar, M.: GI 4
Makepeace, W.: FM19
Malalasekena, G. P.: RB12
Malay States, Federated: ZM5
Malay States Information Agency: FM2, FM3
Malaya (Fed.): DM3, ZM15
Malaya (Fed.) Chief Registration Office: ZM9
Malaya (Fed.) Dept. of Agriculture: XM1, XM2, XM5
Malaya (Fed.) Dept. of Information: EM15
Malaya (Fed.) Dept. of Inland Revenue: YM5
Malaya (Fed.) Dept. of Mines: YM6
Malaya (Fed.) Dept. of Statistics: WM2-WM5, XM3, XM4, YM7-YM12, YM14, ZM15, ZM16
Malaya (Fed.) Dewan Bahasa dan Pustaka: PH62, PH65, PH186
Malaya (Fed.) Election Commission: HM4, WM6
Malaya (Fed.) Embassy. U.S.: AM9
Malaya (Fed.) Income Tax Dept.: YM13
Malaya (Fed.) Museums Dept.: QM1
Malaya (Fed.) Parliament. House of Representatives: HM3
Malaya (Fed.) Permanent Mission to the United Nations: AM1
Malaya (Fed.) Registrar of Societies: IM1
Malaya (Fed.) Survey Dept.: MM2
Malayan Union. Registrar General of Births and Deaths: ZM10
Malaysia: EM18
Malaysia. Dept. of Statistics: WM8-WM11, XM6-XM8, YM17-YM22
Malaysia. Dept. of Tourism: FM1, FM11
Malaysia. Dewan Bahasa dan Pustaka: PH192, PH197
Malaysia. Parliament: DM19
Malaysia. Parliament. House of Representatives: DM23
Malaysia. Parliament. Senate: DM20
Malaysian Airways: FM12, FT18
Mallari, C. B.: PP34
Manalili, B. M.: PP11
Manalili, F. M.: PP37-PP39
Manich Jumsai: PT5, PT15, PT16, PT19, PT22, PT25, PT28
Manila. Far Eastern University. Library: BH4
Manila. Lopez Memorial Museum: BH6, BH7
Manila. National Library: BH1, HP4
Manila. Observatory: NP2
Manila. University of Santo Tomas: LP1

Manit Chumsai: PT5, PT15, PT16, PT19, PT22, PT25, PT28
Manuel, E. A.: DP18, KP2, OP10
March, A. C.: RB3
Maretzki, T. W.: KI 11
Marsden, W.: PH1, PH86, PH140
Martínez de Zúñiga, J.: EP3
Marty, P.: PZ12
Mason, J. B.: AT3
Massachusetts Institute of Technology. Center for International Studies: II 2
Masseron, J.: PV33
Matthes, B. F.: BN2, PI 40, PI 48, PI 49
Matthes, J.: BN9
Matthews, J.: QM2
Matthews, N.: BM5
Maxfield, C. L.: PP15a
Maxwell, L. F.: HA6
Mayer, L. T.: PH95, PH103
Medan, Indonesia. Lembaga Bahasa Indonesia: PH27
Medan, Indonesia. Pathologische Laboratorium: ZI 7, ZI 9
Medan, Indonesia. Stadsgemeente: YJ20a
Medina, I. R.: CP9
Medina, J. T.: AP7-AP9, AP15
Medway, Lord: VA5
Meillier, M.: BF1
Melvill van Carnbee, P.: FI 1, FI 2, NI 2
Meng, C. A.: PH16
Michell, E. B.: PT8
Michigan. State University. Vietnam Advisory Group: JV2, JV3
Michigan. State University. Vietnam Project: AV4, AV5
Middleton, T. C.: AP12
Miller, H.: FM23
Mills, L. A.: AM6
Milne, M. L.: PZ8
Minangkabau Instituut, Amsterdam: AI 7
Mr. Chen & Co.: FI 17
Moluccas (Residency) Gewestelijke Bibliotheek: BE12
Molukken Instituut, Amsterdam: AI 9
Moreno, F. B.: HP10, HP16, HP17
Morère: PZ12
Morey, V.: OP8
Motooka, T.: TA4
Moura, J.: PC3
Mueller, W.: UA4, UA5
Muhammad Shah bin Yusuf, H.: PH52
Muller, F.: KA1
Muller, H. C. A.: BR4
Müller, W. C.: BC2, NZ4
Munaf, H.: EI 37, RI 4
Mundo, C. del: PP27
Munnich, J.: BE4

Munson, F. P.: EC5
Muslimin, K. A.: PH202

Nadanasabathy, V.: BG8
Nana-Tiloka, Bhikku (pseud.): RB5, RB6
Nanyang University. Institute of Southeast Asia: AA27, CA7, JP9
Nasution, A. T.: PH31, PH49, PH70
Nathan, J. E.: ZM6
National Chamber of Malaysian Manufactures: DM21
National Institute of Administration [i.e. Vietnam]: AV11
National Language Books [i.e. Tagalog]: PP7
National Research Council of the Philippine Islands: DP12
Natuurwetenschappelijke Raad voor Nederlandsch-Indië: BR4
Nederlandsch Aardrijkskunding Genootschap, Amsterdam: MI 10, NI 18
Nederlandse Studenten Zendings-Bond: RC4
Neff, K. L.: LA3, LB1
Nellist, G. F. M.: DP11
Nelson, A. M.: PP54
Netherlands (Kingdom, 1815–) Centraal Bureau voor de Statistiek: WI 35
Netherlands (Kingdom, 1815–) Commissie voor het Adatrecht: HI 6
Netherlands (Kingdom, 1815–) Departement van Marine: NZ8
Netherlands (Kingdom, 1815–) Departement van Zaken Overzee: NI 8, WI 36
Netherlands (Kingdom, 1815–) Departement van Zaken Overzee. Bibliotheek: BC1, BC4
Netherlands (Kingdom, 1815–) Regeringsvoorlichtingsdienst, Djakarta: CI 6, DI 13
Netherlands (Kingdom, 1815–) Rijksarchief, The Hague: BC6
Netherlands Forces Intelligence Service: PH118
Neumann, J. H.: PI 39
New York. State University. Foreign Area Materials Center: LP7
New York (City) Public Library. Reference Dept.: BA12
New York University. Burma Research Project: AB4, AB5, EB8
Newberry Library, Chicago: BA11, OP3
Newberry Library, Chicago. Edward E. Ayer Collection: BL1, NZ4a
Ngo-Vu: PV17
Nguyen-Dinh-Hoa: PV19, PV24a
Nguyen-Khac-Kham: RB13
Nguyen-The Anh: HV4
Nguyen-Van-Khon: PV15, PV18, PV24, PV25

Nguyen-Xuan-Dao: CV1
Nicanor, P. M.: DP21
Nicolas, R.: HH3
Nigg, C.: PP22
Nihon Biruma Kyôkai: WB13
Nihon Takushoku Kyôkai: AA9
Noakes, J. L.: ZM12
Noceda, J. J. de: PP44
Noegroho: EI 43
North Borneo: ZM7, ZM13, ZM14, ZM18, ZM19, ZM21
Northern Illinois University. Library: BA20, BA22
Notes et Études Documentaires: AB6
Notoatmodjo, S.: VI 20
Noyer, B.: VH1
Nuh, M.: PH160, PH193
Numismatic Notes and Monographs: SA5
Nunn, G. R.: AA39, TA7
Nuttonson, M. Y.: UB3, VH2

Ockeloen, G.: AI 2
Odenkircher, T. J.: XI 26
Oey, G. P.: BA6
Ohio University. Center for International Studies. Southeast Asia Program: LA8
Oi Ba-Tha: PB19
Onorato, M. P.: LP7
Oostkust van Sumatra-Instituut: BE9
Ophuijsen, C. A. van: PH102, PH105, PH108, PH111
Organisatie voor Natuurwetenschappelijk Onderzoek: BE14, VI 8, VI 9
Organisation for Scientific Research: BE14
Oriental Monograph Series: QA4
Osmena, J.: PH10

PACAF Basic Bibliographies: AA37
Paauw, D. S.: II 2
Pacific Area Bibliographies: VI 10, VM4
Pacific Science Congress: OP4
Pacific Scientific Information Center: VI 16, VM5, VV1
Pacis, M. B.: BH8
Pallegoix, J. B.: PT1, PT2
Pameran Buku Indonesia, Singapore dan Kuala Lumpur: AI 23
Pamuntjak, M. T. S.: PI 51
Panganiban, J. V.: PP26, PP40a, PP42
Panggabean, K.: PH128
Pao, S. C.: PH76–PH78
Papers on Southeast Asian Subjects: CM5, QM2
Papineau, A. J. G.: FM14, FM21
Pardo de Tavera, T. H.: EP6
Paris. Bibliothèque Nationale. Département des Manuscrits: BB7, BM2

Paris. Centre d'Étude des Relations Internationales: JA1
Parish, H. C.: AT3
Parks, O. E.: CV2
Parlaungan: DI 17
Parmentier, H.: FC2, FC3, QC3, QV1
Pavie, A. J. M.: NH2
Pavlenko, A. P.: PH231
Pelzer, K. J.: MA5
Pembina: FI 42
Peña Cámara, J. M. de la: JP8
Penninga, P.: PI 47
Perez, A.: AP15
Perez, C. B.: VP3
Permanent Committee on Geographical Names for British Official Use: MT1
Pernis, H. D. van: PH118, PH126
Peters, T.: DB3
Petitjean, H. C.: HH1
Phan-Gia-Ben: JV4
Phan-Huy-Chu: JV1
Philadelphia. Free Library: AP12
Philippine College of Surgeons, Manila: DP25
Philippine Folklore Society: OP10
Philippine Information Council: EP16
Philippine Islands: FP1, HP3
Philippine Islands. Bureau of Civil Service: DP3, HP2
Philippine Islands. Bureau of Commerce and Industry: YP13, YP14
Philippine Islands. Bureau of Constabulary: DP10
Philippine Islands. Bureau of Education: DP8, DP9
Philippine Islands. Bureau of Forestry: VP2
Philippine Islands. Bureau of Justice: WP5-WP7
Philippine Islands. Bureau of Science: VP4
Philippine Islands. Bureau of Science. Scientific Library: VP3
Philippine Islands. Census Office: ZP5
Philippine Islands. Dept. of Agriculture and Commerce. Division of Statistics: WP8, WP9
Philippine Islands. Dept. of Commerce and Police: FP5
Philippine Islands. Ethnological Survey: PP61
Philippine Islands. Independence Commission: FP6
Philippine Islands. Legislature, 1914: AP20
Philippine Islands. Legislature, 1916- House of Representatives: DP4
Philippine Islands. Louisiana Purchase Exposition Board: EP7
Philippine Libraries: TP1
Philippine Social Sciences and Humanities Review: OP6
Philippines (Commonwealth) Bureau of Customs: YP21
Philippines (Commonwealth) Bureau of the Census and Statistics: WP12
Philippines (Commonwealth) Commission of the Census: UP1, ZP6-ZP8
Philippines (Commonwealth) Dept. of Agriculture: EP12, EP13
Philippines (Commonwealth) Dept. of Agriculture and Commerce: NP3, WP12a
Philippines (Commonwealth) National Assembly: DP14
Philippines (Commonwealth) National Assembly. House of Representatives: DP5
Philippines (Rep.) Agricultural Credit and Cooperative Financing Administration: XP1
Philippines (Rep.) Bureau of Coast and Geodetic Survey: MP4
Philippines (Rep.) Bureau of Commerce: YP18, YP22-YP24, YP27
Philippines (Rep.) Bureau of Lands: EP17, WP13
Philippines (Rep.) Bureau of Mines: VP6
Philippines (Rep.) Bureau of Public Affairs: AP26
Philippines (Rep.) Bureau of Public Libraries: HP12, HP18, TP2
Philippines (Rep.) Bureau of Public Schools: LP5
Philippines (Rep.) Bureau of the Census and Statistics: EP14, WP14-WP21, XP2, XP3, YP25-YP27, ZP1, ZP9-ZP14, ZP16
Philippines (Rep.) Commission on Elections: DP6, HP14
Philippines (Rep.) Commission on National Integration: KP3
Philippines (Rep.) Congress. House of Representatives: DP16
Philippines (Rep.) Cooperatives Administration: YP28
Philippines (Rep.) Dept. of Commerce and Industry: YP19, YP20, YP29
Philippines (Rep.) Dept. of Finance: WP22
Philippines (Rep.) Dept. of Foreign Affairs: EP22
Philippines (Rep.) Dept. of Health: WP23
Philippines (Rep.) Dept. of Labor: YP31
Philippines (Rep.) Division of Agricultural Economics: NP7, UP3, UP4, XP4, XP5

Philippines (Rep.) Institute of National Language: CP4, PP24, PP25, PP31, PP32, PP40
Philippines (Rep.) Labor Statistics Division: YP30
Philippines (Rep.) National Economic Council. Office of Statistical Coordination and Standards: WP24, WP33
Philippines (Rep.) National Employment Service: YP31
Philippines (Rep.) National Institute of Science and Technology: TP1, VP7, VP8
Philippines (Rep.) National Science Development Board: VP1
Philippines (Rep.) Office of Public Information: DP15, EP19
Philippines (Rep.) Office of Statistical Coordination and Standards: WP25-WP30, ZP15
Philippines (Rep.) Office of the President. Program Implementation Agency: IP2
Philippines (Rep.) Official Gazette: HP10
Philippines (Rep.) Philippine Fisheries Commission: WP31
Philippines (Rep.) Philippine Information Agency: EP20
Philippines (Rep.) Program Implementation Agency: IP2, NP8
Phu Nu Moi: EV6
Phu Nu Ngay Mai: EV7
Pigeaud, T.: BN12, PI 16, PI 21, PI 22
Pigneau de Behaine, P. J.: PV50
Pijnappel, J.: NI 3, PH89, PH94
Pino, E.: PH167, PH170, PH182
Pison, D. M. de: NP1
Plang Phloiphrom: PT20, TP24
Pluvier, J. M.: JA7
Poerbatjaraka, Raden Mas N.: BR5, BR6
Poerwadarminta, W. J. S.: PH32, PH36, PH66, PH72a, PH127, PH131, PH196, PH220, PH221, PH227, PI 15, PI 17-PI 20, PI 23
Polin, C.: AV13
Ponce, A. C.: HP13
Porter, R. S.: PP65
Postmus, S.: VI 10
Prop, G.: NI 27
Pudjiadi, R.: LI 6
Purbatjaraka, Raden Mas N.: BR5, BR6
Purbo Hadiwidjojo, M.: VI 19
Purnell, H. C.: PT29
Purwadarminta, W. J. S.: See Poerwadarminta
Pusponegoro, S. D.: WI 37
Pustaka Antara, Kuala Lumpur: OM13

Quezon, M. L.: HP18
Quezon, Philippines. Ateneo de Manila. College of Law: HP1
Quezon, Philippines. Ateneo de Manila. Dept. of History and Government: YP2
Quezon, Philippines. Ateneo de Manila. Institute of Philippine Culture: AP30, GP2, KP5
Quezon, Philippines. University of the Philippines: DP23, LP3
Quezon, Philippines. University of the Philippines. Asian Labor Education Center: IP1
Quezon, Philippines. University of the Philippines. College of Agriculture. Library: UP2
Quezon, Philippines. University of the Philippines. College of Medicine: VP5
Quezon, Philippines. University of the Philippines. Community Development Research Council: HP20, UP6
Quezon, Philippines. University of the Philippines. Graduate School of Arts and Sciences: LP6
Quezon, Philippines. University of the Philippines. Institute of Asian Studies: PP60
Quezon, Philippines. University of the Philippines. Institute of Nutrition: VP5
Quezon, Philippines. University of the Philippines. Institute of Planning: HP22
Quezon, Philippines. University of the Philippines. Institute of Public Administration: CP3, CP6, CP8, HP8, HP9
Quezon, Philippines. University of the Philippines. Institute of Public Administration. Library: HP11, HP13
Quezon, Philippines. University of the Philippines. Inter-Departmental Reference Service: CP3, CP5, CP6, CP8
Quezon, Philippines. University of the Philippines. Library: AP31, BH2, BH3, CP9, CP11, HP15, HP19, OP4, UP5
Quezon, Philippines. University of the Philippines. Social Science Research Center: GP1, LP4
Quezon, Philippines. University of the Philippines. Statistical Center: WP32
Quimba, J. B.: PP6
Quirino, C.: AP32, NZ10

Raffles Museum and Library, Singapore: BG2, BG3, VM2
Rahajoekoesoemah, D.: PH217
Raja Singam, S. D.: MM3
Rajaratnam, S.: FM8

Raliby, O.: PH14
Ranganathan, S. R.: CA2
Rangoon. University. Economics, Statistics and Commerce Departments: ZB10
Rasjidi, C.: LI 5
Rata, A. W.: PH226
Ravier, H.: PV53
Ray-Buc: PC7
Rayner, E. A.: PP68
Rebadavia, C. B.: HP15
Reban, M. J.: CV2
Reinhorn, M.: PL5
Reith, G. M.: FM19
Reitsma, S. A.: FI 13
Renou, L.: SB2
Retana y Gamboa, W. E.: AP5, AP6, AP9, AP10, AP13, AP17, AP19, BB1, BM1, CP2, EP3, RA1
Retizos, I. L.: DP19
Richard, L.: PH204
Rigg, J.: PI 24
Rijkee, W.: FI 14
Roberts, C. F.: EM13
Roberts, T. D.: EL2
Robertson, J. A.: AP16, AP18, JP3
Robson, J. H. M.: AM2, AM3
Rodriguez Moñino, A. R.: AA5
Roff, W. R.: CM5
Romein, J. E.: NA4
Ronkel, P. S. van: BN7, BN8, PH107, PH115, PH150
Ronkel, S. van: BR3
Roolvink, R.: NA3
Roorda, T.: PI 7
Roorda van Eysinga, P. P.: PH85, PH87, PH92
Roorda van Eysinga, W. A. P.: PH88
Rotary Club, Jesselton, North Borneo: FM15
Rotary Club, Saigon: FV7
Rotary Club, Sandakan, North Borneo: FM16
Rotary Club, Singapore: FM20
Rotary International. District 46: DM5
Rouffaer, G. P.: BC2
Royal Asiatic Society of Great Britain and Ireland. Library: BB5
Royal Asiatic Society of Great Britain and Ireland. Malayan Branch: AM6, AM7, BG3, VA5
Royal Commonwealth Society. Library: AA12, BB4, DA5, HA3
Royal Empire Society Bibliographies: AA12
Royal Historical Society, London: JA4
Royal State Railways of Siam: FT2, FT3, FT5, FT6
Royal Steam Packet Company: FI 5
Ruijter, J.: PP55
Rutgers, A. A. L.: UA1, UI 4

Sa'ad Shukry bin Muda: EM16, PH57, PH59
Saaduddin Djambek: EI 18
Sabah: DM6, DM7
Sabah. Dept. of Agriculture: XM9
Sabah. Dept. of Statistics: YM24
Saigon. Archaeological Institute: BP1
Saigon. Chamber of Commerce: YV2
Saigon. National Historical and Literary Institute: BJ3
Saigon. National Institute of Administration: BJ1, BJ2, HV2, HV3
Saito, S.: AA31, AP29, CP12, KM2, KP5
Salayan, A. W.: HI 20
Saleh Subedjo, M.: PH60
Samah, A.: PH33, PH138, PH159
Sanchez, C.: VP8
Sanchez de la Rosa, A.: PP15, PP17
Sanlucar, P. de: PP44
Santos, D. de los: PP43
Santoso, S.: PH189
Sarawak: DM8, YM25, ZM20, ZM22
Sarawak. Dept. of Agriculture: XM10
Sarawak. Dept. of Statistics: WM12, WM16
Sarawak. Dept. of Trade and Customs: YM26
Sarawak. Education Dept.: WM13
Sarawak. Information Service: CM9, DM17, DM22, EM17, LM2
Sarawak. Registration of Births and Deaths Office: ZM1
Sarawak Association: DM18
Sasrasaganda, Raden: PI 12
Sastranegara, R. M.: PH229
Sastrawiria, T.: HI 14
Sastroamidjojo, A. S.: NI 23, UI 7
Satjadibrata, Raden: PI 29- PI 34
Satow, E. M.:TT1
Sauvaget, J.: JA6
Savina, F. M.: OH1, PV1, PZ4, PZ7
Schacht, J.: RI 3
Schleiffer, H.: II 2
Schmidgall Tellings, A. E.: PH44, PH194
Schmidt, K. O.: FT13
Schoel, W. F.: MI 11
Schrieke, B. J. O.: VI 7
Schulze, F.: FI 3
Science and Society Series: KI 10
Scott, J. G.: EB4, EB5, MB2, RA2
Scott, N. C.: PI 56
Seidenfaden, E.: FT2, FT3, FT5, FT6

Sellman, R. R.: NA2
Senny, J.: OA3
Senstius, M. W.: OM5
Serrano, R.: PP45, PP48, PP49
Serrano Laktaw, P.: PP46, PP51
Shadily, H.: PH181
Shamsuddin bin M. Joonoos: PH163
Shan Nu: PH83
Shell Company of Thailand: NT1
Shellabear, W. G.: PH144, PH145, PH151
Shorto, H. L.: OA6, PZ6
Siagian, G.: FI41
Siagian, H.: FI41
Siam Society: MA7
Silpa Birasri: FC4
Sim, V.: DM13
Simandjuntak, G. A.: YI54
Simatupang, R. O.: FI25, FI38, FI47
Simpson, D. H.: DA5
Singapore: DM9
Singapore. Colonial Secretary's Office: DM10
Singapore. Dept. of Information Services: FM9, FM24
Singapore. Dept. of Statistics: WM14, WM15, WM27, ZM17, ZM23
Singapore. Ministry of Culture: CM1, DM16
Singapore. Ministry of Education: LM1
Singapore. Public Relations Office: CM2, CM3
Singapore. Registrar-General of Births and Deaths: ZM2
Singapore. Survey Dept.: FM17, FM22
Singapore (City): YM28
Singapore (City) Nanyang University: AA27, CA7, JP9
Singapore (City) National Library: AM10, AM11, AM13, AM14, BG5
Singapore (City) Polytechnic. Library: CM10
Singapore (City) Raffles Museum and Library: BG2, BG3, VM2
Singapore (City) Teachers Training College. Library: OM11
Singapore (City) University. Library: BG4, BG6, BP3, BP4, CM6, CM8, CM12, LM3
Sithibourn, S.: DL2
Situmorang, F.: PH212
Sjahdana, M.: LI5
Sjahrial-Pamuntjak, R.: GI2
Skeat, W. W.: KM1
Sloan, W. H.: PB3
Smith, C. A.: NZ4a
Smith, G. V.: FC5
Smith, S. J.: PT9

Smithsonian Institution. War Background Studies: KH1
So Sethaputra: PT12, PT17, PT27, PT31, PT32, PT34
Soekarno, C. S.: NI24, NI26
Soemargono, F.: PH210a
Soerjonagoro, M.: PH217
Soewignja, Raden Poerwa: CI5
Southeast Asia Development Advisory Group: DA1
Southeast Asia Institute: OB3, OM6, OP2
Spain. Archivo General de Indias, Seville: BB3
Spain. Instituto Geográfico y Estadístico: ZP2
Spearman, H. R.: MB1
Springer, C.: MA7
Stanford University. Hoover Institution on War, Revolution and Peace: BA7, WA1
Start, L. E.: SB1
Steinberg, D. J.: EC3, EC4
Steller, K. G. F.: PI54
Stemfoort, J. W.: NI8
Sternstein, L.: MA7
Stevens, E. O.: PZ10
Stewart, J. A.: PB11
Straits Settlements: EM4, HM2, YM29, YM30, ZM4, ZM6, ZM8
Straits Settlements. Registrar General of Births and Deaths: ZM3
Straits Settlements. Statistical Office: WM17, YM31
Straub, M.: ZI4
Strout, E.: BA3
Stuart, H. N.: SA4
Stucki, C. W.: LA4, LA7
Studien und Berichte aus dem Forschungs-institut der Friedrich-Ebert-Stiftung: CA5
Sulaiman bin Ahmad: PH173
Sumatra Planters Association: XI27
Summer Institute of Linguistics: OP5, OP7
Sundram, R. M.: ZB10
Sung, L.: PC1
Supardi, Raden: VI20
Supeno, EI42
Surjo Untoro, S.: HI21, PH67
Survey of World Cultures: EC4
Sutter, J. O.: VI16, VM5, VV1
Suvatti, C.: VT1, VT2, VT4
Suzuki, P.: KI8
Swettenham, F. A.: PH146
Syo Sunda Minseibu: PH225
Syracuse University. Library: LA5
Syracuse University. Maxwell Graduate School of Citizenship and Public Affairs: HA8

Taberd, J. L.: PV51, PV52
Tablan, A. A.: PP27, PP34
Taiheiyo Kyokai, Tokyo: AA10, AI11
Tair, M. A.: PH133
Tairas, J. N. B.: TI3
Tamayo, J. P.: PP11
Tan, A. L.: KP3
Tanase, J.: TA4
Tandart, S.: PC5
Tas, H. van der: PH136
Tavera, P. de: BA1
Taylor, E. A.: PH4
Tayona, A. G.: HP8
Te Reo Monographs: OA5
Teeuw, A.: NI22, OM12, PH127
Tennessee Valley Authority: NA6
Tep Yok: PC9
Ternaux-Compans, H.: AA42
Teselkin, A. S.: PH232
Teston, E.: EH3
Teves, J. S.: VP6
Texas. University. Population Research Center: ZA1
Tha Din, M.: PB18
Thai Chamber of Commerce: YT6
Thailand: WT4
Thailand. Central Statistical Office: WT5-WT13, WT15, WT16, XT1, XT2, YT7, YT8, YT13, ZT3-ZT5
Thailand. Customs Dept.: YT9
Thailand. Dept. of Agriculture: VT6
Thailand. Dept. of Commercial Intelligence: YT11
Thailand. Dept. of Industrial Promotion: XT4
Thailand. Dept. of Labor: YT10
Thailand. Dept. of Local Administration: WT14
Thailand. Division of Agricultural Economics: XT3, XT5
Thailand. Fisheries Dept.: VT2, VT4
Thailand. Forestry Dept.: VT3
Thailand. Legation U.S.: MT2
Thailand. Ministry of Economic Affairs: YT12
Thailand. Ministry of National Development: ET2
Thailand. Ministry of the Interior: ZT1, ZT2
Thailand. National Institute of Development Administration: GT3, HT5, YT5
Thailand. Royal State Railways: FT2, FT3, FT5, FT6
Thailand. Sun Borkian Qekkasan Kanwichai: VT5
Thailand. Survey Dept.: FT22

Thailand Management Development and Productivity Center: WT17
Than Htun: JB1, JB3
Thanakhan Haeng Prathet Thai: WT2
Thanh Nghi: PV17, PV43, PV45, PV46
Thani Nayagam, X. S.: OM18
Thao-Kun: PC9
The, L.: LA8
Thebaw, King of Burma: BD4
Thee, T. G.: LI4
Thomas, J. W.: PH4
Thomson, T.: PH2
Thongqin Sunsawal: FT21
Thrombley, W. G.: HT5
Thung, Y.: CI11
Tiele, P. A.: JI1, KA1
Tillema, H. F.: ZI3
Tilman, R. O.: HM5
Tjiptoning: DI14
Tjoi Kakumei: PH224
Tohogakkai: AA1
Tokyo. Institute of Asian Economic Affairs: AA32, AA34, WA2, YA2
Tokyo. Nan'yo Keizai Kenkyusho: AA8
Tokyo. Waseda University. Ohkuma Institute of Social Sciences: JI9
Torres y Lanzas, P.: BB3
Trager, F. N.: AB7
Tran-Thi-Kimsa: AV11, CV4
Tran-Van-Giap: JV1
Tregonning, K. G.: JM1
Tri Amatyakul: FI8, FT10
Tufo, M. V. del: ZM11
Tugault, A.: PH209
Tun Aung Gyaw: PB16
Tun Nyein: PB7, PB16
Tuuk, H. N. van der: BN5, PH91
Tveritinova, A. S.: AA41

Uhlenbeck, E. M.: OM10, OM14
UNESCO: HA5, HA7
UNESCO. Research Center on Social and Economic Development in Southern Asia: GA2, GA3
UNESCO. South Asia Science Corp.: VA2
UNESCO. Bibliographical Handbooks: AA19
United Nations. ECAFE: IA1, NA6
United States. Agency for International Development: JV3, NA6, VC1, WL5, WL7, WL8, WV1
United States. Army. Forces in the Far East: PH150
United States. Army. Forces in the Pacific: JP5
United States. Army Language School: OT2, OV1, PB17

United States. Army Map Service: MH1, MI 15, OH2
United States. Board on Geographic Names: MA6, MB6, MB7, MC1, MI 13–MI 16, MI 18, ML1, MM1, MP2, MT3, MV1, MV2
United States. Bureau of Foreign and Domestic Commerce: YA4
United States. Bureau of Insular Affairs: MP1
United States. Bureau of the Census: ZP3, ZP4
United States. Coast and Geodetic Survey: MP3, NP2
United States. Committee to Aid the National Liberation Front of South Vietnam: AV13
United States. Congress. House of Representatives: NV2
United States. Congress. Senate: AP14, BA1, EP6, NP2
United States. Dept. of Commerce: YJ23
United States. Dept. of Defense: FP13
United States. Dept. of Health, Education and Welfare: LA3, LB1
United States. Dept. of State: AB2, AI 15, AI 24, AV8, AV10, DH2, DM14, DP17, GA1
United States. Dept. of the Army: EB11, EC5, EI 41, EM20, ET10, EV4, EV5
United States. Embassy. Thailand: DT1
United States. Engineer Agency for Resources Inventories: NA6
United States. Information Service, Bangkok: CT1
United States. Information Service, Vientiane: OL1
United States. Library of Congress: AP14, BA1, EP6, HP7
United States. Library of Congress. American Libraries Book Procurement Center, Djakarta: BA16
United States. Library of Congress. Division of Bibliography: AI 12, AM4, AP22, JP2, JP4
United States. Library of Congress. General Reference and Bibliography Division. Netherlands Studies Unit: AI 13
United States. Library of Congress. Orientalia Division: AA13, AA15, AA36, BA5, BA17
United States. Library of Congress. Reference Dept.: AH6, JP8
United States. Military Assistance Institute. Library: AT6, AV12

United States. Office of Armed Forces Information and Education: FV12
United States. Office of Foreign Agricultural Relations: UA2
United States. Office of Geography: MA6, MB6, MB7, MC1, MI 16, MI 18, ML1, MM1, MT3, MV1, MV2
United States. Operations Mission to Thailand: HT1
United States. Operations Mission to Vietnam: WV2
United States. Waterways Experiment Station, Vicksburg, Miss.: GT2
Urbain-Gabriel, Brother: PT20
Usui, J.: TA4
Utrecht. Rijksuniversiteit. Bibliotheek: LA1

Vajiranana National Library, Bangkok: BI 1
Valenzuela, W. P.: DA4
Van Gisteren Tot Morgen: DI 19
Vanoverbergh, M.: PP19, PP62
Verbeek, R. D. M.: VI 2
Verdoorn, F.: VI 6
Verea, F. G.: FP4
Vereeniging Toeristenverkeer: FI 11, FI 43
Vereeniging Tot Bevordering van het Bibliotheekwezen in Nederlandsch-Indië: KI 3
Veröffentlichungen des Seminars für Indonesische und Südseesprachen der Universität Hamburg: OM17
Veth, P. J.: MI 1
Veur, P. van der: LA8
Vietnam. Archaeological Institute: NV1
Vietnam. Do Cong-Chanh Va Giao-Thong: PV5a
Vietnam. Embassy. France: AV2
Vietnam. Embassy. United States: FV11
Vietnam. National Archives and Libraries: RB13
Vietnam. National Commission of UNESCO: KV1
Vietnam. National Institute of Administration: HV2, HV3
Vietnam. National Statistical Institute: WV3–WV5, ZV1–ZV4
Vietnam. National Tourist Office: FV3–FV5, FV9, FV10, FV13, FV14
Vietnam. Nha Thong Gian Doc Quan-Thue: YV3
Vietnam. So Thong-Ke Va Kinh-Te Nong-Nghiep: XV1–XV3
Vietnam. Tax Directorate General: YV4
Villamor, I.: WP6, WP7
Villasin, O. S.: YP34

Vindel, F.: NZ9
Virata, E. T.: UP6
Vlieland, C. A.: ZM8
Voorhoeve, P.: BB8, OM7
Vreede, A. C.: BN3, PI 7
Vreeland, H. H.: EC4
Vromans, A. G.: BC5, JA2
Vuuren, L. van: KI 3

Wade, J.: PZ3
Wainwright, M. D.: BM5
Wall, H. T. F. K. E. W. A. C. van de: PH91
Wall, V. I. van de: DI 9
Wang, H. C. C.: LM3
Waseda University. Ohkuma Institute of Social Sciences: JI 9
Waworuntu, J.: FI 27
Wellan, J. W. J.: AI 6
Wells, M. B.: FT11, FT12, FT17, FT19
Welsh, D. V.: BA11, OP3
Wenn, H. T.: PH75
Werndly, G. H.: OM2
West-Java (Province) Kantor Urusan Agama: PH40
Widjojo Nitisastro: ZI 24
Wieringa, B.: MI 7, MI 9
Wilkinson, R. J.: PH143, PH147, PH148, PH155, PH157, PH195
Williams, H. P.: PP63
Winstedt, R. O.: PH63, PH153, PH157, PH165, PH168, PH169, PH174, PH177, PH187, PH198, PH200
Winter, C. F.: PI 4
Wira Bunyanurak: WT17
Wirasatisna, H.: HI 14
Wit Sidogura Publications: FI 27
Wit Siwasariyanon: PT21

Wittermans, T.: PH167, PH170, PH182
Wittermans-Pino, E.: PH167, PH170, PH182
Wojowasito, S.: PH166, PH176, PH178, PH179, PH196
World Education Series: LT2
Wright, H. M.: EP8
Wu, C. H.: JP6, JP7, JP9

Yabes, L. Y.: OP1, OP6
Yale Anthropological Studies: KI 6
Yale University. Southeast Asia Studies: EI 40, KA4, KA5, MA5
Yale University. Southeast Asia Studies. Bibliography Series: AB7, CP7, II 3, II 4, KA3, KP4
Yale University. Southeast Asia Studies. Cultural Report Series: KA5
Yamada, Y.: PP60
Yamin, M.: NI 25
Yatco, J. C.: HP13
Yeh, S. C.: PH22
Yi Yi, D.: JB4
Yip, W. K.: LM5
Yule, H.: EA6
Yunesuko Higashi Ajia Bunka Kenkyu Senta, Tokyo: AA40, TP3, TT3

Zadrozny, M. G.: EC2
Zain, S. M.: PH29, PH64, PH175
Zainal Abidin bin Safarwan: PH201
Zeini: EI 25
Zending der Nederlandse Hervormde Kerk: NI 19
Zendingsbureau, Oegstgeest: NI 19
Zenker, J. T.: AA2
Zuid Sumatra Instituut: AI 6

Z
3221
J63